Explore new ideas!

Welcome to Reading/Writing Workshop

Read exciting literature, science and social studies texts!

Become an expert writer!

Build vocabulary and knowledge to unlock the Wonders of reading!

Use your student login to explore your interactive Reading/Writing Workshop, practice close reading, and more.

Go Digital!   www.connected.mcgraw-hill.com

Wonders

Program Authors

Diane August

Donald R. Bear

Janice A. Dole

Jana Echevarria

Douglas Fisher

David Francis

Vicki Gibson

Jan Hasbrouck

Margaret Kilgo

Jay McTighe

Scott G. Paris

Timothy Shanahan

Josefina V. Tinajero

McGraw Hill Education

Cover and Title Pages: Nathan Love

www.mheonline.com/readingwonders

Send all inquiries to:
McGraw-Hill Education
2 Penn Plaza
New York, NY 10121

ISBN: 978-0-07-676573-7
MHID: 0-07-676573-3

Printed in the United States of America

4 5 6 7 8 9 QVS 20 19 18 17 16   **B**

Unlock the
Wonders of Reading

With your *Reading/Writing Workshop* you will:

- Closely read and reread literature and informational text

- Discuss what you have read with your peers

- Become a better writer and researcher

- Look for text evidence as you respond to complex text

Get Ready to Become:

- Lifelong Learners
- Critical Thinkers
- Part of the Community of Learning

READ and REREAD

Exciting Literature

Open your book and fire up your imagination! You'll find myths, stories, historical fiction, mysteries, and poems. They're all there waiting for you to explore and share.

Informational Texts

Build knowledge with many kinds of informational texts, including biographies, science and social studies selections, and news articles. Sometimes the real world is more exciting than fiction.

Access Complex Text

Different genres of text can be challenging in various ways. First you need to figure out what kind of text you are reading: narrative, informational, or argument. If you are finding the text difficult, refer to the tips below to move you in the right direction.

VOCABULARY

If you come across an unfamiliar word, look for context clues. Some texts contain technical terms. You might want to look these up in a dictionary or other reference source.

MAKE CONNECTIONS

Often the text does not come out and state everything. You have to make inferences. In fiction, a character's motivations are not always directly stated. Figure out what the motivations are by looking at other characters' actions and dialogue. In expository text, you might have to connect several pieces of information and analyze them to find the essential idea.

ILLUSTRATIONS AND TEXT FEATURES

Are there any illustrations that can give you clues about the plot or character development? In nonfiction, are there any maps or diagrams that can help you understand information?

TEXT STRUCTURE

How is the text organized? Does the author compare and contrast information? Is there a series of problems presented? Are there steps in a process?

How might a diagram or graph help you understand information in a nonfiction text?

L👀k for Text Evidence

When you answer a question about your reading, you often have to look for evidence in the text to support or even find the answer. Here are some tips to help you find what you are looking for.

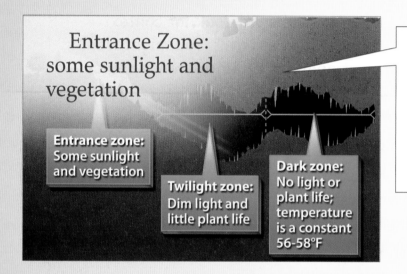

Entrance Zone: some sunlight and vegetation

Entrance zone: Some sunlight and vegetation

Twilight zone: Dim light and little plant life

Dark zone: No light or plant life; temperature is a constant 56-58°F

Stated
I can locate specific information here about the three types of cave zones.

Most Troglobites have ghostly white skin. Some even have skin you can see through. They don't need pigment in their skin to protect them from the sun's rays.

Unstated
This sentence allows me to infer that these creatures never see the sun.

Text Evidence

Evidence will either be stated directly or implied. You have to make inferences based on your general comprehension. Here is how to tell if a question will have a stated or unstated answer:

It's Stated — Right There!

The answers to questions that ask you to find a certain fact, date, event, setting, or quantity can usually be found in a single sentence.

To answer broader questions you need to combine stated information from more than one place. A question such as, "How are the three cave zones different?" would require you to synthesize stated information from all parts of the text.

It's Unstated — Here Is My Evidence

The answers to some questions are not stated. For example, the question, "Why is each cave zone perfect for its inhabitants?" asks you to analyze information, put the answer in your own words, and support it with text evidence.

How do you find text evidence? To make inferences, locate the facts, figures, and specialized vocabulary and then think about what they mean. In a fiction text think about what the characters do and say to figure out the theme.

. . . .

 Point to additional stated information that tells about the three cave zones.

Be an Expert Writer

Remember that good writing represents clear ideas, is well organized, and contains text evidence and details from reliable sources. See how Abby answered a question about a text she read.

Abby's Model

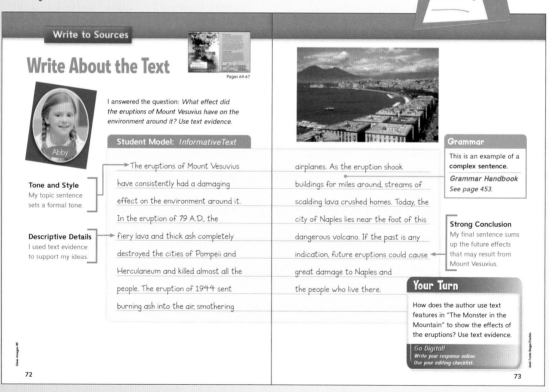

Write About the Text

Pages 64-67

Abby

I answered the question: *What effect did the eruptions of Mount Vesuvius have on the environment around it? Use text evidence.*

Student Model: *Informative Text*

Tone and Style
My topic sentence sets a formal tone.

Descriptive Details
I used text evidence to support my ideas.

The eruptions of Mount Vesuvius have consistently had a damaging effect on the environment around it. In the eruption of 79 A.D, the fiery lava and thick ash completely destroyed the cities of Pompeii and Herculaneum and killed almost all the people. The eruption of 1944 sent burning ash into the air, smothering airplanes. As the eruption shook buildings for miles around, streams of scalding lava crushed homes. Today, the city of Naples lies near the foot of this dangerous volcano. If the past is any indication, future eruptions could cause great damage to Naples and the people who live there.

Grammar
This is an example of a **complex sentence.**
Grammar Handbook
See page 453.

Strong Conclusion
My final sentence sums up the future effects that may result from Mount Vesuvius.

Your Turn
How does the author use text features in "The Monster in the Mountain" to show the effects of the eruptions? Use text evidence.

Go Digital!
Write your response online.
Use your editing checklist.

72

73

Write About the Text

When you write about something you have read closely, you should answer the question clearly and use an appropriate tone. Use supporting details as text evidence. These details should strengthen your answer. If you have to do research, make sure to use multiple, reliable sources and then provide a bibliography or Works Cited list. Use the question checklist below.

Arguments Did I support my opinions with facts and details?

Informative Texts Did I clearly group information in paragraphs? Did I make a closing statement to create a strong conclusion that brings together all of my information?

Narrative Texts When you write a narrative, use your imagination to develop real or fictional events. The checklist below will help make your work more memorable.

- Sequence Did I use a sequence of events that unfolds naturally and effectively? Did I make use of clue words and transitions?

- Dialogue Did I use dialogue and descriptions to develop characters, theme, and events? Does my dialogue accurately represent my characters' personalities? Does it show the characters' responses to situations in a believable manner?

 What is your favorite genre to write in? Share with a partner.

Unit 1

The Big Idea

How can changes transform the way people look at the world?............**16**

SOCIAL STUDIES

(t to b) Greg Newbold; Tristan Elwell

🔷 **Go Digital!** www.connected.mcgraw-hill.com.

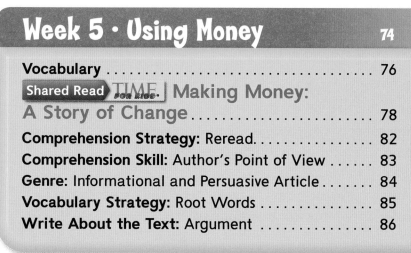

Unit 2

Excursions Across Time

The Big Idea

What can we gain from reading about past civilizations? **88**

(t to b) KHALED AL-HARIRI/Reuters/Corbis; Ocean/Corbis

Go Digital! www.connected.mcgraw-hill.com.

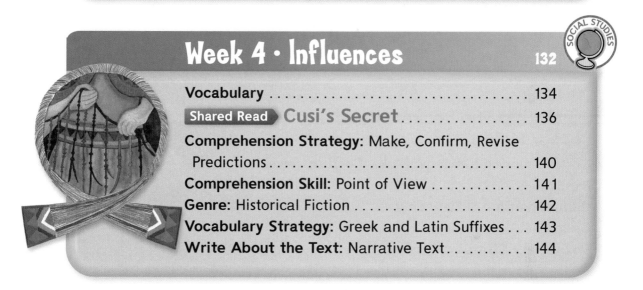

Week 4 · Influences 132

Week 5 · Past and Present 146

(t to b) Janet Broxon; Chris Deeney/Alamy

Unit 3

ACCOMPLISHMENTS

The Big Idea

What does it take to accomplish a goal?...**160**

Peter Ferguson

 Go Digital! www.connected.mcgraw-hill.com.

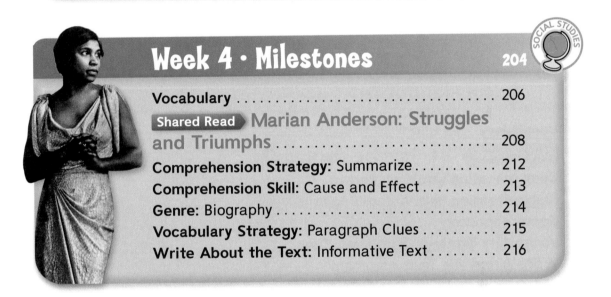

(t to b) Popperfoto/Getty Images; Brand X Pictures

9

Unit 4

Challenges

The Big Idea

How do people meet challenges and solve problems? **232**

(t to b) NASA; Jerry Cooke/Corbis

SOCIAL STUDIES

Unit 5 Discoveries

The Big Idea

(t to b) Design Pics/Richard Wear; Jago; London Ladd

Go Digital! www.connected.mcgraw-hill.com.

Week 3 · Innovations 334

Week 4 · Breakthroughs 348

Week 5 · Exploration 362

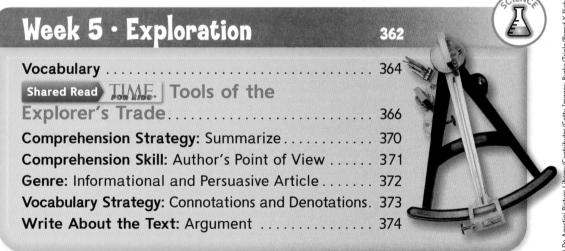

Unit 6

Taking ACTION

The Big Idea

Week 1 · Resources   378

Week 2 · Witnesses   392

Week 3 · Investigations 406

Week 4 · Extraordinary Finds 420

Week 5 · Taking a Break 434

(t to b) Courtesy of Antonio A. Mignucci-Giannoni, PhD; Adam Niklewicz

CHANGES

The BIG Idea

How can changes transform the way people look at the world?

The Tide **Rises,**
The Tide **Falls**

The tide rises, the tide falls,
The twilight darkens, the curlew calls;
Along the sea-sands damp and brown
The traveler hastens toward the town,
    And the tide rises, the tide falls.

Darkness settles on roofs and walls,
But the sea, the sea in darkness calls;
The little waves, with their soft, white hands,
Efface the footprints in the sands,
    And the tide rises, the tide falls.

The morning breaks; the steeds in their stalls
Stamp and neigh, as the hostler calls;
The day returns, but nevermore
Returns the traveler to the shore,
    And the tide rises, the tide falls.

— Henry Wadsworth Longfellow

Essential Question

How do new experiences offer new perspectives?

Go Digital!

18

A New Point of View

My visit to this beautiful Tlingit clanhouse in Alaska really changed my perception of how people interact with each other and nature.

► Several families would live in a clanhouse, sharing an indispensable fire for warmth and cooking, but sleeping in separate areas.

► The carvings and paintings outside show the significance to Tlingit culture of local animals: ravens, eagles, weasels, sea lions, and others.

It's all so different from what I'm used to!

Talk About It

Write words you have learned about gaining a new perspective. Then compare life in a Tlingit clan house with family life today.

Alike	Different

Vocabulary

Use the picture and the sentences to talk with a partner about each word.

consolation

One **consolation** of losing was knowing he had done his best.

How do people provide consolation to their relatives and friends?

glimmer

My dog shows a **glimmer** of excitement when he knows it is time to play.

How are the meanings of glimmer and trace related?

heinous

The children's **heinous** table manners made it unpleasant to eat with them.

What are examples of heinous table manners?

indispensable

Binoculars are **indispensable** to bird watchers.

What item do you find indispensable during the school day?

perception

Our **perception** that our friend Lea was happy made us smile.

What might cause you to have the perception that a friend is sad?

phobic

Many people are **phobic** about going to the dentist.

Describe something you are phobic about.

sarcastic

Her **sarcastic** comment hurt Aaron's feelings.

Why are sarcastic comments often hurtful?

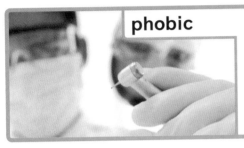

threshold

A welcome mat is always found at the **threshold** of their home.

What else is often found at the threshold of a home?

COLLABORATE

Your Turn

Pick three words. Write three questions for your partner to answer.

Go Digital! *Use the online visual glossary*

(t to b) Getty Images/Brand X Pictures/SW Productions; Stockbyte/PunchStock; Angela Hampton Picture Library/Alamy; Comstock Images/Getty Images

CITY music

Essential Question

How do new experiences offer new perspectives?

Read about the way a girl's outlook changes when she moves to a new home.

Greg Newbold

Farewell to Me

I crammed one last box into the back seat and slammed the car door. It felt as if I were slamming the door on my whole life. At first, I was thrilled when Mom told me she'd gotten a fantastic new job as a veterinarian at an animal hospital. Then, because she always saves the bad news for last, she told me the really **heinous** part. The hospital wasn't in our city; it was miles away in the middle of nowhere. And I'm definitely *not* a country girl.

I slouched against the car, taking a last look at our building. To most people, it probably just looks like any other old apartment house, but I love every grimy brick. Soon I'd be staring at piles of hay.

Just then, I heard a bright blast of music and saw my best friends, Hana and Leo, come charging up to me. While Hana played a cool riff on her trumpet, Leo sang, "We will miss you, Celia . . . At least you won't be in Australia." I raised my eyebrows.

Laughing, Leo said, "Hey, *you* find something to rhyme with *Celia*!"

"You guys are utterly **indispensable**!" I blurted out. "How will I live without you?"

"Ever hear of texting?" asked Hana, punctuating her question with a loud trumpet honk. I jumped into the car fast so no one could see me tear up. As Mom pulled away, I waved goodbye to my friends, my neighborhood, and my life.

We rode a while in silence, and I wedged my violin case beneath my legs for comfort. Leo, Hana, and I had been writing songs for our band, but that was all over now. "Don't think of this as an ending," Mom said, with her knack for reading my mind. "It's an exciting beginning, and we're on the **threshold** of a breathtaking new adventure."

"Yeah, it'll be great. I couldn't be happier," I said glumly.

"Don't be **sarcastic**, *mija*," Mom said. "It's so unattractive."

23

Being attractive wasn't a big goal at the moment, but annoying Mom wasn't either. So I clammed up and looked out the window as crowded, exciting city streets turned first into bland suburban shopping strips and then into endless, boring trees and fields of corn.

"Look: cows!" Mom said, as we cruised past some black-and-white blotches in a pasture.

"Sure, they seem sweet," I said, "but I bet they have a mean streak when you're not looking."

"It's normal to be a bit **phobic** about unfamiliar things," Mom said, in her best patient-parent tone. "But you don't need to be afraid of cows. They're harmless."

"Harmless . . . and boring," I thought to myself. "Like everything in the country."

Not So Bad?

We finally arrived at our new home, a two-story wooden farmhouse. It had a crooked roof, a rickety front porch, and too many places for bats to hide. "Would you mind if I don't go in yet?" I asked.

Mom looked overwhelmed. She just nodded and said I could go explore. I felt a **glimmer** of hope, a small hint that country life might turn out okay. Mom never let me go out alone in the city, so maybe a bit more freedom would be one **consolation** of living here.

I wandered off, clutching my violin and not paying attention to where I was going. It didn't matter; it was all just a blur of green and brown. I imagined that a big Saturday night here meant sitting around talking about corn . . . or watching it grow.

Suddenly I heard something I wasn't expecting—a blaring, jazzy tune. I pushed through some corn only to come face-to-face with an enormous cow. Then another hot jazz riff floated through the air. I spun around and saw a tall kid playing a beat-up old saxophone in the clearing. His music was fantastic, and he didn't dress the way I figured a country kid would. Where were the muddy dungarees and plaid bandana? This guy was wearing clothes that made him look cool, like a famous performer.

Not Bad at All!

I couldn't resist, so I took out my violin and began to play along. The boy looked surprised, but he didn't miss a beat. We improvised a cool duet, and by the end—no kidding—the big cow's tail was swishing to the rhythm. "I'm Jason," he said when we finished. "I play out here because the cows don't complain when I mess up. You must be Celia. My dad said you were moving in. I can't believe you play violin! I've been looking for someone to write songs with."

I looked at Jason and his dented sax, the cheerful cow and tall corn, the majestic trees in the distance, and the sun shining in the brilliant blue sky. I could feel my **perception** of country life already changing, and I had a feeling it would change a lot more.

Make Connections

Talk about how Celia's first experience in her new home gives her a new perspective. **ESSENTIAL QUESTION**

Describe a time when trying something new or unfamiliar changed your perspective. **TEXT TO SELF**

Visualize

To visualize something is to form a mental picture of it. Use the descriptions of settings, characters, and events in a story to imagine what they look like. As you read on, use new details from the text to add to or change your mental images.

 Find Text Evidence

You may not be sure why Celia reacts the way she does to having to move to the country. Reread the first paragraph on page 24. Look for details that help you visualize the differences Celia sees between her old neighborhood and her new one.

---

page 24

Being attractive wasn't a big goal at the moment, but annoying Mom wasn't either. So I clammed up and looked out the window as crowded, exciting city streets turned first into bland suburban shopping strips and then into endless, boring trees and fields of corn.

I read that, from the car, Celia could see "crowded, exciting city streets" change to "endless, boring trees and fields of corn." From this, I can infer that Celia thinks the country will be very different from, and much less interesting than, the city.

Your Turn

Reread the section "Not So Bad?" on pages 24–25. Make a list of descriptive words and phrases that help you form a mental picture of Celia's new house. As you read, remember to use the strategy Visualize.

Character, Setting, Plot

In fiction, changes to the **setting** often affect the **characters** and shape the events in the **plot**. As you read a story like "Cow Music," comparing and contrasting details from the different settings can help you make inferences about the ways the characters act and understand the most important plot events.

 Find Text Evidence

As I reread the first section of "Cow Music," I see that Celia thinks leaving the city means waving "goodbye to . . . my life." Though her mother calls the move "a breathtaking new adventure," Celia feels during the car ride that everything in the country will be "boring."

Characters
Celia, Celia's mother

Setting
city street, traveling in the car

Beginning
Celia says goodbye to friends then watches the changing landscape.

↓

Middle

↓

End

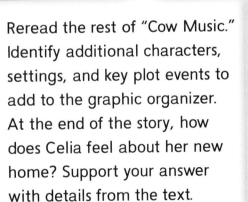

Your Turn

Reread the rest of "Cow Music." Identify additional characters, settings, and key plot events to add to the graphic organizer. At the end of the story, how does Celia feel about her new home? Support your answer with details from the text.

Go Digital!
Use the interactive graphic organizer

Realistic Fiction

"Cow Music" is realistic fiction. It has characters who look and act like real people. It takes place in settings that could be real.

Realistic Fiction:

- Has a narrator, who is sometimes one of the characters
- Usually has dialogue to show what the characters say

Find Text Evidence

As I started reading "Cow Music," I wondered who "I" was. As I read on, I understood that the character Celia is telling the story. She is the narrator. I also learn about the characters from their dialogue.

page 23

Farewell to Me

I crammed one last box into the back seat and slammed the car door. It felt as if I were slamming the door on my whole life. At first, I was thrilled when Mom told me she'd gotten a fantastic new job as a veterinarian at an animal hospital. Then, because she always saves the bad news for last, she told me the really **heinous** part. The hospital wasn't in our city; it was miles away in the middle of nowhere. And I'm definitely *not* a country girl.

I slouched against the car, taking a last look at our building. To most people, it probably just looks like any other old apartment house, but I love every grimy brick. Soon I'd be staring at piles of hay.

Just then, I heard a bright blast of music and saw my best friends, Hana and Leo, come charging up to me. While Hana played a cool riff on her trumpet, Leo sang, "We will miss you, Celia . . . At least you won't be in Australia." I raised my eyebrows.

Laughing, Leo said, "Hey, *you* find something to rhyme with *Celia!*"

"You guys are utterly **indispensable**!" I blurted out. "How will I live without you?"

"Ever hear of texting?" asked Hana, punctuating her question with a loud trumpet honk. I jumped into the car fast so no one could see me tear up. As Mom pulled away, I waved goodbye to my friends, my neighborhood, and my life.

We rode a while in silence, and I wedged my violin case beneath my legs for comfort. Leo, Hana, and I had been writing songs for our band, but that was all over now. "Don't think of this as an ending," Mom said, with her knack for reading my mind. "It's an exciting beginning, and we're on the **threshold** of a breathtaking new adventure."

"Yeah, it'll be great. I couldn't be happier," I said glumly.

"Don't be **sarcastic**, *mija*," Mom said. "It's so unattractive."

23

Narrator The narrator is the "voice" that tells the story.

Dialogue Dialogue is what the characters say. Their exact words are placed inside quotation marks.

Your Turn

COLLABORATE

Tell how the story would be different if the author had chosen Celia's mother to be the narrator instead of Celia. Then find two examples of dialogue. Explain what each tells you about the character who is speaking.

Sentence Clues

When you read an unfamiliar word in a story, carefully reread the sentence in which it appears. Look for context clues in the sentence to help you figure out the word's meaning.

Find Text Evidence

I'm not sure what the word riff *means on page 23 of "Cow Music." I see that the word* played *comes before it in the sentence. The phrase* on her trumpet *follows right after it. If a riff is something Hana plays on her trumpet, it must be part of a piece of music.*

While Hana played a cool riff on her trumpet, Leo sang, "We will miss you, Celia. . ."

COLLABORATE

Your Turn

Use context clues in sentences to find meanings of these words in "Cow Music."

breathtaking, *page 23*

rickety, *page 24*

majestic, *page 25*

Write About the Text

Pages 22–25

I responded to the prompt: *Write an email from Celia's mom to a friend about Celia's mood on the car ride to the country. Use details from the story.*

Teresa

Student Model: *Narrative Text*

Hi Paula,

I feel completely overwhelmed

by this move! I just drove four hours

with a daughter who only spoke two

sentences to me. From the start, she

made it clear that I was ruining her life

by moving to the country. I understand

that she's unhappy about leaving her

friends and the only home she's ever

known. It's hard for me, too. I told

her to think of the move as a great

Strong Opening

My first sentence grabs the reader's attention.

Inferences

I used details from the story to determine how Celia's mother would feel.

30

adventure. She said, "Yeah, it'll be great," in a sarcastic tone of voice. Then she stared out the window, looking like a convict on the way to prison. She even found fault with some cows! I hope I'm doing the right thing. I want this move to be good for her too.

Talk to you soon,

Mia

Supporting Details
I used text evidence from the story to describe how Celia acted.

Grammar

This **exclamatory sentence** expresses strong emotion.

Grammar Handbook See page 450.

Your Turn

Write an email from Celia to her friend Hana telling about how she feels after her first day at the new house. Use details from the story.

Go Digital!
Write your response online.
Use your editing checklist.

Essential Question

Why do people form alliances?

Go Digital!

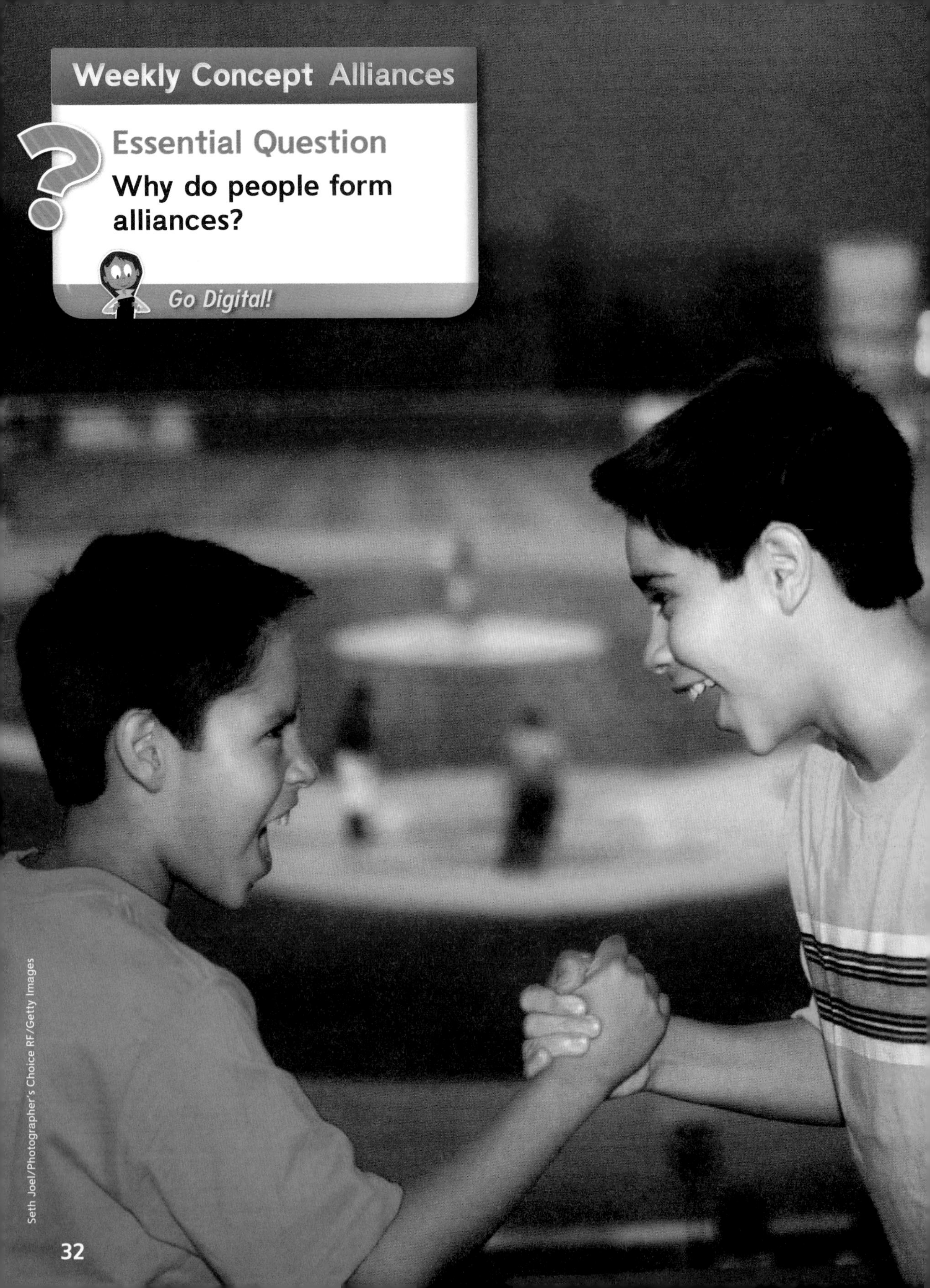

Seth Joel/Photographer's Choice RF/Getty Images

32

FORMING ALLIANCES

My brother Hector and I support our local minor league baseball team, but we can't always afford tickets to the games. So we formed an alliance.

▶ I sometimes do yard work for neighbors.

▶ With Hector helping me, we clean twice as many yards in a week as I can by myself.

Our partnership means we save up money for tickets much faster!

Talk About It

Write words you have learned about forming alliances. Then talk with a partner about what makes an alliance successful.

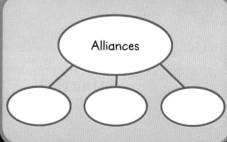

Alliances

Vocabulary

Use the picture and the sentences to talk with a
partner about each word.

adversity

A lack of rain ruins crops and brings
adversity to farmers.

What qualities can help people face
adversity?

alliance

The two nations agreed to form an
alliance for common goals.

Describe some advantages of forming
an alliance.

confinement

They felt a feeling of **confinement**
inside the tiny tree house.

What is an antonym for confinement?

inflicted

The hurricane **inflicted** damage in
many towns.

Describe a time that weather inflicted
harm in your area.

reminisce

My aunts like to **reminisce** about their summer vacations.

What do you like to reminisce about?

retrieved

The dog always **retrieved** whatever his owner tossed for him.

What things have you seen that a dog has retrieved?

smuggle

We had to **smuggle** my mother's gift into the house.

When might you smuggle a gift?

spindly

The weight of the birds bent the **spindly** branches.

Describe plants with spindly branches that you have seen.

Your Turn

COLLABORATE

Pick three words. Write three questions for your partner to answer.

Go Digital! **Use the online visual glossary**

Drumbeat of Freedom

Essential Question

Why do people form alliances?

Read how a brother and sister form an alliance with a soldier in the War of Independence.

On a cold December evening in 1777, the deep blue curtain of night had begun to drop over the snow-covered hills and fields of Valley Forge, Pennsylvania. As always at this time, Sarah Bock lit a lantern and walked to the barn to check on the animals. Though she had only just turned twelve, she shouldered many responsibilities on her family's farm.

As she crossed the yard, Sarah could see smoke rising above the encampment barely a mile away. She had often wondered about General George Washington and his Continental Army wintering there. The soldiers faced great adversity during this bitterly cold winter. They were poorly clothed, and many were hungry or ill.

Sarah hurried toward the barn to seek refuge from the wind that bit at her cheeks. She took a shortcut through a stand of spindly trees. Their thin branches could barely support the weight of the snow. Suddenly, she saw something that made her heart leap to her throat. A trail of footprints led from the trees to the barn. Some were smudged with blood.

When Sarah reached the barn, she took a few wary steps inside. All at once, the lantern's glow caught a shadowy figure huddled in the corner. Sarah held her breath and slowly stepped backward, her heart pounding. Just as she made it back to the barn door, she heard a young man's voice.

"Don't be afraid," the man said, limping barefoot out of the shadows. "I will do you no harm."

"Who are you?" Sarah asked. There was fear in her voice, but the sight of this poor soldier, half starved and hurt, had already lessened her alarm.

"My name is Charles Kent," he said. "I'm stationed with General Washington. The men are starving. Might you spare a little food?"

In recent weeks, word had spread that some of the soldiers had taken to begging. Not all of the farm families were sympathetic to their cause, however. Sarah's own father had told her he wasn't sure the soldiers could succeed in this conflict with the British. He didn't want anyone in his family to become involved in the war.

Sarah had a difficult decision to make. Should she obey her father, or should she help the soldiers? A moment later, Sarah spoke in a quiet voice. "I can see how hungry you are. Stay here. I'll try to **smuggle** out some of the salt beef we keep in our cellar for hard times." Sarah ran back to the house, and a short time later she returned to the barn with the food hidden under her cloak.

After that first night, Charles came back to the barn many times. Sarah would bring him beef or bread when she went out to do her evening chores.

One evening, Sarah had time to sit with Charles while he ate. He began to **reminisce** about his family back home. He spoke about life in the army and why he felt this fight for freedom was a worthy one.

Suddenly, they heard a creak. It was the barn door. Sarah jumped to her feet as her 18-year-old brother John walked in. She saw surprise and then anger cross his face. Before he could say a word, Sarah swiftly introduced her new friend.

"But Sarah, you know Father doesn't want us involved in this war," John scolded. Then, a bit uncertainly, he added, "This fight is none of our business."

"I know that's how Father feels," she answered. "But I believe the war is important. These men are fighting for us, for our freedom. We can't just stand by while they suffer from hunger and disease. How is it fair that soldiers fighting for such a just cause should have these harsh conditions **inflicted** on them?"

Sarah's brave words erased the anger from her brother's face. John hesitated a moment and then sat down with Sarah and Charles. He listened eagerly to the soldier's tales of battles against the British. Later that night, John brought Charles a pair of old shoes to wear.

Soon, the harsh winter melted away into spring, and Sarah noticed that the army encampment seemed increasingly busy with activity. The troops, who had been held prisoners by the cold, were breaking free from the **confinement** of their winter quarters. Were they getting ready to fight the British again?

Sarah knew John was sneaking away to speak with the soldiers, and she was sure he had formed an

alliance with Charles and the others. Now, when Sarah and John knew their parents couldn't hear, they even spoke about their growing loyalty to the cause of independence.

One sunny morning in June, Sarah awoke to the steady thump of drumbeats echoing through the sleepy valley like a heartbeat. She dressed quickly and ran outside to join her parents. Just beyond the farm, General Washington's troops were marching out of Valley Forge. Though their uniforms were tattered, they all stood as straight as arrows. They had **retrieved** the resolve that had been tested during the long, difficult winter.

Sarah suddenly realized that her brother was missing. "Where is John?" she asked. Without answering, her mother stifled a sob and wiped tears from her eyes. A feeling of worry rose in Sarah's heart, but it was mixed with pride.

Just then, more soldiers strode by. In their ranks were John and Charles. When John waved, Sarah could see in his eyes that he was a true supporter of the cause. Now Sarah stood straight and tall. She waved to her brother as he marched away to the drumbeat of freedom.

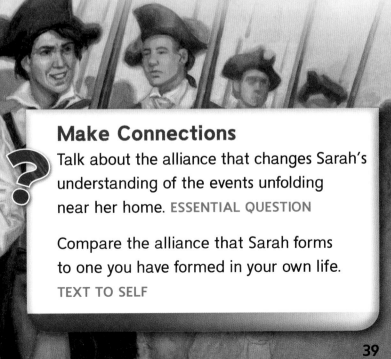

Make Connections

Talk about the alliance that changes Sarah's understanding of the events unfolding near her home. ESSENTIAL QUESTION

Compare the alliance that Sarah forms to one you have formed in your own life. TEXT TO SELF

Visualize

When reading fiction, readers form pictures in their minds of the setting, characters, and events. Look for descriptive details to help you visualize characters' actions.

Find Text Evidence

To understand Sarah's reaction to finding Charles in the barn, use the descriptive details on page 37 of "Drumbeat of Freedom" to visualize how she felt.

page 37

When Sarah reached the barn, she took a few wary steps inside. All at once, the lantern's glow caught a shadowy figure huddled in the corner. Sarah held her breath and slowly stepped backward, her heart pounding. Just as she made it back to the barn door, she heard a young man's voice.

The phrases "held her breath" and "heart pounding" describe the reaction of someone who is afraid. I can infer from them that Sarah was startled to find a stranger in the barn.

COLLABORATE

Your Turn

Make a list of descriptive words and phrases on page 37 of "Drumbeat of Freedom" that help you visualize John's reaction to Sarah's alliance with Charles. As you read, remember to use the strategy Visualize.

Character, Setting, Plot

In fiction, the events in the plot occur in a certain sequence, or order. The plot often begins with a description of a problem the main characters have. The sequence of events shows what the characters do to solve the problem.

 Find Text Evidence

When I reread "Drumbeat of Freedom," I think about how the setting affects the characters. Then I look for time-order words and phrases, such as "suddenly" and "all at once," that signal main plot events. Using those, I can identify the sequence of events.

> The harsh winter causes the problem that the characters face.

Characters
Sarah Bock, Charles Kent, John Bock
Setting
a farm near Valley Forge, winter 1777
Problem
Sarah and John must decide whether to form an alliance with Charles.
Event
Sarah finds Charles in the barn.
Event
Solution

Your Turn

Reread "Drumbeat of Freedom." Identify words and phrases that signal important events in the plot. List those events in the graphic organizer. Then use them to identify the characters' solution.

Go Digital!
Use the interactive graphic organizer

Historical Fiction

"Drumbeat of Freedom" is historical fiction. It has a real setting drawn from history and presents actual events from the point of view of fictional people living in a historical time period.

Find Text Evidence

The first sentence of "Drumbeat of Freedom" says that the year is 1777. I know the War of Independence was an actual event, and George Washington was a real person. However, the main characters are people the author has imagined living at that time. The illustrations show them dressed in clothing of the period.

page 39

alliance with Charles and the others. Now, when Sarah and John knew their parents couldn't hear, they even spoke about their growing loyalty to the cause of independence.

One sunny morning in June, Sarah awoke to the steady thump of drumbeats echoing through the sleepy valley like a heartbeat. She dressed quickly and ran outside to join her parents. Just beyond the farm, General Washington's troops were marching out of Valley Forge. Though their uniforms were tattered, they all stood as straight as arrows. They had **retrieved** the

resolve that had been tested during the long, difficult winter.

Sarah suddenly realized that her brother was missing. "Where is John?" she asked. Without answering, her mother stifled a sob and wiped tears from her eyes. A feeling of worry rose in Sarah's heart, but it was mixed with pride.

Just then, more soldiers strode by. In their ranks were John and Charles. When John waved, Sarah could see in his eyes that he was a true supporter of the cause. Now Sarah stood straight and tall. She waved to her brother as he marched away to the drumbeat of freedom.

Make Connections
Talk about the alliance that changes Sarah's understanding of the events unfolding near her home. ESSENTIAL QUESTION

Compare the alliance that Sarah forms to one you have formed in your own life. TEXT TO SELF

39

Illustrations The characters are shown wearing clothing that people might have worn at the time of the War of Independence.

COLLABORATE

Your Turn

List two details in "Drumbeat of Freedom" that show it is historical fiction. Decide with your partner which parts of the story are factual and which are made up.

Paragraph Clues

Sometimes there aren't enough context clues within the sentence that contains an unfamiliar or multiple-meaning word. When this is the case, you can look for context clues in nearby sentences to help you figure out the word's meaning.

 Find Text Evidence

The sentence, Sarah hurried toward the barn to seek refuge from the wind that bit at her cheeks, *on page 37 of "Drumbeat of Freedom," doesn't have clues that help me find the meaning of the word* refuge. *In nearby sentences, I read that it's a bitterly cold winter, and that Sarah takes a shortcut past snow-covered trees. So refuge must mean* "a place to escape from harsh conditions."

> Sarah hurried toward the barn to seek
> refuge from the wind that bit at her cheeks.

COLLABORATE

Your Turn

Use context clues in nearby sentences to find or verify the meanings of the following words in "Drumbeat of Freedom":

encampment, *page 37*
stand, *page 37*
sympathetic, *page 37*
resolve, *page 39*

43

Write About the Text

Pages 36–39

Miles

I answered the question: *Is it wrong for the soldiers to beg for food from the farmers? Support your argument with details from the story.*

Student Model: *Argument*

Introduce a Claim
My opening sentence clearly states my opinion.

> It is not wrong for the soldiers to beg for food. They do not have enough food in their camp, and they are starving. They do not steal food from the farmers. They simply explain why they need food, which is an

Relevant Evidence
I gave details from the story to support my opinion.

Word Choice

I used strong words such as *honorable* to make it clear how the soldiers acted.

honorable thing to do. The farmers are free to choose whether or not to help the soldiers. If the soldiers must beg in order to get the food they need to survive, then it is not wrong for them to beg. Everyone must eat.

Grammar

The **subject** of this sentence is *everyone* and the **predicate** is *must eat*.

Grammar Handbook See page 451.

Your Turn

Was Sarah right to help Charles Kent? Include details from the story to support your argument.

Go Digital!
Write your response online.
Use your editing checklist.

Essential Question

How do life forms vary in different environments?

Go Digital!

Living Environments

Scientists use a classification system based on the environmental layers in a rainforest to talk about the plant and animal species living there.

- The top, or emergent, layer hosts primates and one-third of the world's bird species.

- The shady canopy layer has the most species, including frogs, some birds, and large cats.

- Reptiles, bats, owls, and broad-leafed plants thrive in the mostly dark understory.

- Insects, amphibians, and certain large mammals live on the dark, moist forest floor.

Talk About It

Write words you have learned about the different rainforest environments. Then talk with a partner about why animals might live in a particular layer.

Rainforest Environments

Vocabulary

Use the picture and the sentences to talk with a
partner about each word.

classification

Classification of grocery items by
category makes them easier to find.

What is a synonym for classification?

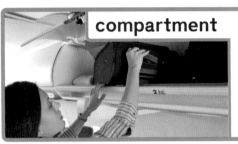

compartment

She placed her luggage in the plane's
overhead **compartment**.

What things do you store in a
compartment?

engulfs

Fog often **engulfs** parts of the bridge in
the morning.

What is a synonym for engulfs?

flanked

Cheering fans **flanked** the road as the
marathon runner ran past.

How are the words flanked and
bordered similar?

maneuvering

Maneuvering his bicycle up the twisting and rocky path was easy for him.

What might make maneuvering a bicycle difficult?

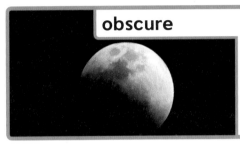

obscure

Earth's shadow will **obscure** the moon during the eclipse.

What is an antonym for obscure?

species

Dogs are among the most popular **species** that people keep as pets.

Name two other popular pet species.

submerged

A scuba diver explored the **submerged** shipwreck.

Where might you find a submerged object?

Your Turn

COLLABORATE

Pick three words. Write three questions for your partner to answer.

Go Digital! *Use the online visual glossary*

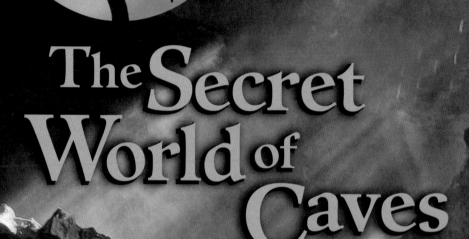

The Secret World of Caves

Essential Question

How do life forms vary in different environments?

Read how plant and animal life varies in different parts of caves.

In the Mouth of the Cave

Stepping into a cave is like entering an entirely new world. The environment is suddenly cooler and damper. Though there is some light here, it is dimmer than the light outside. There is a sense of stillness and quiet. This outermost area is called the *entrance zone*. It is a hallway leading to the many secrets of life in a cave.

An animal that uses the entrance zone of a cave belongs to the classification known as *trogloxenes*. Creatures in this category may seek shelter in caves but don't spend their whole life cycles in them. They also spend time on the surface. Some entrance zone organisms are called *accidentals* because they often find their way in accidentally. These cave guests stay for a while but not for long.

Bats are among the most common trogloxenes. Hanging upside down from a cave's ceiling, they are protected and sleep undisturbed. Bats also hibernate this way during the coldest months. In warm months, bats search for food outside the cave.

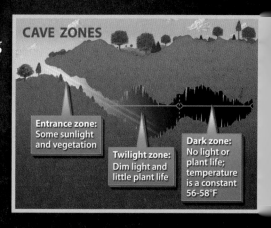

CAVE ZONES

Entrance zone: Some sunlight and vegetation

Twilight zone: Dim light and little plant life

Dark zone: No light or plant life; temperature is a constant 56-58°F

Other species make use of the entrance zone for protection, too. Pack rats build nests using twigs and leaves from the outside. Their big eyes and long whiskers help in maneuvering through the dim light. Small gray birds called phoebes seek safety inside cave doorways. They make their nests in a compartment, or nook, in the cave walls. These small spaces hide the birds from animals that prey on them.

Twilight Time

Deeper inside a cave, the walls and ceiling obscure most of the light from outside. This shadowy area is known as the *twilight zone*. The light in this zone is so dim that everything appears to be bathed in a bluish glow. This part of a cave feels even damper and cooler than the entrance zone.

Animals that rely on the environment of the twilight zone are called *troglophiles*. Their eyesight is often poor, and they usually have less colorful bodies than animals living outside of caves. These creatures spend their entire life cycles inside moist caves, but many can also survive in similar habitats outside of caves. Animals commonly found living in the twilight zones of caves are centipedes, fish, beetles, earthworms, and spiders.

Some twilight zone animals live **submerged** under water. This spring cavefish lives on microscopic organisms.

Totally in the Dark

Deeper still inside a cave, beyond the twilight zone, is the *dark zone*. Here passageways are flanked on either side by steep stone walls. There is no light at all. Darkness engulfs this place, and moist air envelops everything.

It is hard to believe that any animals could live their whole lives in total darkness. Yet many strange creatures live in the dark zones of caves. These animals, known as *troglobites*, include rare species of frogs, salamanders, spiders, worms, insects, and crabs. Cave biologists believe that these unusual creatures are distantly related to animals that once lived near caves. But they look only slightly similar to their surface relatives. Troglobites even need food that is unavailable outside of caves.

Troglobites are adapted to living with the absence of light. Most of them are completely sightless. So it is only logical that these unusual cave dwellers have heightened senses of smell and touch. For example, their bodies can detect the slightest vibrations. They can also sense changes in the air pressure around them. When something is moving nearby, these creatures can feel it. This special ability helps them catch food. It also helps them avoid becoming another animal's meal.

Most troglobites have ghostly white skin. Some even have skin you can see through. They don't need pigment in their skin to protect them from the sun's rays. And they don't need skin coloring to help them blend in with their surroundings for safety. These unusual adaptations mean that troglobites can never leave the dark zones of caves.

Scientists now know that cave animals are vulnerable to even minor changes in their environment. So their work includes protecting these least known and fascinating creatures.

This crayfish has see-through skin.

Make Connections

Talk about how different life forms are well suited to living in each of the three cave zones. ESSENTIAL QUESTION

What other animals have you seen or learned about that live in unusual habitats? TEXT TO SELF

Reread

Some informational texts include scientific information that may be difficult to understand the first time you read it. As you read "The Secret World of Caves," you can pause and reread difficult sections to make certain you understand them.

 Find Text Evidence

It may not be clear to you why bats live only part of their lives in the entrance zone of a cave. Reread the section "In the Mouth of the Cave" on page 51 of "The Secret World of Caves."

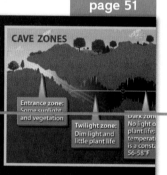

page 51

Bats are among the most common trogloxenes. Hanging upside down from a cave's ceiling, they are protected and sleep undisturbed. Bats also hibernate this way during the coldest months. In warm months, bats search for food outside the cave.

Other species make use of the entrance zone for protection, too. Pack rats build nests using twigs and leaves from the outside. Their big eyes and long whiskers help in maneuvering through the dim light. Small gray birds called

CAVE ZONES

Entrance zone: Some sunlight and vegetation

Twilight zone: Dim light and little plant life

Dark zone: No light or plant life; temperature is a constant 56-58°F

I read that bats hibernate in caves "during the coldest months" and search for food outside caves in warm months. From this, I can infer that bats spend more time in caves when the weather is cold and food is hard to find.

COLLABORATE

Your Turn

Why is *accidental* a good name for some entrance zone creatures? Reread "In the Mouth of the Cave" on page 51 to answer the question. As you read, remember to use the strategy Reread.

Main Idea and Key Details

The main idea is the most important point an author makes about a topic. When the main idea is not stated directly, use the key supporting details to help you identify it.

Find Text Evidence

When I reread the section "Twilight Time" on page 52 of "The Secret World of Caves," I will look for important details about the twilight zone of a cave. Then I can think about what the details have in common to identify the main idea.

These details are all related to one idea.

Main Idea   A variety of species rely on the twilight zone's special environment.
Detail   The twilight zone is darker and damper than the entrance zone.
Detail   Twilight zone animals spend their whole lives in caves, but many could live outside, too.
Detail   Spiders, beetles, centipedes, fish, and worms live in the twilight zone.

COLLABORATE

Your Turn

Reread the section "Totally in the Dark." Identify the key details and list them in the graphic organizer. Use the details to determine the main idea of the section.

Go Digital!
Use the interactive graphic organizer

Expository

"The Secret World of Caves" is an expository text. It explains what life is like in underground caves using factual information and visual images.

Find Text Evidence

"The Secret World of Caves" explains how creatures live in or use caves. The headings tell me what each section is about. The photos with captions show me what caves and cave creatures look like. The diagram helps me understand the different cave zones.

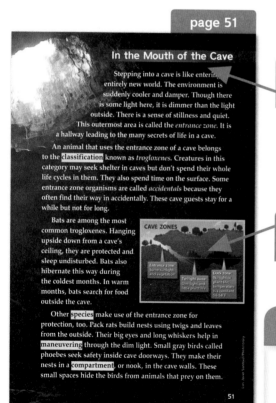

page 51

In the Mouth of the Cave

Stepping into a cave is like entering an entirely new world. The environment is suddenly cooler and damper. Though there is some light here, it is dimmer than the light outside. There is a sense of stillness and quiet. This outermost area is called the *entrance zone*. It is a hallway leading to the many secrets of life in a cave.

An animal that uses the entrance zone of a cave belongs to the classification known as *trogloxenes*. Creatures in this category may seek shelter in caves but don't spend their whole life cycles in them. They also spend time on the surface. Some entrance zone organisms are called *accidentals* because they often find their way in accidentally. These cave guests stay for a while but not for long.

Bats are among the most common trogloxenes. Hanging upside down from a cave's ceiling, they are protected and sleep undisturbed. Bats also hibernate this way during the coldest months. In warm months, bats search for food outside the cave.

Other species make use of the entrance zone for protection, too. Pack rats build nests using twigs and leaves from the outside. Their big eyes and long whiskers help in maneuvering through the dim light. Small gray birds called phoebes seek safety inside cave doorways. They make their nests in a compartment, or nook, in the cave walls. These small spaces hide the birds from animals that prey on them.

CAVE ZONES

Entrance zone
Some sunlight and vegetation

Twilight zone
Dim light and little plant life

Dark zone
No light or plant life, temperature is constant 55–56°F

51

Text Features

Headings Headings identify the topic of each section of text.

Photographs and Captions Photographs illustrate information in the text. Captions explain what is shown in the photographs.

Diagrams Labeled diagrams show a visual representation of ideas.

Your Turn

COLLABORATE

Find and list three text features in "The Secret World of Caves." Tell what you learned from each feature.

Greek Roots

An unfamiliar word in a scientific text may contain a Greek root you know. Use the meaning of the root to help you define the word. Here are some common Greek roots and their meanings.

Root	Meaning	Root	Meaning
cycl-	circular, wheel	*log-*	word, study
scop-	look, examine	*zon-*	area, section

 Find Text Evidence

I see the phrase entrance zone *on page 51 of "The Secret World of Caves." If I know the root* zon- *means "area" or "section," I can figure out that an entrance zone is the section where you enter.*

> This outermost area is called the
> *entrance zone.* It is a hallway leading
> to the many secrets of life in a cave.

Your Turn

Use Greek roots to define each word or phrase:
   life cycles, *pages 51 and 52*
   microscopic, *page 52, caption*
   logical, *page 53*
Tell how you used the Greek root to help you
understand the meaning of each word.

Pages 50–53

Write About the Text

Tyler

I answered the question: *How does the author help us understand what* trogloxenes *means? Include text evidence.*

Student Model: *Informative Text*

Focus on a Topic
My topic sentence explains how the author answers the question.

The author helps us understand

what *trogloxenes* means by defining

the word, expanding the definition,

and giving examples. The author first

defines *trogloxenes* as a classification

of animals that use the entrance zone

of caves. The author then tells the

reader more about trogloxenes.

Details
I provided evidence from the text to support the topic.

These animals may seek shelter in caves, but they don't spend their entire lives in them. Trogloxenes also spend time on the surface. Finally, the author provides examples by discussing how trogloxenes such as bats, pack rats, and small gray birds called phoebes seek protection in cave entrances.

Grammar

A **compound sentence** like this combines two sentences into one.

Grammar Handbook See page 452.

Transitions

I used the word *finally* to make clear the relationship among ideas.

Your Turn

How do the details in the diagram of the cave on page 51 help us understand the text better? Include text evidence.

Go Digital!
Write your response online.
Use your editing checklist.

Essential Question

How do natural forces affect Earth?

Go Digital!

Arctic-Images/Getty Images

SURFACE CHANGES

Unless you live near a volcano, you aren't likely to witness a scene like this. But forces within our Earth often produce dramatic surface changes.

► Earth's crust is continually moving, causing volcanism and earthquakes. There are many active volcanoes in the United States.

► During certain types of eruptions, jets of molten rock called lava fountains reach temperatures of 2,000° F and spray as high as 1,600 feet into the air.

You won't want to get too close!

Talk About It

Write words you have learned about Earth's surface changes. Then talk with a partner about why volcanoes are so dangerous.

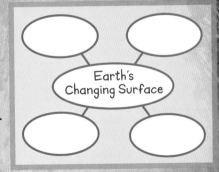

Earth's Changing Surface

Vocabulary

Use the picture and the sentences to talk with a
partner about each word.

cascaded

As the sink overflowed, water **cascaded**
onto the floor.

What else have you seen that cascaded?

documentation

The scientist hoped that careful
documentation of experiment results
would support her theory.

Why is documentation important?

dynamic

Because a tornado is so **dynamic**, it can
quickly change course.

Why are dynamic weather events often
dangerous?

exerts

Sunny weather often **exerts** a positive
effect on a person's mood.

What exerts a positive effect on your
mood?

plummeting

We watched the meteors **plummeting** through the night sky.

What is a synonym for plummeting?

pulverize

The chef needed to **pulverize** the spice into a fine powder.

Why might a cook pulverize food for a recipe?

scalding

You should let **scalding** soup cool before trying to eat it.

What might happen if you eat or drink something that is scalding?

shards

The vase fell off the shelf and broke into many **shards**.

What else might break into shards?

COLLABORATE

Your Turn

Pick three words. Write three questions for your partner to answer.

Go Digital!   *Use the online visual glossary*

The MONSTER in the MOUNTAIN

Essential Question

How do natural forces affect Earth?

Read how a scientist studies forces that cause volcanic activity at Mount Vesuvius.

Bettmann/CORBIS

64

Meet Marta Ramírez

As a young girl during World War II, Marta Ramírez saw newsreels that showed B-25 airplanes flying near the smoky plume of a volcanic eruption. The year was 1944, and Mount Vesuvius in Italy was erupting! Blankets of burning ash were seen smothering the airplanes. **Shards** of volcanic rock came **plummeting** from the sky. Soldiers on the ground ran for cover. Each glowing splinter of rock was like a deadly bullet.

Those images never left Marta. She has been fascinated by volcanoes ever since. When she got older, Marta earned degrees in geology and volcanology. Though she has studied many of the world's volcanoes, she returns again and again to Mount Vesuvius. Marta has climbed down into its smoking crater many times. In the following memoir, she describes one of her visits and why this volcano still inspires her work.

At the Monster's Mouth

I recently went to see this **dynamic** volcano again. I decided to climb its slope along with the dozens of curious tourists visiting that day. As we walked, our shoes crunched on cinders that had been dropped there long ago. Finally reaching the rim, we gazed at the spectacular view. We stared 800 feet down into the crater. It was quiet for now, but I knew it was only sleeping. Frequent tremors and small earthquakes prove that this monster is not dead. Did the others standing there with me know about the danger beneath their feet?

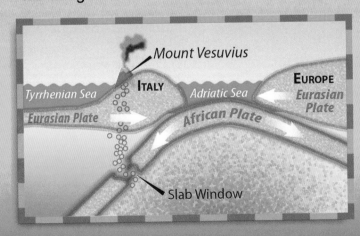

This model shows how Mount Vesuvius formed where one plate of Earth's crust pushes against another. Molten rock at this collision point **exerts** pressure upward until lava explodes from the volcano.

Every time I see this volcano up close, I think about how it had roared like a lion back in 1944. The trembling earth shook buildings for miles around, and streams of **scalding** lava flowed down the sides. Like glowing red fingers, they stretched out to crush defenseless homes below. It must have been terrifying to witness in person. Today, the lava that once **cascaded** down the mountain is hard and dry. It looks a bit like the skin of an elephant.

When the Monster Awakens

There is a lot of **documentation** of Vesuvius's past. Geologists have gathered this evidence of earlier eruptions by studying the rocks that were formed. Before 1944, the most catastrophic eruption occurred in 79 A.D. A Roman writer named Pliny the Younger described it in detail in his letters. On the morning of that tragic day, no one guessed that an enormous volcanic explosion was about to **pulverize** tons of rock and send it raining down on the city. People couldn't know

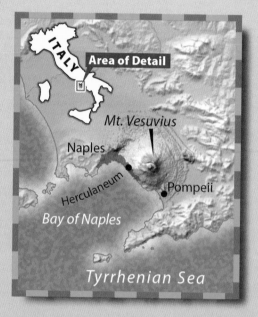

that thick, dark ash and fiery lava would completely destroy the nearby cities of Pompeii and Herculaneum. By evening, few people had survived.

Many smaller eruptions have occurred since then, including the one in 1944. Volcanologists believe that another major eruption could occur at any time. The probability grows with each passing year. To watch for geological changes within Vesuvius, we have set up seismographs on the slopes of its cone. These instruments measure the slightest shifts in the rock beneath the mountain.

During one dangerous but exciting mission, I climbed down into the crater itself. My crew and I worked on mapping what was going

on underground. We also measured the gases leaking from small vents. Any sudden increase in carbon dioxide and other gases might signal an eruption.

Looking Ahead

I don't go into the crater anymore, but I often think about how Vesuvius threatens the environment around it. Today, the city of Naples lies at the foot of Mount Vesuvius. If an eruption occurred tomorrow, the city would not be ready. Tons of ash and rock would once more be hurled into the air. This volcanic debris would keep cars, planes, and trains from operating. People would try escaping on foot. Sadly, no one can outrun such an eruption.

The only sure way to protect people who live near this volcano is to give them enough warning. The city of Naples has detailed evacuation plans. For the plans to work, however, officials need to be warned seven days before an eruption occurs. I hope the work that volcanologists do will help to give people the warning they need. Until then, I'll be watching this sleeping monster, just in case it starts to wake up.

Make Connections

Talk about how Earth's natural forces affect the environment around Mount Vesuvius. **ESSENTIAL QUESTION**

What natural occurrences have you experienced that could pose a danger to people? **TEXT TO SELF**

Behind Vesuvius are the remains of Mount Somma, a volcano that erupted 25,000 years ago. Vesuvius formed inside Somma's crater.

Reread

Rereading portions of "The Monster in the Mountain" can help you better understand the factual information about Mount Vesuvius and its volcanic eruptions.

 Find Text Evidence

You may not be sure why volcanologists study a volcano even when it isn't erupting. Reread "When the Monster Awakens" on page 66 of "The Monster in the Mountain."

page 66

When the Monster Awakens

There is a lot of **documentation** of Vesuvius's past. Geologists have gathered this evidence of earlier eruptions by studying the rocks that were formed. Before 1944, the most catastrophic eruption occurred in 79 A.D. A Roman writer named Pliny the Younger described it in detail in his letters. On the morning of that tragic day, no one guessed that an enormous volcanic explosion was about to **pulverize** tons of rock and send it raining down on the city. People couldn't know that thick, dark ash and fiery lava would completely destroy the nearby cities of Pompeii and Herculaneum. By evening, few people had survived.

ITALY
Area of Detail

Mt. Vesuvius
Naples
Herculaneum
Pompeii
Bay of Naples
Tyrrhenian Sea

I read that scientists gather historical and geological documentation about the volcano's past. From this I can tell that learning about past eruptions helps predict when it may erupt again.

Your Turn

COLLABORATE

How does information about past eruptions affect people living near Vesuvius today? Reread "Looking Ahead" on page 67. Remember to use the strategy Reread.

Main Idea and Key Details

The main idea is the most important point an author makes about a topic or in a section of text. The main idea may be stated or unstated. If it is not stated, readers use key details to identify the main idea.

Find Text Evidence

When I reread "Meet Marta Ramírez" on page 65, I can ask myself what this section is mainly about. All of the key details together help me figure out the main idea.

All the details connect to the unstated main idea.

Main Idea
Ramírez's childhood fascination with Mount Vesuvius led to a lifelong career as a volcanologist.
Detail
As a child, Ramírez saw dramatic newsreel images of Mount Vesuvius erupting in 1944.
Detail
Ramírez earned degrees in geology and volcanology.
Detail
Ramírez has studied many volcanoes, and Vesuvius in particular.

Your Turn

Reread the rest of "The Monster in the Mountain." Find the key details in each section and list them in the graphic organizer. Use what the details have in common to find the main idea of each section.

Go Digital!
Use the interactive graphic organizer

Narrative Nonfiction

"The Monster in the Mountain" is mostly a first-person narrative by a scientist. Narrative nonfiction:

- Gives factual information about a topic
- May tell one person's experiences related to that topic

 Find Text Evidence

"The Monster in the Mountain" is a scientist's memoir written with the first-person pronouns I and we. A map shows the location of Vesuvius. A model adds information about how Vesuvius formed.

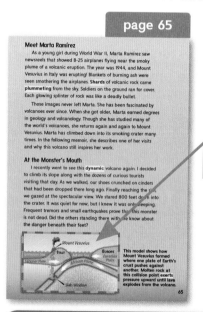

page 65

Meet Marta Ramírez

As a young girl during World War II, Marta Ramírez saw newsreels that showed B-25 airplanes flying near the smoky plume of a volcanic eruption. The year was 1944, and Mount Vesuvius in Italy was erupting! Blankets of burning ash were seen smothering the airplanes. **Shards** of volcanic rock came **plummeting** from the sky. Soldiers on the ground ran for cover. Each glowing splinter of rock was like a deadly bullet.

Those images never left Marta. She has been fascinated by volcanoes ever since. When she got older, Marta earned degrees in geology and volcanology. Though she has studied many of the world's volcanoes, she returns again and again to Mount Vesuvius. Marta has climbed down into its smoking crater many times. In the following memoir, she describes one of her visits and why this volcano still inspires her work.

At the Monster's Mouth

I recently went to see this **dynamic** volcano again. I decided to climb its slope along with the dozens of curious tourists visiting that day. As we walked, our shoes crunched on cinders that had been dropped there long ago. Finally reaching the rim, we gazed at the spectacular view. We stared 800 feet down into the crater. It was quiet for now, but I knew it was only sleeping. Frequent tremors and small earthquakes prove that this monster is not dead. Did the others standing there with me know about the danger beneath their feet?

This model shows how Mount Vesuvius formed where one plate of Earth's crust pushes against another. Molten rock at this collision point exerts pressure upward until lava explodes from the volcano.

65

Text Features

Maps Maps show the locations of places discussed in the text.

Models Models provide simple visual explanations of detailed factual information.

COLLABORATE

Your Turn

Find and list two text features in "The Monster in the Mountain." Tell your partner how each contributes to your understanding of the factual information.

Metaphor and Simile

A simile compares two things or ideas using the words *like* or *as*. A metaphor is a direct comparison that refers to one thing as another. It does not use *like* or *as*.

 Find Text Evidence

On page 65, *I see the word* like *in the sentence,* Each glowing splinter of rock was like a deadly bullet. *This comparison is a simile. In the sentence,* Soon blankets of burning ash were smothering the airplanes, *the burning ash is compared to smothering blankets without using* like *or* as. *This is a metaphor.*

Each glowing splinter of rock was like a deadly bullet.

Soon blankets of burning ash were smothering the airplanes.

Context clues help you understand the comparisons.

Your Turn

Reread the first sentence on page 66. Tell whether it contains a simile or a metaphor. Identify the things being compared. Then identify one more simile and one more metaphor. Tell how the comparisons add to your understanding of the text.

71

Write About the Text

Pages 64–67

Abby

I answered the question: *What effect did the eruptions of Mount Vesuvius have on the environment around it? Use text evidence.*

Student Model: *InformativeText*

Tone and Style
My topic sentence sets a formal tone.

Descriptive Details
I used text evidence to support my ideas.

The eruptions of Mount Vesuvius have consistently had a damaging effect on the environment around it. In the eruption of 79 A.D., the fiery lava and thick ash completely destroyed the cities of Pompeii and Herculaneum and killed almost all the people. The eruption of 1944 sent burning ash into the air, smothering

airplanes. As the eruption shook

buildings for miles around, streams of

scalding lava crushed homes. Today, the

city of Naples lies near the foot of this

dangerous volcano. If the past is any

indication, future eruptions could cause

great damage to Naples and

the people who live there.

José Fuste Raga/Corbis

Grammar

This is an example of a **complex sentence.**

*Grammar Handbook
See page 453.*

Strong Conclusion

My final sentence sums up the future effects that may result from Mount Vesuvius.

Your Turn

How does the author use text features in "The Monster in the Mountain" to show the effects of the eruptions? Use text evidence.

Go Digital!
Write your response online.
Use your editing checklist.

Essential Question

What factors influence how people use money?

Go Digital!

TIME FOR KIDS®

MONEY MATTERS

I don't enjoy shopping, especially during crowded sales. But after my wife and I had twin sons, we learned quickly how to take advantage of cost-saving opportunities.

▶ Besides price, we consider many factors before we spend our money. Among them are how long our family will use an item and how well it is made.

▶ Because prices fluctuate, we try to keep track and plan ahead. That way we spend our money wisely.

Living within our means is important to us, and we plan to teach our children to do the same.

Talk About It

Write words you have learned about using money. Then talk with a partner about what influenced a decision you had to make about using money.

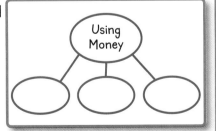

Using Money

Vocabulary

Use the picture and the sentences to talk with a
partner about each word.

available

The school's running track is made
available to local residents on weekends.

What is an antonym of available?

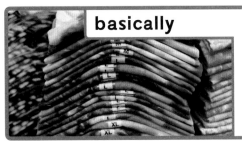

basically

Most of the t-shirts at the street fair
looked **basically** the same.

What is a synonym for basically?

factors

People consider such **factors** as location
and price when choosing a place to live.

What factors do you consider when
choosing a book to read?

fluctuate

The prices of vegetables may **fluctuate**
depending on when they are in season.

What causes the outdoor temperature
to fluctuate?

formula

The guitarist's **formula** for success was a combination of lessons and practice.

What is your formula for doing well on a quiz?

inventory

The store clerk checked to see whether there was enough **inventory** to cover expected sales over the next month.

What is in your inventory of school supplies?

manufactured

The gift shop sold both **manufactured** goods and hand-made items.

Name a manufactured product that you use regularly.

salaries

The annual increase in workers' **salaries** is meant to cover rising costs of living.

What happens when salaries decrease?

Your Turn

COLLABORATE

Pick three words. Write three questions for your partner to answer.

Go Digital!   *Use the online visual glossary*

Essential Question

What factors influence how people use money?

Read how currency has evolved in response to changing needs.

At the U.S. mint in Philadelphia, these "blanks" will soon become pennies.

Stephen Higer/Bloomberg via Getty Images

MAKING MONEY

What do cows, sacks of grain, seashells, strings of beads, and swaths of deerskin have in common? They have all been used as money. Currency in the form of coins and bills is a fairly recent development. And before there was any currency at all, there was barter.

Let's Make a Deal

Barter is **basically** a cashless system for exchanging goods or services. People likely bartered from the earliest days of human society. Maybe someone was good at making tools but needed help hunting for food. Another person was a good hunter but needed an axe to build a shelter. When they bartered, the toolmaker got help hunting, and the hunter got a new axe. Today, the give-and-take of bartering with a neighbor can be a useful **formula** for exchanges of goods and services, but most of us use money to buy what we need.

How Many Cows Does That Cost?

About 9000 B.C., humans developed agriculture and started living in communities. They grew crops and raised animals for food. So the first form of currency was probably livestock. People could pay for goods and services with cattle, sheep, goats, pigs, or camels. Grain and other crops served as money, too. As societies developed, however, ships and caravans made a growing **inventory** of goods **available** for trade over great distances. Suddenly, big live cows and huge sacks of grain were no longer practical to use as currency. People needed money that would not die or spoil after a short time.

Shopping with Shells

About 1200 B.C., the Chinese began using cowrie shells as money. Cowries are animals that live along many coastlines, so people in Africa and India used this more convenient form of currency, too. On the other side of the world, Native Americans made money by stringing beads carved from clamshells. They called their currency *wampum*.

Wampum made from quahog clams

Metal Money

The Chinese were the first to use metal for making currency. At first, they cast bronze or copper into shapes that resembled cowrie shells or small tools. These **manufactured** "coins" later became flat and, eventually, round. Before long, the use of round metal coins was adopted in other parts of the world, including Asia Minor, Greece, and Rome. Many early coins were stamped with images of animals, deities, or kings.

A number of **factors** gave metal coins an advantage over earlier forms of currency. They lasted a long time, were easily recognized and counted,

Examples of coins from the ancient world

and had values based on the metals from which they were made. The rarest metals, such as silver and gold, had the highest values.

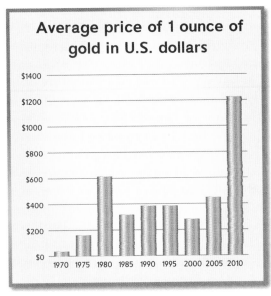

Average price of 1 ounce of gold in U.S. dollars

Paying with Paper

The Chinese developed yet another form of money about 100 B.C. It was flat, like today's paper money, but each "bill" was actually made of deerskin. In the seventh century A.D., the Chinese even started printing the very first paper money. Its popularity in China didn't last, but the idea really caught on in Europe by the eighteenth century.

Money Now

The key idea about money today is that it is issued by governments. In the U.S., your one-dollar bill is worth the same as anyone else's. The same is true for the South African *rand,* the Chinese *yuan,* the Brazilian *real,* and the *euro* of the European Union. However, the value of one nation's currency in relation to others can **fluctuate** daily.

Today's money is far more versatile than ancient varieties. In addition to exchanging actual coins and bills, we can write checks that represent the money we have in the bank. We also use the least physical form of money: electronic, or computer-based, currency. When employers deposit **salaries** directly into their workers' bank accounts, or when we charge an online purchase to a debit or credit card, the exchange is made entirely in the digital realm.

Barter or Bucks?

POINT COUNTERPOINT

Barter Is Better by Jonah M.

I've learned how to get things I need without spending a dime! Officially, it's called "bartering," but it's as simple as trading what I don't need anymore for something I want. Last week I traded my in-line skates for my friend Robert's guitar. It's a lot like recycling: things you were going to throw away will be used by somebody else. Another way to barter is to trade your time and some work for something you want.

The Case for Cash by Haylee D.

Cash lets me choose exactly what I want to buy. I can also compare prices of similar items at different stores. I don't always spend my money right away. My mom helped me open a savings account when I was 7 years old. Whenever I receive some cash, I go straight to the bank to deposit at least half of it. Over time, the money I save, and any interest it earns, will help me buy things I wouldn't be able to afford otherwise.

Make Connections

Talk about how people's changing needs caused them to develop various currencies. ESSENTIAL QUESTION

What are some of the different forms of currency you have used to pay for goods and services? TEXT TO SELF

aincamerastock/Alamy

Reread

Some expository texts include details that are difficult to understand at first. You can pause to reread sections of "Making Money" that are unclear to you.

Find Text Evidence

You may not be sure why metal coins have been a successful form of currency. Reread the section "Metal Money" on page 80.

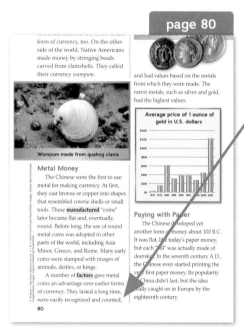

page 80

I read that the shapes of metal currencies had changed over time and that round coins lasted and were "easily recognized and counted." I can infer from this that the advantages of using coins as currency have led people to keep using them even today.

Your Turn

Why is today's money more versatile than money in the past? Reread "Money Now" on page 81 to answer the question. As you read, remember to use the strategy Reread.

Author's Point of View

The author of an expository text may convey a certain attitude toward the topic. This point of view may be mostly objective or show some bias. To identify the author's point of view, list key details and decide what overall attitude they reveal.

 Find Text Evidence

When I reread "Making Money," I can look for the most important points the author is making in each section. Then I can decide whether all the ideas reveal a general point of view about the topic.

Details
Most people today use money instead of bartering.
Long-distance trade made using livestock as currency impractical.
Metal coins had many advantages over earlier forms of currency.

Author's Point of View
Forms of currency have evolved over time. Today's currencies are more versatile and serve people better than ever before.

How are all the details related?

Your Turn

Reread the rest of "Making Money." Identify other key details and list them in the graphic organizer. Then tell how all the details support the author's point of view toward the topic.

Go Digital!
Use the interactive graphic organizer

83

Expository

"Making Money: A Story of Change" is an expository text.

An **Expository** text:

- Often includes photographs to illustrate the text
- May use graphs to show relationships among data
- May include sidebars to provide information from differing points of view

 Find Text Evidence

"Making Money: A Story of Change" explains why people developed various types of currency throughout history. The bar graph provides further information about an idea discussed in the text. The sidebar provides opinions related to the topic.

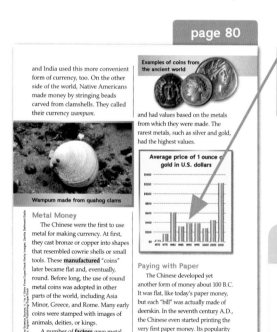

page 80

and India used this more convenient form of currency, too. On the other side of the world, Native Americans made money by stringing beads carved from clamshells. They called their currency *wampum*.

Wampum made from quahog clams

Metal Money

The Chinese were the first to use metal for making currency. At first, they cast bronze or copper into shapes that resembled cowrie shells or small tools. These **manufactured** "coins" later became flat and, eventually, round. Before long, the use of round metal coins was adopted in other parts of the world, including Asia Minor, Greece, and Rome. Many early coins were stamped with images of animals, deities, or kings.

A number of **factors** gave metal coins an advantage over earlier forms of currency. They lasted a long time, were easily recognized and counted,

80

Examples of coins from the ancient world

and had values based on the metals from which they were made. The rarest metals, such as silver and gold, had the highest values.

Average price of 1 ounce of gold in U.S. dollars

Paying with Paper

The Chinese developed yet another form of money about 100 B.C. It was flat, like today's paper money, but each "bill" was actually made of deerskin. In the seventh century A.D., the Chinese even started printing the very first paper money. Its popularity in China didn't last, but the idea really caught on in Europe by the eighteenth century.

Text Features

Graphs Graphs may expand on information in the text and present data visually.

Sidebars Sidebars provide more information related to the topic, often from a different perspective.

 COLLABORATE

Your Turn

Find and list two text features in "Making Money." Tell your partner how each added to your understanding of the topic.

Root Words

Adding a prefix or a suffix to a word changes the word's meaning. When you read an unfamiliar word, first look to see if you recognize its root. Use the meaning of the root word, along with context clues, to help you find the word's meaning.

 Find Text Evidence

I wasn't sure of the meaning of the word directly *on page 81 of "Making Money." I recognize the letters* –ly *as a suffix, so the root word is* direct. Direct *can mean "straight" or "nonstop." The phrase* into their workers' bank accounts *provides a context clue. I think* directly *must mean "in a straight or nonstop way."*

Employers deposit salaries directly into their workers' bank accounts.

Your Turn

COLLABORATE

Use root words and context clues to help you find the meaning of each word from "Making Money."

popularity, *page 80*
relation, *page 81*
varieties, *page 81*

(l to r) Silvio Fiore/SuperStock/Getty Images; Danita Delimont/Gallo Images/Getty Images; Ingram Publishing/SuperStock

Write About the Text

Pages 78–81

Victor

I answered the question: *Is bartering better than using cash in some cases? Support your argument with relevant evidence and clear reasons.*

Student Model: *Argument*

Bartering is better than using cash in some cases. This is especially true for kids. We may not have a lot of money, but we often have things we can barter. For example, suppose I have a key chain my friend wants. She has a phone case I like. We exchange the items, and we're both happy. People can

Introduce a Claim
My opening sentence clearly states my opinion.

Grammar

The writer avoided a **run-on sentence** by inserting the word *and* after the comma in this sentence.

Grammar Handbook See page 453.

Clear Reasons
I supported my argument with relevant details from the text.

also barter their time and work.
For example, I might help a friend
practice her soccer kicks in exchange
for her helping me with homework. In
cases like these, bartering is a way of
saving money, recycling, and getting
things done!

Transitions

I used the phrase *For example* to make the relationship between ideas clear.

Your Turn

What is the easiest form of money to use and why? Support your argument with relevant evidence and clear reasons.

Go Digital!
Write your response online.
Use your editing checklist.

Excursions Across Time

The Big Idea

What can we gain from reading about past civilizations?

The Past

The Past! the dark, unfathom'd retrospect!
The teeming gulf! the sleepers and the shadows!
The past! the infinite greatness of the past!
For what is the present, after all, but a growth out
    of the past?

    —Walt Whitman, from "Passage to India"

Essential Question

What contributions were made by early civilizations?

Go Digital!

(b) Jean Dominique Dallet/Alamy

CRADLES OF CIVILIZATION

If you had any doubt that ancient peoples were skilled engineers, a visit to the Temple of Amun-Re at Karnak in Luxor, Egypt, (at left) would be enough to convince you.

▶ Archaeologists believe the massive sandstone blocks utilized in constructing the 134 carved columns were hauled to Karnak from 100 miles away.

▶ Modern engineers are still puzzling over how beams weighing 140,000 pounds were lifted onto the tops of the 69-foot columns.

Talk About It COLLABORATE

Write words you have learned about the skills of ancient builders and artisans. Then talk with a partner about what ancient buildings and artifacts tell us about the people who made them.

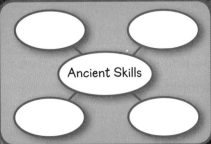

Ancient Skills

(c) Image Source/Getty Images; (it) John Miles/Getty Images ; (ib) ©Dewitt Jones/Corbis

91

Vocabulary

Use the picture and the sentences to talk with a
partner about each word.

artifact

We examined the ancient **artifact** to
figure out how it was made.

Describe the oldest artifact you
have seen.

communal

At the picnic, we all ate together at a
communal table.

What is a synonym for communal?

derived

Lemonade is **derived** from lemons.

What types of foods and drinks can be
derived from apples?

inscription

The **inscription** that goes with her statue
quotes one of her famous speeches.

What else might a statue's inscription
include?

millennium

After ten centuries, a new **millennium** began in the year 2000.

How many decades are there in one millennium?

stationery

Kyle wrote formal thank-you notes on special **stationery**.

How are the words stationery and paper related?

utilize

You should **utilize** all tools safely.

Describe some tools that are dangerous if you utilize them incorrectly.

yields

Farmers use special plant food to increase crop **yields**.

Why would farmers want to produce large yields of crops?

COLLABORATE

Your Turn

Pick three words. Write three questions for your partner to answer.

Go Digital! *Use the online visual glossary*

Empire of the Sea

Essential Question

What contributions were made by early civilizations?

Read about the contributions made by the ancient Phoenicians.

Between the Mountains and the Sea

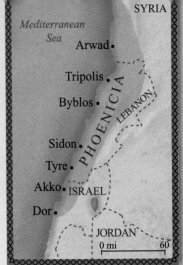

Around 1500 B.C., a remarkable civilization began to develop. Squeezed between tree-covered mountains to the east and the Mediterranean Sea to the west, tiny Phoenicia would flourish for more than 1,000 years. During that **millennium**, the Phoenicians would explore far beyond their homeland and establish a trading empire. It was their clever solutions to key problems that enabled them to thrive.

Resource Rich

*Imagine what it was like to live in Phoenicia. Although your country is not big in size, it is rich in resources. Cedar trees cover the hills. Farmers grow many crops, including large **yields** of grapes, olives, and wheat. There are more than enough resources for your own people. How will you profit from what you don't use?*

To benefit from their resources, the Phoenicians began producing various goods. For example, they cut cedar trees to use as timber for building. They used the shells from a type of snail called the murex to make a highly prized purple dye. And as more than one ancient **artifact** shows, they also made beautiful objects of glass. The Phoenicians believed they could find buyers for all of these goods.

From Cedar Trees to Cargo Ships

Because of Phoenicia's location, your neighbors include Greeks, Egyptians, Hebrews, and other groups. These people are all possible trading partners. The most practical way of reaching them is to cross the Mediterranean. But your merchants have access only to small boats, which cannot hold much cargo. How will you transport your goods to the people who want them?

◀ Modern shipbuilders reproduce the designs of Phoenician ships.

Archaeologists have been able to **utilize** written records from other civilizations to learn about the Phoenicians. From those records, they have **derived** evidence that the Phoenicians constructed enormous cargo ships from cedar wood. They used a method called "keeling the hull." The keel was a large wooden beam forming the central spine of the ship. The ship's curved hull, or frame, was built around the keel. This technique kept the ship strong and stable in the water. As a result, Phoenician ships could safely carry large, heavy loads.

The Phoenicians also became skilled navigators. In earlier times, traders had sailed only during the daytime. They stayed close to the coast for fear of losing their way. But the Phoenicians learned how to find their way using the stars. They could chart a course and steer their ships by locating the North Star, which soon became known as the "Phoenician star."

Trade Routes and Trading Posts

Your work as a Phoenician merchant includes exporting timber, dyed fabrics, glassware, and some foods. You also want to import copper, tin, silk, spices, horses, and papyrus for making **stationery** *to write on. How will you create a system of trade routes for buying and selling these goods?*

At first, there were few set trade routes for the Phoenicians to follow. So they developed their own. They traveled west and south around Africa and north to Europe. Phoenician routes helped other people trade, too. As Phoenician merchants sailed from place to place, they exchanged goods, ideas, and customs among people in many cultures. Their routine ports even developed into cities. Carthage in northern Africa provided a safe harbor for Phoenician merchants over many years.

Timeline of Phoenician History

1300 B.C.
Phoenicians establish treaties with Egypt.

810 B.C.
The port city of Carthage is founded.

600 B.C.
Phoenicians sail as far as present-day Great Britain.

332 B.C.
The Greek army conquers the key Phoenician city of Tyre.

Phoenician Letters.		
K K	A
9 9 9	Bh or B
1	Gh or G
△ 9 △	Dh or D
9 9 N	H
9 9	V or W
1	Z or Ds
□ 日	CH or Hh
⊘ ⅋ *Syriac*	T
⫫ ⫫	J or I
J ﹂	CH or K
∠ >	L
⊐ ⫝	M
9 9 5 ⫝ ⫵	N
⫫	S
O ⊙ ◎	Aa or Gn
﹁ ﹁	Ph or P
Y ⅄	Ts or Ss
▷	K or Q
9 ợ	R
Ш ш	Sh or S
厂	Th or T

▲ The Phoenician alphabet used letters to represent sounds.

From Aleph to Zayin

With trade going well, you need to keep accurate records of sales. But writing systems were complicated. Egyptian writing involved making an **inscription**, *or carving, of symbols called hieroglyphs. Mesopotamian writing, called cuneiform, grouped wedge-like shapes to represent ideas and numbers. What simpler,* **communal** *system of writing could you use to help everyone understand your records?*

The Phoenicians found a solution: an alphabet. This new system of writing used combinations of the same letters to represent different sounds. Beginning with the letter *aleph*, their alphabet included 22 consonants. Because of its simplicity, it was soon widely adopted in many places. It also became the basis for alphabets used in many modern languages, including ours.

By 300 B.C., the Phoenician trading civilization had fallen into decline. But the Phoenicians' alphabet, navigational methods, and shipbuilding designs lived on. Thousands of years later, the contributions of ancient Phoenicia continue to enrich our world.

Make Connections

Talk about the important contributions of the Phoenicians. **ESSENTIAL QUESTION**

Describe how one Phoenician innovation affects your everyday life. **TEXT TO SELF**

North Wind/North Wind Picture Archives

97

Ask and Answer Questions

Asking and answering questions about key details in an expository text can help you understand them. Ask yourself questions as you read each section of "Empire of the Sea."

 Find Text Evidence

When a text includes headings, use them to ask yourself a question before reading each section. If you can answer your question easily, continue on. If not, reread the section.

page 95

Resource Rich

Imagine what it was like to live in Phoenicia. Although your country is not big in size, it is rich in resources. Cedar trees cover the hills. Farmers grow many crops, including large **yields** of grapes, olives, and wheat. There are more than enough resources for your own people. How will you profit from what you don't use?

To benefit from their resources, the Phoenicians began producing various goods. For example, they cut cedar trees to use as timber for building. They used the shells from a type of snail called the murex

Before reading "Resource Rich" I asked, "What does resource rich mean?" <u>I read that Phoenicians had more than enough trees and food and could sell some.</u> Now I know resource rich means having more than you need.

Your Turn

COLLABORATE

Ask yourself a question before reading "From Cedar Trees to Cargo Ships." If you cannot answer the question after reading the section, reread it. Remember to use the strategy Ask and Answer Questions as you read.

Problem and Solution

The structure of an informational text may highlight several problems and the solutions to them. A text about a historical topic may discuss the ways people solved problems in the past.

 Find Text Evidence

When I reread "Empire of the Sea," I note that the author says that the Phoenicians' "clever solutions to key problems . . . enabled them to thrive." I can identify each problem and then look for the solution they found.

Problem	Solution
The Phoenicians needed ways to profit from their many resources.	They produced goods that they believed they could sell.
The Phoenicians needed a way to transport their products.	

Each problem has its own solution.

 COLLABORATE

Your Turn

Reread "Empire of the Sea." For each section, identify the problem that the Phoenicians faced and list it in the graphic organizer. Then identify the solution the Phoenicians found for each problem.

Go Digital!
Use the interactive graphic organizer

Expository

The selection "Empire of the Sea" is an expository text.

An **Expository** text:
- May provide information about people and places in history
- May include timelines and maps

 ### Find Text Evidence

"Empire of the Sea" gives me information about the history and technology of Phoenicia. A timeline provides context by showing dates of important events in Phoenician history. A map shows where this ancient civilization was located.

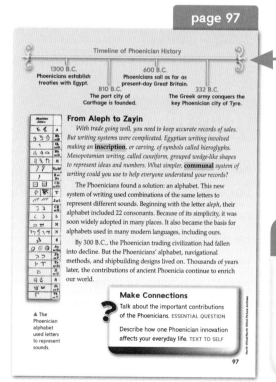

page 97

Timeline of Phoenician History

1300 B.C.
Phoenicians establish treaties with Egypt.

810 B.C.
The port city of Carthage is founded.

600 B.C.
Phoenicians sail as far as present-day Great Britain.

332 B.C.
The Greek army conquers the key Phoenician city of Tyre.

From Aleph to Zayin

With trade going well, you need to keep accurate records of sales. But writing systems were complicated. Egyptian writing involved making an **inscription**, *or carving, of symbols called hieroglyphs. Mesopotamian writing, called cuneiform, grouped wedge-like shapes to represent ideas and numbers. What simpler,* **communal** *system of writing could you use to help everyone understand your records?*

The Phoenicians found a solution: an alphabet. This new system of writing used combinations of the same letters to represent different sounds. Beginning with the letter *aleph*, their alphabet included 22 consonants. Because of its simplicity, it was soon widely adopted in many places. It also became the basis for alphabets used in many modern languages, including ours.

By 300 B.C., the Phoenician trading civilization had fallen into decline. But the Phoenicians' alphabet, navigational methods, and shipbuilding designs lived on. Thousands of years later, the contributions of ancient Phoenicia continue to enrich our world.

Make Connections

Talk about the important contributions of the Phoenicians. ESSENTIAL QUESTION

Describe how one Phoenician innovation affects your everyday life. TEXT TO SELF

▲ The Phoenician alphabet used letters to represent sounds.

97

Text Features

Timelines Timelines show important dates and events in sequence.

Maps Maps may show the location of historical places in relation to present-day national boundaries.

COLLABORATE

Your Turn

Identify two text features in "Empire of the Sea." Tell your partner what information you learned from each of the features.

Latin Roots

As you read "Empire of the Sea," you may come across words you don't recognize. Knowing the meanings of common Latin roots can help you define an unfamiliar word.

 Find Text Evidence

I read the word civilization *in the first sentence on page 95 of "Empire of the Sea." If I know the Latin root* civ- *means "citizen," I can figure out that* civilization *means "a collection of citizens."*

> **Around 1500 B.C., a remarkable civilization began to develop.**

Below are Latin roots for other words in "Empire of the Sea."

Latin Root	Meaning
-struct-	build
nav-	ship
-port-	carry

Your Turn

Use the Latin roots from the chart to help you find the meanings of the following words in "Empire of the Sea."

transport, *page 95*
constructed, *page 96*
navigators, *page 96*

Write About the Text

Pages 94–97

Isabel

I responded to the prompt: *Based on what you have read, describe a typical scene in Carthage during the time of the Phoenicians. Include sensory details.*

Student Model: *Informative Text*

Sensory Details
I mentioned sights and sounds that make it easier to visualize the scene.

Supporting Details
I included text evidence about trade in ancient Carthage.

> The morning sun sparkled on the Mediterranean Sea. Large cargo ships were tied up along the shore of the North African city of Carthage. The ships creaked as the waves rocked them back and forth. Merchants talked, laughed, and bargained with each other. Containers of Phoenician glassware

were placed carefully into carts to be

taken to market. Horse-drawn wagons

were loaded with fragrant cedar wood

from the mountains of Phoenicia.

Trading with Phoenicia helped the

people of Carthage and merchants

from other lands get goods they weren't

able to produce themselves.

Grammar

This sentence includes **common nouns** such as *wagons* and a **proper noun**, *Phoenicia*.

Grammar Handbook See page 454.

Strong Conclusion

My final sentence summarizes the importance of Carthage to the Phoenicians.

Your Turn

How does the author use reasons and evidence to support the claims that Phoenician civilization was a remarkable one?

Go Digital!
Write your response online.
Use your editing checklist.

Essential Question

How did democracy develop?

Go Digital!

Democratic Concepts

This curious arrangement of stacked seats is all that remains of the Bouleuterion, a building built around 175 B.C. for a very special purpose.

▶ People in the ancient Ionian city of Priene governed themselves. The Demos was an annual assembly of all citizens, but the Boule was a smaller elected council of 640 people.

▶ The Bouleuterion was a place for the council to meet and decide important issues, much as the U.S. Senate chamber is today.

Talk About It

COLLABORATE

Write words you have learned about the structure of Priene's government. Then talk with a partner about why you think it was organized this way.

Priene's Government

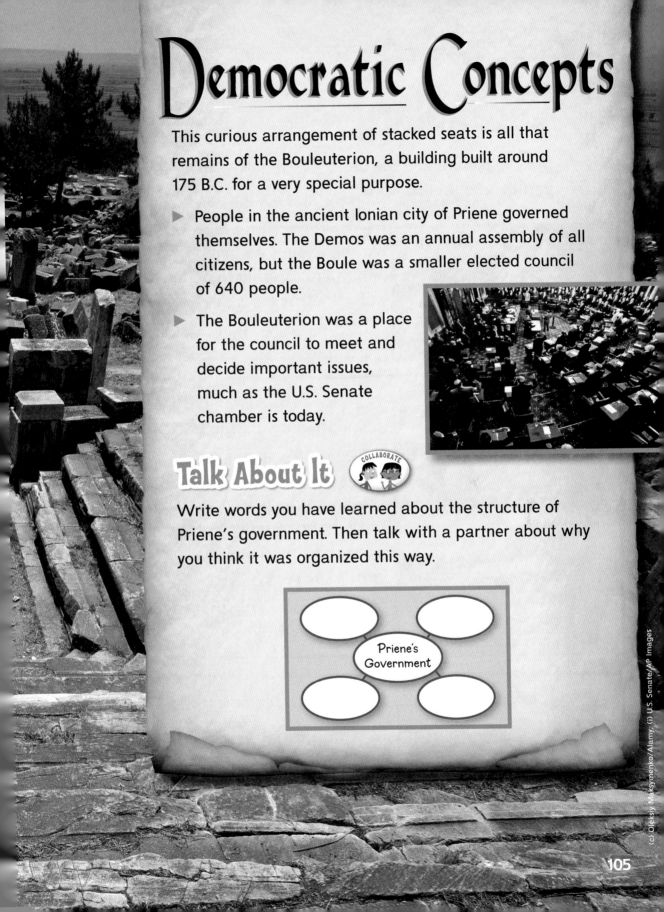

(c) Oleksiy Maksymenko/Alamy, (i) U.S. Senate/AP Images

Vocabulary

Use the picture and the sentences to talk with a
partner about each word.

aspiring

At the tryouts, we heard many singers
who were **aspiring** to perform in our
school talent show.

What is a synonym for aspiring?

foundation

Learning to dribble the ball is a good
foundation for playing basketball.

What is a foundation for playing
baseball?

preceded

The grand marshal's float **preceded** the
rest of the parade.

If you preceded a friend to class, who
would arrive first?

principal

The **principal** ingredients of an omelet
are eggs.

What is the principal ingredient in your
favorite meal?

promote

Many zoos today **promote** the idea of animal conservation.

What idea do you think is important to promote?

restrict

Using a leash can help **restrict** a dog's movements.

How else might you restrict a dog's movements?

speculation

Cloudy skies lead to **speculation** over the chance of rain.

What speculation happens in a detective story?

withstood

The lighthouse **withstood** the hurricane's force.

How are the meanings of withstood and survived similar?

Your Turn

COLLABORATE

Pick three words. Write three questions for your partner to answer.

Go Digital! **Use the online visual glossary**

The Democracy DEBATE

Essential Question

How did democracy develop?

Read about the ideas that philosophers in ancient Greece and Rome had about democracy.

Ocean/Corbis

108

Born and Raised in Greece

Have you ever heard the phrase "government by the people?" That is the meaning of the word *democracy*. The United States is a democratic republic, as are many countries around the world. But where did democracy come from? Some of the earliest ideas about democracy arose in the city of Athens in ancient Greece. But how should democracy be put into practice? The answer to that question has been strongly debated for centuries.

Even when democracy was a new idea, people argued about how it should work. How should power be shared? Should *all* people be allowed to vote and make important decisions? Among the first people to think about these key issues were the ancient Greek philosophers.

Great Minds

The word *philosopher* means "lover of wisdom," a person who seeks knowledge and is able to make good and fair decisions. One of the best-known Greek philosophers, Socrates, lived nearly 2,500 years ago. He valued wisdom highly, and he thought deeply about democracy. Socrates was one of the **principal** critics of government run by the people. He felt that only fair and wise individuals should be allowed to decide things.

Socrates

The ideas that Socrates had about democracy were considered dangerous to the existing democracy in Athens. The current Athenian leaders did not want some other "fair and wise" people **aspiring** to run their city. Socrates was a famous teacher. And **speculation** among the city's leaders included worries that he would encourage young students to pick up his radical ideas. So they chose to execute him.

Students of Philosophy

The philosopher Plato had studied with Socrates. He also thought seriously about democracy. In 380 B.C., Plato shared his ideas about government in his book *The Republic.* He agreed with Socrates that rule by the people would bring

Plato

about poor decisions and a weak government. But, unlike his teacher, he believed that three different groups of people could share the responsibility of governing. The "highest" group would be philosopher-kings guided only by what is best for the state. The second group would be soldiers who protected the state. The last group would be common people who provided goods and services.

Around 388 B.C., Plato formed a school called the Academy. A star pupil there was the philosopher Aristotle, who believed in balance and moderation. About 350 B.C., Aristotle wrote in his book *Politics* that a government that tries to **restrict** power to a few educated men would not work. It would benefit only the rich. A democracy run by common people would not work either, because such people might not make wise decisions.

Aristotle

Aristotle's solution was combining the two. This would give people from all parts of society a voice.

Changes in Rome

About 400 years after Aristotle, the influence of Greek thinking was still felt by philosophers in Rome. Cicero is the best known Roman philosopher. Like Aristotle, he believed a balance of power brought peace and prosperity. That was because different types of people took part in government.

Cicero believed that the Roman republic was the best model for government because it was mixed. It combined features of a monarchy, an aristocracy, and a democracy. Cicero saw that the Roman republic was breaking down, mostly because the aristocracy had gained too much power. In his book, *On the Republic,* he urged a return to a more balanced government.

Cicero

Philosopher Kings

Soldiers

Producers of Goods and Services

Philosopher	Place	Time Period	Ideas About Democracy
Socrates	Greece	469–399 B.C.	Only wise and just people should govern.
Plato	Greece	427–347 B.C.	Rule should be shared by philosopher-kings, soldiers, and providers of goods.
Aristotle	Greece	384–322 B.C.	Educated and common people should each have a role in government.
Cicero	Rome	106–43 B.C.	The Roman republic—a monarch, an aristocracy, and the people—is best.

The Debate Continues

The founders of the United States also thought about how a democracy should be organized. They studied governments that had **preceded** ours and believed that the **foundation** of any new government should revisit Greek and Roman ideas. For example, Thomas Paine wrote booklets to **promote** the idea that people should govern themselves. James Madison admired Aristotle's and Cicero's beliefs in balancing power among different groups.

In 1787, Madison helped Alexander Hamilton write a set of essays called *The Federalist* to encourage states to ratify the Constitution. They made the case for having a *pair* of law-making groups. The smaller Senate would be similar to Rome's senate, while the House of Representatives would give more people a voice. They also endorsed having one president and a system of courts to interpret the laws.

Today, people are still debating what the meaning of *democracy* is and how our government should be organized. The U.S. Constitution has been amended more than 25 times to reflect changing ideas. Yet it is important to remember that our government has roots in ideas from ancient times. Democracy has **withstood** the test of time.

Make Connections

Talk about how the philosophers' ideas influenced our democracy.
ESSENTIAL QUESTION

How does your understanding of democracy compare to the ideas the philosophers had? **TEXT TO SELF**

Ask and Answer Questions

Before reading an informational text such as "The Democracy Debate," use the title and any headings to ask yourself questions that will set your purpose for reading. Answering those questions as you read can help you understand the text.

 Find Text Evidence

Sometimes the author of an informational text introduces an idea right at the beginning that helps you ask a purpose-setting question. Reread the section "Born and Raised in Greece" on page 109 of "The Democracy Debate."

page 109

Born and Raised in Greece

Have you ever heard the phrase "government by the people?" That is the meaning of the word *democracy*. The United States is a democratic republic, as are many countries around the world. But where did democracy come from? Some of the earliest ideas about democracy arose in the city of Athens in ancient Greece. But how should democracy be put into practice? The answer to that question has been strongly debated for centuries.

Even when democracy was a new idea, people argued about how it should work. How should power be shared? Should *all* people be allowed to vote and make important decisions? Among the first people to think about these key issues were the ancient Greek philosophers.

principal crit
government r
the people. H
that only fair
wise individu
should be all
to decide thir

The ide
Socrates had
were conside
existing dem
The current A
not want som
wise" people
their city. Soc
teacher. And
the city's lead
worries that h
young studer
radical ideas.
execute him.

Near the end of the first paragraph, I read the author's question, But how should democracy be put into practice? *I think this is a good question to set my purpose for reading.*

Your Turn

How did you answer the purpose-setting questions you had before you read the section "Great Minds?" If you could not answer your questions, reread the section.

Compare and Contrast

Authors of some informational texts organize their ideas by comparing and contrasting them. A text about history often presents differing views that people had about a topic.

 Find Text Evidence

When I reread "The Democracy Debate," I can look for the ways the author compares and contrasts the ideas that ancient philosophers had about government. Signal words and phrases, such as "unlike" and "agreed with" help me identify how the philosophers' ideas were the same and how they were different.

The center section shows what both have in common.

SOCRATES
believed that only wise people should govern

BOTH
believed that common people should not govern by themselves

PLATO
believed philosopher kings should govern with soldiers and common people

COLLABORATE

Your Turn

Reread "The Democracy Debate." Compare and contrast ideas about government that Plato and Aristotle had. Use the graphic organizer to help you organize the information.

Go Digital!
Use the interactive graphic organizer

113

Expository

"The Democracy Debate" is an expository text.

An **Expository** text:

- May be about a topic from history
- May include headings, diagrams, and charts

Find Text Evidence

"The Democracy Debate" presents different views held by various thinkers in the past. The diagram on page 110 provides a visual representation of one idea. The chart on page 111 shows information from the text in a simple, organized way.

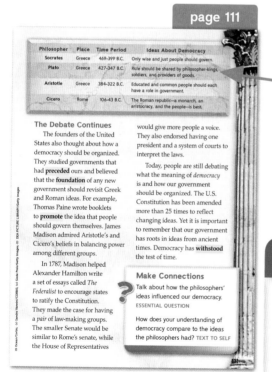

page 111

Philosopher	Place	Time Period	Ideas About Democracy
Socrates	Greece	469-399 B.C.	Only wise and just people should govern.
Plato	Greece	427-347 B.C.	Rule should be shared by philosopher-kings, soldiers, and providers of goods.
Aristotle	Greece	384-322 B.C.	Educated and common people should each have a role in government.
Cicero	Rome	106-43 B.C.	The Roman republic—a monarch, an aristocracy, and the people—is best.

The Debate Continues

The founders of the United States also thought about how a democracy should be organized. They studied governments that had **preceded** ours and believed that the **foundation** of any new government should revisit Greek and Roman ideas. For example, Thomas Paine wrote booklets to **promote** the idea that people should govern themselves. James Madison admired Aristotle's and Cicero's beliefs in balancing power among different groups.

In 1787, Madison helped Alexander Hamilton write a set of essays called *The Federalist* to encourage states to ratify the Constitution. They made the case for having a *pair* of law-making groups. The smaller Senate would be similar to Rome's senate, while the House of Representatives would give more people a voice. They also endorsed having one president and a system of courts to interpret the laws.

Today, people are still debating what the meaning of *democracy* is and how our government should be organized. The U.S. Constitution has been amended more than 25 times to reflect changing ideas. Yet it is important to remember that our government has roots in ideas from ancient times. Democracy has **withstood** the test of time.

Make Connections

Talk about how the philosophers' ideas influenced our democracy. ESSENTIAL QUESTION

How does your understanding of democracy compare to the ideas the philosophers had? TEXT TO SELF

Text Features

Charts Charts often summarize information and compare related details from the text.

Diagrams Diagrams often illustrate specific ideas from the text.

Your Turn

Find and list two text features in "The Democracy Debate." Tell your partner what information you learned from each of the features.

Greek and Latin Prefixes

Knowing the meanings of common prefixes can help you define unfamiliar words. Below are some prefixes and their meanings.

Prefix	Meaning	Example	
en-	"in, into"	*enforce*	→ "put in force; make happen"
pro-	"in front"	*proclaim*	→ "claim or say in front of"
re-	"back, again"	*recall*	→ "call back; think again"

 Find Text Evidence

I am not sure of the meaning of the word encourage *on page 109 of "The Democracy Debate." If I know that the prefix* en- *means "in" or "into," I can figure out that* encourage *means "to put courage into."*

> And speculation . . . included worries that he would
> en|courage young students to pick up his radical ideas.

Your Turn

Use Greek and Latin prefixes from the list above to help you find the meanings of these words from "The Democracy Debate."

protected (*-tect-* means "cover"), *page 110*

reflect (*-flect* means "bend"), *page 111*

Pages 108–111

Write About the Text

Kevin

I responded to the prompt: *Pretend you are Plato. Write an editorial that shows why your ideas about democracy are the best. Support your argument with details from the text.*

Student Model: *Argument*

Introduce a Claim
My thoughts about democracy are addressed in the opening of my editorial.

People of Greece, hear me! When a government is too large, poor decisions often get made. Bad decisions create a weak republic. I have an idea about democracy. Let's divide the people into three groups. Each group will have a role in governing. Philosopher-kings, who are wise and educated, will be

Development
I organized and developed my ideas clearly.

guided by what is best for our state.

Strong, brave soldiers will protect our

state from attacks. Common people will

produce goods and services. All three of

these groups are important to Greece.

So all three groups will help govern and

make Greece stronger.

Grammar

State and *attacks* are examples of **singular** and **plural nouns**.

Grammar Handbook See page 455.

Strong Conclusion
I summarized the importance of a shared government.

Your Turn

Pretend you are one of the founders of the United States. Write an editorial arguing that the proposed United States form of democracy is better than Greek and Roman democracy.

Go Digital!
Write your response online.
Use your editing checklist.

Essential Question

What was life like for people in ancient cultures?

Go Digital!

Living in the Ancient World

When you look at this fresco, or wall painting, from a town in ancient Rome, you can't help wondering what these people were like.

▶ Both the woman and girl are dressed up. Is this a special family occasion? Is the girl the woman's daughter, or her younger sister?

▶ The woman is playing a kind of harp called a *kithara*. What does her expression show? How does she feel about performing?

Do these two remind you of people you know?

Talk About It

Write words you have learned about studying the everyday lives of people who lived in ancient times. Then talk with a partner about what this painting tells you about the ancient Romans.

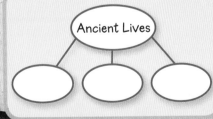

Ancient Lives

Vocabulary

Use the picture and the sentences to talk with a
partner about each word.

alcove

We moved our table into the **alcove** in
our kitchen.

Describe an indoor or outdoor alcove
that you have seen.

commerce

All **commerce** involves trading goods or
services for money.

What types of commerce are you
familiar with?

domestic

The sisters' **domestic** chores include
cleaning up after meals.

What domestic responsibilities do
you have?

exotic

In my city, owning an **exotic** pet, such
as a dangerous snake, is illegal.

What is an antonym for exotic?

fluent

Having lived in Spain, she is **fluent** in English and Spanish.

What people are often fluent in two languages?

stifling

Splashing in a wading pool is one way to cool off in this **stifling** heat.

What is a synonym for stifling?

upheaval

An energetic new puppy can cause some **upheaval** in a home.

How might a puppy cause upheaval?

utmost

A good doctor treats patients with the **utmost** care.

What is a synonym for utmost?

Your Turn

COLLABORATE

Pick three words. Write three questions for your partner to answer.

Go Digital! *Use the online visual glossary*

Yaskul's Mighty Trade

Essential Question

What was life like for people in ancient cultures?

Read about the importance of trade along the Silk Road in the ancient Kushan Empire.

Winson Trang

Located in what is now Afghanistan, the ancient city of Bactra in the Kushan Empire was a key market for merchants traveling the Silk Road trade route. In AD 110, lively commerce attracted merchants from east and west to the famous market in Bactra. In the following, Yaskul, the 12-year-old son of a Bactrian merchant, is eager to make his first official trade.

I Make Plans

It is early, but I am awake. Though we are only in the month of *Hyperberetaios*, it is a cold autumn day. As I quickly dress, I think about how the Chinese caravan arrived last night. If winter comes early, we may not see another caravan for months, as snow will close the passes. My family must have success at the market tomorrow.

Tomorrow I become a trader, I think. Father says I will be there only to watch and learn, but Grandfather says that Father is too cautious. He says Father makes timid trades and does not obtain the best prices, especially for lapis lazuli.

Lapis lazuli! How I love the brilliant blue stone that comes from the mines up north. Grandfather says that even the Egyptians prized this stone. He has awarded me some beads of my own and is instructing me on how to price them. "You listen, and you learn from me. Always watch the eyes of the man you bargain with. The eyes say when he is willing to pay more and when he will walk away."

Thieves!

When Grandfather and I reach our storage room today, Father is already there. "Thieves!" he cries. "They took everything!" Grandfather surveys the room and says it is not everything. I too spot yarn and metal cups tossed on the floor.

Father points to a small **alcove**, a shelf we have carved in the wall. "The thieves missed our wool rugs and sacks of salt. But all our lazuli stones are gone!" I comprehend how little is left for the market tomorrow. What remains are **domestic** items, and common home goods will not fetch many *drachm* coins. The merchants from China will likely dismiss our wares. Quickly, I remind Father that I still have my lazuli beads.

Grandfather peers at me, thinking. "Yes," he says, nodding. "Your stones are now of the **utmost** importance, our only hope for a successful trade. You must convince the Chinese that your stones are of the highest quality, or we will not get the best price."

I swallow hard. Grandfather smiles and puts his hand on my shoulder. "Don't fret, Yaskul. You possess the skill to make this trade a mighty one."

I Make a Friend

In the evening, I slip away to observe the Chinese traders before we meet them at market. I feel my eyes widen when the traders draw close to their fire's light. Their **exotic** robes truly glow with color. They are so much finer than my clothes.

Suddenly, one man of perhaps 19 years walks toward me. I jump back, but he smiles and waves at me. "Do not be frightened." His voice is friendly. "Is Bactra your home?" I am amazed that he is so **fluent** in my language. This young man has traveled much already, I think. "Are you a trader?" he asks me.

"I am Yaskul," I say. "My family are traders." He introduces himself as Zhang. "I have heard that name," I answer. "Did not a great man named Zhang come to Bactra long ago?"

Zhang nods. "Zhang Qian was sent to find allies for us. But he found instead your marvelous marketplace.

He called your people 'shrewd traders.'" We smile. I tell him of the **upheaval** caused today by the theft of our goods. "Your luck was hard. Even so, you will trade well," Zhang says. I hope he is right.

Market Day

I have strung my beads as a necklace, which shows the stones well. Father has guarded our remaining merchandise all night. With Grandfather, we transport it to the marketplace. Today's bright sun will make the stalls grow hot and **stifling**.

I am amazed by all the goods for sale: tea, almonds, elegant ceramics, carved ivory and jade, and the finest Chinese silk. We reach our stall as the Chinese traders arrive. Zhang nods to me as Father begins bartering with the oldest Chinese merchant, but this elder does not seem impressed by our offerings.

Then Zhang speaks. "Do you have any of the vivid blue stones your people are known for?" Grandfather gently pushes me forward. Nervously, I hold out my necklace. I notice the oldest merchant's eyes light up, and I hear myself tell him how particularly fine these beads are. The trading grows lively, and before I realize it, we agree on a high price. I hand him the necklace, and Father collects a handful of drachms.

Zhang winks at me, but says not a word. After the Chinese traders depart, Grandfather embraces me, and even Father thumps me on the back. Now I can truly call myself a trader!

Make Connections

Talk about the importance of trade in the lives of people living in the ancient city of Bactra. **ESSENTIAL QUESTION**

Describe a time when you overcame nervousness to succeed at something important to you. **TEXT TO SELF**

Make Predictions

Pausing occasionally to predict what will happen next can help you understand a story. As you read "Yaskul's Mighty Trade," identify clues in the text that help you **confirm** or **revise** your predictions.

 Find Text Evidence

You may have wondered how Yaskul would be affected by the theft of the lazuli stones. Reread "Thieves!" on pages 123.

page 123

Thieves!

When Grandfather and I reach our storage room today, Father is already there. "Thieves!" he cries. "They took everything!" Grandfather surveys the room and says it is not everything. I too spot yarn and metal cups tossed on the floor.

Father points to a small **alcove**, a shelf we have carved in the wall. "The thieves missed our wool rugs and sacks of salt. But all our lazuli stones are gone!" I comprehend how little is left for the market tomorrow. What remains are **domestic** items and common home goods will not fetch many drachm coins. The merchants from China will likely dismiss our wares. Quickly, I remind Father that I still have my lazuli beads.

I read that Yaskul's beads are the only lazuli stones the family has left. From this I predicted that Yaskul must help his family. When I read that Yaskul would trade the beads himself, it confirmed my prediction.

Your Turn

Reread "I Make a Friend" on page 124. What clues did you use to predict the role Zhang would play during Yaskul's trade the next day? As you read, remember to use the strategy Make Predictions.

Point of View

In fiction, a narrator tells the story. When one of the characters is the narrator, the story has a first-person point of view.

 Find Text Evidence

When I reread "I Make Plans" on page 123, I see that the narrator uses the first-person pronouns I, me, and my. This shows that the story is narrated by one character. I know I will learn about other characters and events only from the narrator's perspective.

Details	Point of View
Yaskul is telling the story, so he is the narrator.	The story has a first-person point of view.
Yaskul uses the pronouns "I," "me," and "my."	

Your Turn

COLLABORATE

Reread "Yaskul's Mighty Trade." Decide what you can and cannot know about the characters and events, and list the information in the graphic organizer. Then tell how you know the story has a first-person point of view.

Go Digital!
Use the interactive graphic organizer

127

Historical Fiction

The story "Yaskul's Mighty Trade" is historical fiction.

Historical Fiction:

- Takes place in a real setting from history and may refer to real people from the past
- May include foreign words that reflect the setting

 Find Text Evidence

I can tell "Yaskul's Mighty Trade" is historical fiction, because the story takes place in a real city in the past. The characters mention a real person in history. Words from other languages, such as drachms, *show that the characters live in a foreign place.*

page 124

Father points to a small **alcove**, a shelf we have carved in the wall. "The thieves missed our wool rugs and sacks of salt. But all our lazuli stones are gone!" I comprehend how little is left for the market tomorrow. What remains are **domestic** items, and common home goods will not fetch many *drachm* coins. The merchants from China will likely dismiss our wares. Quickly, I remind Father that I still have my lazuli beads.

Grandfather peers at me, thinking. "Yes," he says, nodding. "Your stones are now of the **utmost** importance, our only hope for a successful trade. You must convince the Chinese that your stones are of the highest quality, or we will not get the best price."

I swallow hard. Grandfather smiles and puts his hand on my shoulder. "Don't fret, Yaskul. You possess the skill to make this trade a mighty one."

I Make a Friend

In the evening, I slip away to observe the Chinese traders before we meet them at market. I feel my eyes widen when the traders draw close to their fire's light. Their **exotic** robes truly glow with color. They are so much finer than my clothes.

Suddenly, one man of perhaps 19 years walks toward me. I jump back, but he smiles and waves at me. "Do not be frightened." His voice is friendly. "Is Bactra your home?" I am amazed that he is so **fluent** in my language. This young man has traveled much already, I think. "Are you a trader?" he asks me.

"I am Yaskul," I say. "My family are traders." He introduces himself as Zhang. "I have heard that name," I answer. "Did not a great man named Zhang come to Bactra long ago?"

Zhang nods. "Zhang Qian was sent to find allies for us. But he found instead your marvelous marketplace.

124

Historical Setting The setting places the plot in the past.

Foreign Language Words The characters use ancient words from another language.

COLLABORATE

Your Turn

Find two passages in "Yaskul's Mighty Trade" that show it is historical fiction. Tell your partner how each adds to the setting or the plot.

Connotations and Denotations

In a story like "Yaskul's Mighty Trade," the author may use certain words that have a positive or negative tone. The tone that a word has in context is called its **connotation**. A word's straightforward dictionary meaning is called its **denotation**.

 Find Text Evidence

On page 123 of "Yaskul's Mighty Trade," Yaskul uses the words cautious *and* timid *to describe Grandfather's view of Father's trades. Both words have similar meanings, or denotations. But the tone, or connotation, of* timid *is negative, as in "always fearful."* Cautious *has the positive connotation of "being careful."*

> **Grandfather says that Father is too cautious.**
>
> **He says Father makes timid trades.**

Your Turn

Decide whether the connotation of each word, as used in "Yaskul's Mighty Trade," is more positive or negative.
- **tossed,** *page 123*
- **common,** *page 124*
- **shrewd,** *page 125*

Write About the Text

Pages 122–125

Paige

I responded to the prompt: *Add an event to the story. Write a scene in which Yaskul sells a rug to a merchant and gets a good price for it. Include dialogue.*

Student Model: *Narrative Text*

Develop Characters

A new merchant appears in my scene and develops a relationship with Yaskul.

Dialogue

My scene includes a realistic conversation.

> Several other merchants in bright robes stroll past. I call out boldly, "You are passing up fine items!" I surprise myself with my newfound courage and hold my head high as one merchant turns back to look.
>
> "What items?" he asks.
>
> "These fine wool rugs are just what you need," I continue. "Look at the craftsmanship and colors."
>
> "I've seen many rugs today," he says.

130

"But none as handsome as these. See?"

The merchant steps up and examines

the rugs. His interest attracts a crowd.

The merchant runs his fingers across the

rugs slowly. Then he bargains with me for

one large rug and at last offers a good

price. I take his *drachms*, proud of my

second profitable trade.

Grammar

Rugs is a **plural noun**, and *crowd* is a **collective noun**.

Grammar Handbook See page 455.

Strong Conclusion
My ending wraps up the events of the scene.

Your Turn

Add an event to the story in which Yaskul and Zhang talk to each other after Yaskul sells the beads. Make sure to use details from the story.

Go Digital!
Write your response online.
Use your editing checklist.

Essential Question

What influences the development of a culture?

Go Digital!

Cultural Legacies

The rice fields curving along the slopes of Longji Mountain in China are often called "Dragon's Backbone" because of their appearance.

▶ The legacy of terrace farming by the Yao people began here some 700 years ago.

▶ Because rice fields must be flooded each spring, flat "steps" are needed to hold the water.

This agricultural expertise ensures the food supply in a region not well suited to farming.

Talk About It

Write words you have learned about the influence of a landscape on its inhabitants. Then talk with a partner about how the culture of the Yao people is affected by living on Longji Mountain.

Life on Longji Mountain

Vocabulary

Use the picture and the sentences to talk with a
partner about each word.

benefit

One **benefit** of being tall is that you can
see over high walls.

What is a benefit of studying hard?

deftly

The juggler **deftly** kept the apples in the
air for several minutes.

Describe something that you do deftly.

derision

When the team played badly, fans
reacted with **derision**.

How might people show derision for a
sports team?

eaves

The birds built a nest under the **eaves**
of our roof.

Why might birds build a nest under the
eaves?

expertise

The carpenter's **expertise** could be seen in the fine detailing.

What expertise does a chef in a fine restaurant have?

impudence

Laughing at someone shows a lot of **impudence**.

How are the meanings of the words impudence and behavior related?

legacy

My grandmother's scrapbooks preserve a **legacy** of family memories.

How else might a legacy be preserved?

symmetry

The butterfly's wings show beautiful **symmetry**.

What else in nature shows symmetry?

Your Turn

COLLABORATE

Pick three words. Write three questions for your partner to answer.

Go Digital!   *Use the online visual glossary*

(t to b) Vladimir Godnik/beyond/Corbis; MBI/Alamy; Walter B. McKenzie/Getty Images; cs9/ZUMA Press/Newscom

Cusi's Secret

Janet Broxon

? Essential Question

What influences the development of a culture?

Read about how an Incan girl's skill with weaving helps her learn about her culture.

Beautiful textiles had great value to the Inca, whose empire arose in what is now Peru. The year is 1430, and 11-year-old Cusi is an Incan girl with a special talent for weaving. Although few girls were allowed to receive an education in Inca society, Cusi dreams of going to school.

A Family Tradition

As they did most mornings, Cusi and her mother were working at their handheld looms. A curious girl, Cusi asked, "Tell me again, Mama: How is it that our family became such fine weavers?"

"When I was a girl, your grandmother taught me to shear wool from the alpaca in our herds and then to weave with it," Cusi's mother patiently responded. "It was *her* mother—your great grandmother—who had passed our family's **legacy** on to her."

When the sun grew warm, Cusi took her loom to the shadows beneath the **eaves** of their house. Alone now, she gazed over at the girls' schoolhouse gleaming on a nearby hill. "How I wish I could go there," she said longingly. "I do not understand why there are schools for all the boys but so few girls have a chance to learn. It is not fair!"

A Special Invitation

As Cusi was voicing her thoughts, she spied one of the school's *mamaconas*, or teachers, walking along a nearby path. Cusi fell silent as the woman stopped to watch her weave. Pretending not to see the teacher, she did her very best to show off her skills.

Cusi began working a vibrant pattern into the perimeter of the cloth. Her hands **deftly** glided over the woolen strands, darting as quickly as a hummingbird flies. The teacher watched in amazement, impressed by the loveliness and **symmetry** of Cusi's design.

Then Cusi's concentration was broken by a knocking sound. She looked up to see her parents greeting Mamacona at the door. Humbly, the teacher said to them, "I watched your daughter working at her loom. She is young to have such **expertise**. Will you allow her to become one of my students?"

ILLUSTRATIONS: Janet Broxon

Hearing this, Cusi wanted to rush forward and shout for joy, but she knew Incan girls should not display such **impudence**. So she remained still. After what seemed like hours, Cusi's father spoke. "We will miss her, but yes, we would be honored to have Cusi attend school. An education will be of great **benefit** to her."

That night, Cusi's parents made the arrangements for her to begin school. She would leave them in just one week. Cusi felt such optimism, but she was nervous, too.

Much to Learn

Cusi found living at the school so different from being at home. She had to memorize the essentials of Incan history and beliefs, and she also learned to prepare foods, including *chicha morada*, a special drink made from purple corn.

But the highlight of Cusi's new life was weaving class. She relished learning to spin yarn from the precious wool of *vicuñas*. Cusi had glimpsed the tiny camels roaming distant hills, and once on market day she had even secretly stroked a garment made from their silky wool. She knew only royal people could wear such robes. "It is a privilege just to touch fibers as fine as these," she sighed contentedly.

One afternoon, while the other girls were practicing techniques she had already mastered, Cusi began to daydream. Her thoughts drifted back to a day when she had seen a village elder using a *quipu* to count and record the number of alpacas in the herds. The counting tool, made by knotting strands of wool, had fascinated her.

"Excuse me, sir," she had said to the man. "Will you please show me how to use the counting threads?"

With a sneer of **derision**, the man had shouted angrily at Cusi. "Foolish girl! Has no one told you only men may use the *quipu?* Never speak such nonsense again!"

Cusi had run away as fast as her legs would take her, yet she never forgot about the *quipu*. Even now, as she recalled that long ago scene, her fingers worked at tying knots in a wool cord. She was convinced the secrets of this forbidden tool were the key to great knowledge.

Suddenly, a classmate's shout startled Cusi from her thoughts. "Cusi has fallen asleep!" The girls broke into laughter and, blushing, Cusi hid the knots in her lap.

"Enough!" the teacher said to quiet the class. "Cusi, please step outside."

A Secret to Treasure

When they were alone, Mamacona gestured toward the knotted wool that Cusi held behind her back. "Show me what you have made," she said sternly. When Cusi gave her the knots, the woman's eyes widened in alarm. "Is this a *quipu?* Women should not possess these things. You take great risk!"

"But if I knew how to use the *quipu,*" Cusi pleaded, "I could keep school records, and the royal merchants could no longer cheat us when buying our *vicuña* robes."

Mamacona struggled with her thoughts. She knew well the ban against women using the *quipu*, but she herself had possessed this thirst for knowledge when she was a girl. She recalled how her brother had secretly taught her to keep accounts with the *quipu*. In the end, she was won over by Cusi's hopeful plea.

"I will teach you to make a *quipu* properly," she whispered. Cusi's face lit up. "*But*...you must promise never to tell anyone!"

Cusi hugged her teacher. "Thank you, Mamacona. I promise. I will not disappoint you. I will learn, and I will forever keep our secret!"

Make Connections

Talk about the importance of wool and weaving in the Inca culture. **ESSENTIAL QUESTION**

Describe a time when you learned something you had wanted to know for a long time. **TEXT TO SELF**

Make Predictions

As you read a story, use what you learn about the characters, setting, and plot to **confirm** or **revise** predictions you make. After each section of "Cusi's Secret," predict what will happen next. Use text evidence to confirm or revise your predictions.

 Find Text Evidence

You may have used what the introduction says about the lives of Incan girls to predict whether Cusi will be able to attend school. Reread "A Special Invitation" to help you confirm or revise your prediction.

> **page 138**
>
> remained still. After what seemed like hours, Cusi's father spoke. "We will miss her, but yes, we would be honored to have Cusi attend school. An education will be of great **benefit** to her."
>
> That night, Cusi's parents made the arrangements for her to begin school. She would leave them in just one week. Cusi felt such

It surprised me when Cusi's father agreed to let Cusi attend school. I had predicted that Cusi, like most Incan girls, would not get a formal education. So I revised my predictions about the rest of the story.

Your Turn

What prediction did you make after reading "Much to Learn"? Identify the passages in the story that you used to confirm or revise your prediction.

Point of View

When a narrator who is *not* one of the characters tells the story, the story has a **third-person point of view**. A third-person narrator lets readers know what *each* of the characters thinks.

 Find Text Evidence

When I reread "A Family Tradition" on page 137 of "Cusi's Secret," I see that neither Cusi nor her mother is telling the story. The narrator is not participating in the action. I will learn about the events from the perspectives of more than one character.

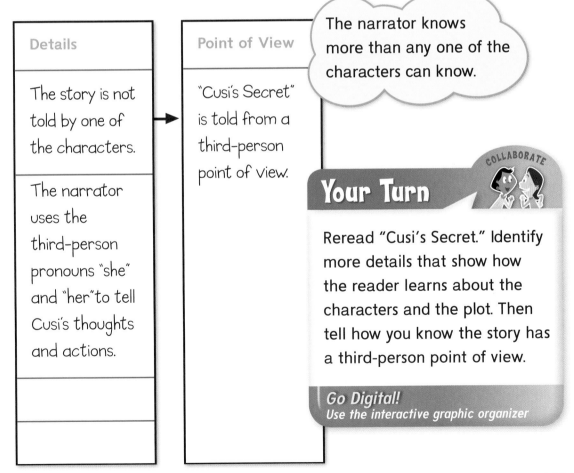

Details	Point of View
The story is not told by one of the characters.	"Cusi's Secret" is told from a third-person point of view.
The narrator uses the third-person pronouns "she" and "her" to tell Cusi's thoughts and actions.	

The narrator knows more than any one of the characters can know.

Your Turn COLLABORATE

Reread "Cusi's Secret." Identify more details that show how the reader learns about the characters and the plot. Then tell how you know the story has a third-person point of view.

Go Digital!
Use the interactive graphic organizer

141

Historical Fiction

The author of "Cusi's Secret" uses what historians know about the past to create a realistic setting and plot.

Historical Fiction:
- Usually includes dialogue
- May include flashbacks to earlier times in the characters' lives

 Find Text Evidence

"Cusi's Secret" uses historical facts about life in the Inca Empire, but the characters and dialogue are imagined by the author. It includes flashbacks to tell us more about the characters' pasts.

page 138

Hearing this, Cusi wanted to rush forward and shout for joy, but she knew Incan girls should not display such **impudence**. So she remained still. After what seemed like hours, Cusi's father spoke. "We will miss her, but yes, we would be honored to have Cusi attend school. An education will be of great **benefit** to her."

That night, Cusi's parents made the arrangements for her to begin school. She would leave them in just one week. Cusi felt such optimism, but she was nervous, too.

Much to Learn

Cusi found living at the school so different from being at home. She had to memorize the essentials of Incan history and beliefs, and she also learned to prepare foods, including *chicha morada*, a special drink made from purple corn.

But the highlight of Cusi's new life was weaving class. She relished learning to spin yarn from the precious wool of *vicuñas*. Cusi had glimpsed the tiny camels roaming distant hills, and once on market day she had even secretly stroked a garment made from their silky wool. She knew only royal people could wear such robes. "It is a privilege just to touch fibers as fine as these," she sighed contentedly.

One afternoon, while the other girls were practicing techniques she had already mastered, Cusi began to daydream. Her thoughts drifted back to a day when she had seen a village elder using a *quipu* to count and record the number of alpacas in the herds. The counting tool, made by knotting strands of wool, had fascinated her.

"Excuse me, sir," she had said to the man. "Will you please show me how to use the counting threads?"

With a sneer of **derision**, the man had shouted angrily at Cusi. "Foolish girl! Has no one told you only men may use the *quipu*? Never speak such nonsense again!"

Cusi had run away as fast as her legs would take her, yet she never forgot about the *quipu*. Even now, as she recalled that long ago scene, her fingers worked at tying knots in a wool cord. She was convinced the secrets of this forbidden tool were the key to great knowledge.

Dialogue Dialogue lets characters speak for themselves.

Flashback Flashbacks are events that happened before the current plot events.

 COLLABORATE

Your Turn

Find two examples of information that is based on historical fact in "Cusi's Secret." Then identify one example of a flashback.

138

Greek and Latin Suffixes

Common suffixes can help you define an unfamiliar word. Below are some Greek and Latin suffixes and their meanings:

Suffix	Meaning	Example
-ion, -tion, -sion	"the state of"	*educating → education*
-ism	"the state of"	*being real → realism*
-ize	"to make"	*a summary → summarize*
-ous	"full of"	*fame → famous*

 ## Find Text Evidence

I read the word concentration *on page 137. If I know that the suffix* -ion *means "the state of," I can figure out that* concentration *means "the state of concentrating."*

Then Cusi's <u>concentration</u> was broken by a knocking sound.

Your Turn

Use a suffix from the chart above to help you find the meaning of each of these words from "Cusi's Secret."

optimism (*optim-* means "best, favorable"), *page 138*

nervous, *page 138*

memorize, *page 138*

Tell how you used the suffix to help you understand the meaning of each word.

Write About the Text

Pages 136–139

Nicolás

I responded to the prompt: *Write a paragraph from Mamacona's point of view telling how she feels about the Incan tradition of weaving. Use details from the text.*

Student Model: *Narrative Text*

I watched from the doorway as the girls wove silky yarn into their handheld looms. Some were struggling, but Cusi was doing exceptionally well. Her pattern was intricate with intense reds and yellows, making me think of a bright sunrise over the mountains. As the girls worked, I recalled learning

Point of View

I wrote the story in first person to show that it is from Mamacona's perspective.

Descriptive Details

I used words like *intricate* and *intense* to help the reader picture what I am describing.

Transitions

I used words and phrases to tell when a scene takes place.

Jose Luis Pelaez Inc/Blend Images/Getty Images

144

to weave on my mother's loom until

I was given my own. My mother had

explained that fine weaving was an

Incan tradition going back many years.

I had been proud to learn of my people's

tradition, and it made me happy to

share it with my students.

Grammar

Possessive nouns such as *mother's* and *people's* show ownership of something.

Grammar Handbook *See page 456.*

Your Turn

Write a paragraph from Cusi's point of view about the next time she sells her vicuña robes to the royal merchants. Use text evidence for support.

Go Digital!
Write your response online.
Use your editing checklist.

Essential Question

What can the past teach us?

Go Digital!

LISTENING TO THE PAST

I'd seen photographs of ruins like this.
But it wasn't until we were standing
right inside this Greek temple in Sicily
that I started contemplating what people
might have been thinking 2,400 years ago.

▶ Why did they choose this place? How did
they decide on the number of columns?

▶ And what can something that has survived all
these years tell us about ourselves?

As we looked at the beautiful scene, it was as
if we could hear the voices of people from long ago,
commemorating their job well done.

Talk About It

Write words you have learned
about examining objects made
long ago. Then talk with a
partner about a time you learned
something from the past.

Lessons from
the Past

Vocabulary

Use the picture and the sentences to talk with a
partner about each word.

commemorate

We watch fireworks as a way to
commemorate the Fourth of July.

How do you commemorate
Thanksgiving Day?

contemplate

The girls had to **contemplate** whether
they should go out or stay home.

What decision have you had to
contemplate?

forlorn

Lisa felt **forlorn** when her best friend
moved away.

What is an antonym of forlorn?

majestic

The grand, snow-topped mountain range
looked **majestic** in the distance.

What is a synonym for majestic?

Poetry Terms

lyric poetry

I like reading **lyric poetry** because it expresses the poet's strong personal feelings.

What might the topic of a lyric poem be?

sonnet

Each of the 14 lines in a **sonnet** contains pairs of stressed and unstressed syllables.

Tell why you think a sonnet would be easy or hard to write.

rhyme scheme

A poem's **rhyme scheme** is the pattern made by its end rhymes.

Why must you read an entire poem to identify its rhyme scheme?

meter

You can hear stressed and unstressed syllables when a poem with strong **meter** is read.

How could you determine the meter in a poem?

COLLABORATE

Your Turn

Pick three words or poetry terms, and write a question about each for your partner to answer.

Go Digital! **Use the online visual glossary**

Essential Question
What can the past teach us?

Read how two poets
experience the past and
what they learn from it.

Ozymandias

I met a traveler from an antique land

Who said: "Two vast and trunkless legs of stone

Stand in the desert . . . Near them, on the sand,

Half sunk, a shattered visage lies, whose frown,

And wrinkled lip, and sneer of cold command,

Tell that its sculptor well those passions read

Which yet survive, stamped on these lifeless things,

The hand that mocked them, and the heart that fed:

And on the pedestal these words appear:

'My name is Ozymandias, king of kings:

Look on my works, ye Mighty, and despair!'

Nothing beside remains. Round the decay

Of that colossal wreck, boundless and bare

The lone and level sands stretch far away."

—Percy Bysshe Shelley

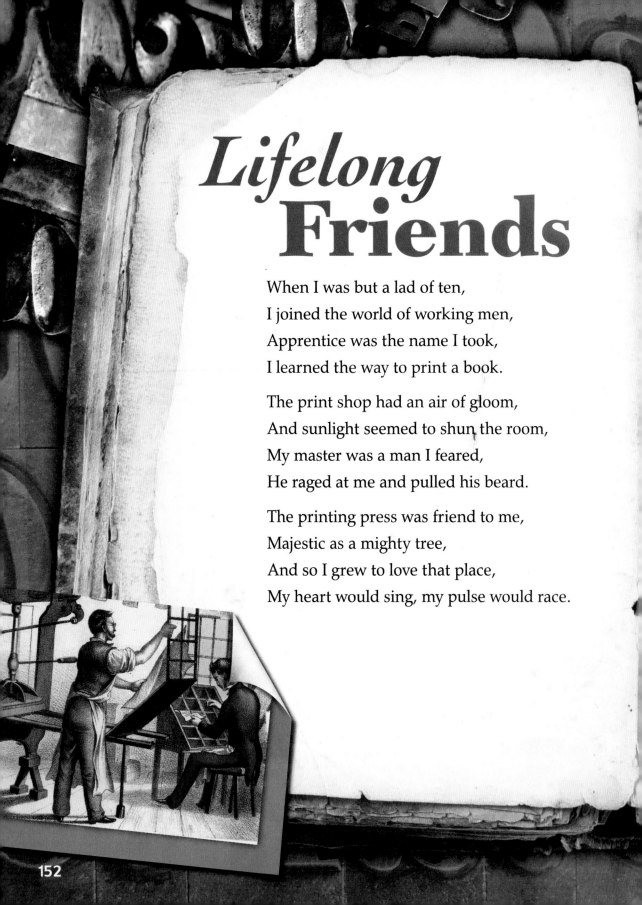

Lifelong Friends

When I was but a lad of ten,
I joined the world of working men,
Apprentice was the name I took,
I learned the way to print a book.

The print shop had an air of gloom,
And sunlight seemed to shun the room,
My master was a man I feared,
He raged at me and pulled his beard.

The printing press was friend to me,
Majestic as a mighty tree,
And so I grew to love that place,
My heart would sing, my pulse would race.

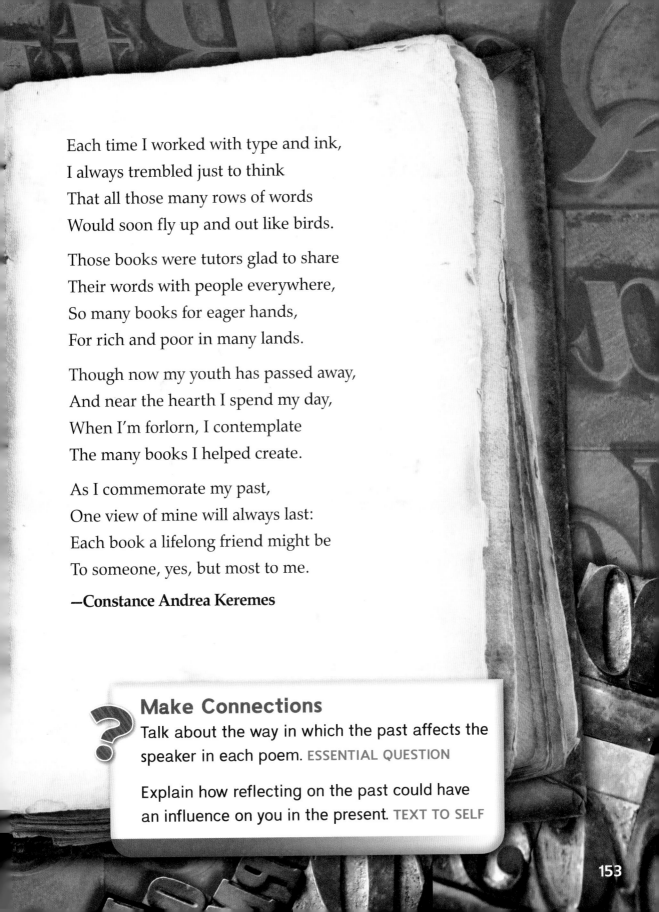

Each time I worked with type and ink,
I always trembled just to think
That all those many rows of words
Would soon fly up and out like birds.

Those books were tutors glad to share
Their words with people everywhere,
So many books for eager hands,
For rich and poor in many lands.

Though now my youth has passed away,
And near the hearth I spend my day,
When I'm forlorn, I contemplate
The many books I helped create.

As I commemorate my past,
One view of mine will always last:
Each book a lifelong friend might be
To someone, yes, but most to me.

—Constance Andrea Keremes

Make Connections

Talk about the way in which the past affects the speaker in each poem. ESSENTIAL QUESTION

Explain how reflecting on the past could have an influence on you in the present. TEXT TO SELF

Lyric Poetry and Sonnet

Lyric poetry:
- Expresses the speaker's thoughts or personal feelings
- Has a musical quality but does not always rhyme

A **sonnet**:
- Has fourteen lines and a pattern to its end rhymes
- Uses pairs of stressed and unstressed syllables

 Find Text Evidence

The speaker in "Ozymandias" describes a reaction to a ruined statue. When I read the poem out loud, it sounds almost like a song, so I think it's a lyric poem. It has fourteen lines, a pattern of rhyming words, and a pattern of stressed and unstressed syllables in each line. This structure tells me it's also a sonnet.

page 151

I met a traveler from an antique land
Who said: "Two vast and trunkless legs of stone
Stand in the desert . . . Near them, on the sand,
Half sunk, a shattered visage lies, whose frown,
And wrinkled lip, and sneer of cold command,
Tell that its sculptor well those passions read
Which yet survive, stamped on these lifeless things,
The hand that mocked them, and the heart that fed:
And on the pedestal these words appear:
'My name is Ozymandias, king of kings:
Look on my works, ye Mighty, and despair!'
Nothing beside remains. Round the decay
Of that colossal wreck, boundless and bare
The lone and level sands stretch far away."

—Percy Bysshe Shelley

Rhyming words may be at the ends of every other line.

Your Turn

COLLABORATE

Reread "Lifelong Friends" on pages 152–153. Decide if it is an example of a lyric poem. Then determine if it is a sonnet and explain why.

Theme

The theme of a poem is the overall idea, or message about life, that the poet wants to communicate. Usually, the poet does not state the theme directly. To determine a poem's theme, look for key details that provide clues about the message the poet wants to convey.

Find Text Evidence

In "Lifelong Friends," the speaker describes the "gloom" of the print shop and how his master "raged." Yet he loves working with the "majestic" printing press and the idea of making books for people to read. I can look for more details about this contradiction to infer the poet's message and identify the theme of poem.

> What message does the poet want to share?

Detail
The print shop had an air of gloom

↓

Detail
My master was a man I feared

↓

Detail
When I'm forlorn, I contemplate, The many books I helped create.

↓

Theme
Challenging work can be fulfilling.

COLLABORATE

Your Turn

Reread "Ozymandias." Identify key details and record them in the graphic organizer. Then use the details to determine the theme.

Go Digital!
Use the interactive graphic organizer

155

Rhyme Scheme and Meter

The **stanzas,** or groups of lines in a poem, often contain sound patterns. One pattern is a **rhyme scheme,** which places rhyming words at the ends of lines. Another pattern involves a combination of stressed and unstressed syllables called **meter.** Rhyme schemes and meter give poetry a lyrical, musical quality.

 Find Text Evidence

Reread "Lifelong Friends" on pages 152–153. Listen for sound patterns within the poem. Pay attention to both rhyming patterns and patterns of stressed and unstressed syllables.

page 152

Lifelong Friends

When I was but a lad of ten,
I joined the world of working men,
Apprentice was the name I took,
I learned the way to print a book.

The print shop had an air of gloom,
And sunlight seemed to shun the room,
My master was a man I feared,
He raged at me and pulled his beard.

The printing press was friend to me,
Majestic as a mighty tree,
And so I grew to love that place,
My heart would sing, my pulse would race.

152

The last words in each pair of lines rhyme. If I use letters to represent this pattern, each stanza has a rhyme scheme of aabb. *Each line has four pairs of syllables. The first syllable in each pair is unstressed and the second is stressed.*

Your Turn

Reread "Ozymandias." Use letters to represent the rhyme scheme in lines 11-14. Then tell whether the pattern of stressed and unstressed syllables is the same in each line.

Personification

Personification is a kind of figurative language that poets use to make descriptions and images more vivid. When poets use this device, which gives human abilities or feelings to nonhuman objects, animals, or ideas, we see ordinary things in a new way.

 Find Text Evidence

In the sixth line of "Lifelong Friends," And sunlight seemed to shun the room, *the poet gives a human ability to the sunlight. This personification of sunlight gives me a mental image of sunlight purposely avoiding the room, the way a person might.*

The print shop had an air of gloom,
And sunlight seemed to shun the room,
My master was a man I feared,
He raged at me and pulled his beard.

Your Turn

Find two more examples of personification in the poem "Lifelong Friends." Tell how each helps you understand an idea the poet is trying to convey with figurative language.

157

Tetra Images/Getty Images

Write About the Text

Pages 150–153

Brianna

I responded to the prompt: *Write a lyric poem about a place you love to visit. Use precise language.*

Student Model: *Narrative Text*

In the Mountains

Look at the mighty mountains,

In shades of green and blue.

I think that they are smiling

As they call to me and you.

So up into the mountains,

My happy family hikes,

Sometimes we take a picnic lunch,

Sometimes we bring our bikes.

Precise Language

I used vivid words to help readers visualize my observations.

Narrator

I introduced myself as the narrator of the poem.

Transitions
I used phrases such as *At other times* to set some events apart in time.

At other times I like to sit

Upon a rocky ridge,

With no one there for company

Except for my dog, Midge.

Grammar

The word *Midge* is an example of an **appositive**.

Grammar Handbook See page 456.

We listen to the chipmunks play

And watch soft, white clouds roam,

We feel the wind blow through

our hair,

And then we head for home.

Your Turn

Write a lyric poem about an important event from your past. Use precise language.

Go Digital!
Write your response online.
Use your editing checklist.

ewg3D/Getty Images

ACCOMPLISHMENTS

The Ballad of Malcolm McBride

They said, "You can't do it," to Malcolm
   McBride,
"It's a goal too complex to attain."
But twelve-year-old Malcolm had hopes and
   a dream
And a plan he that he soon would make
   plain:

"The kids around here need a safe spot to
   play in,
A site we can call 'our own space.'
Since nobody uses the lot by the river,
It seems like it's just the right place."

The land was for sale, but the city said, "No,
This year's budget can stand no more debt.
Remaking a lot that's all ragged and rough
Would take funds we don't have, we
   regret."

Not ready for softball or football or soccer,
The lot was all thistles and rocks,
Strewn with garbage: glass jars, plastic
   bottles, and boxes,
And even some worn-out old socks.

But Malcolm McBride sent appeals to
   The News:
"Is there no one to whom we can turn?
Will no businesses step in to help with
   some money?
The rest of the funds we can earn."

Then Malcolm McBride asked a few of
   his buddies
To set up a table in town.
While most passed them by, there were
   some volunteers
Who said, "Sure, you can put our names
   down."

Then a company offered to buy the old lot,
Volunteers truly did come to clean it.
When done, it looked great; with a cheer
   Malcolm said,
"Look what happens when you really
   mean it!"

—Carlos Jackson

MIXA next/Getty Images

The BIG Idea

What does it take to accomplish a goal?

Essential Question

What happens when people share ideas?

Go Digital!

Jim West/PhotoEdit Inc.

162

Sharing Ideas

When the city finally approved funding for our mural project, we realized we had to negotiate with each other over which design to use.

▶ We tossed around lots of ideas. Finding common ground was the hard part.

▶ It came down to a silhouette of our city's skyline or a sunburst. Then someone had the insight that we could combine both designs!

When everybody shares ideas, it makes all the difference.

Talk About It

COLLABORATE

Write words you have learned about finding common ground. Then talk with a partner about a time when sharing ideas had a positive outcome.

Finding Common Ground

163

Vocabulary

Use the picture and the sentences to talk with a
partner about each word.

capacity

This car has a seating **capacity** of
four people.

How are the meanings of capacity and
full related?

enthralled

The new parents are **enthralled** by
their baby.

Describe something that has enthralled
you in the past.

fallow

The farmer left the field **fallow** for a
year before planting another corn crop.

What is a synonym for fallow?

insight

Artifacts made by people long ago give
scientists **insight** into ancient cultures.

Tell how the books you have read would
give people insight into your personality.

negotiate

My mother was able to **negotiate** a lower price for the car.

What other situations often require people to negotiate?

regulation

All the players must wear **regulation** uniforms during a game.

What regulation procedures must you follow at school?

resemblance

A frog's **resemblance** to a certain type of toad may make it hard to tell them apart.

What other animals bear a close resemblance to one another?

unseemly

The old, abandoned house had an **unseemly** appearance.

What might make an old house look unseemly?

Your Turn

COLLABORATE

Pick three words. Write three questions for your partner to answer.

Go Digital! *Use the online visual glossary*

The Rockers Build a Soccer Field

Essential Question
What happens when people share ideas?

Read how all members of a team contribute toward reaching their goal.

Peter Ferguson

166

A Dream to Share

"*Buenos días*, Mariana," Mr. Sanchez greeted his daughter at the breakfast table. "*¿Dormiste bien?*"

"I slept very well, Papa. I had a dream that I scored the winning goal on a brand new soccer field!"

Mr. Sanchez smiled and said, "Your dream could be a sign that River Edge will finally get a **regulation** soccer field. Maybe you have special **insight** into what will happen at tonight's Town Council meeting. Remember, we must get the whole team there to convince them we need a better field."

That night, Mariana and her father arrived at the meeting hall to find it filled to **capacity**. They sat with the other River Edge Rockers, their community soccer team. Councilwoman Maloof opened the discussion, and Mr. Boyd, the Rockers' manager, spoke first. "Our team currently practices in a tiny school yard, and only when it's not already booked." The team nodded briskly.

Mrs. Yamagata, owner of Something Sushi, walked to the podium. "I believe the town owns an empty lot next to my restaurant," she said. "Couldn't that be a soccer field?" The Rockers applauded.

"A soccer field would be a good use for that lot," Councilwoman Maloof said. "But the town simply doesn't have the money to build and maintain one."

"The Rockers can do it!" Jamil spoke up.

"Jamil's right," Mr. Sanchez said. He began to **negotiate** with the Council. "If the town lets the Rockers use the vacant lot, *we* will turn it into a soccer field."

After some discussion, the Council reached a decision. "We hereby approve using the vacant lot adjacent to Something Sushi for a community soccer field!" Mariana looked nervously at her cheering teammates, then at her father. Mr. Sanchez winked at her, as if to say, "Didn't you have a dream?"

Dirty Dogs Raise Funds

The following day, at Something Sushi, the team got together to share ideas for raising money. "A karaoke night would be fun," said Mariana.

"Cool!" Jamil shouted. "I'll get to show off my incredible voice."

"Next idea—*please!*" the team's goalie, Benny Chan, joked.

"What about a car wash?" suggested Mr. Boyd.

"That's good," Benny said, "except the Environment Club is already having one." Then suddenly he shouted, "Hey, let's have a DOG wash!" Everyone thought it was a great idea—until they met the dirty dogs.

On the day of the dog wash, dog owners lined up in the middle school parking lot, where six wading pools had been set up. Mariana began washing a large shaggy dog, shielding herself from the suds that flew each time the dog shook himself off. Suddenly, a poodle Jamil was washing jumped out of the pool to chase a dachshund. Then several others took off, barking and tangling their leashes.

Mr. Boyd was not amused. "Owners, control your dogs!" After this near disaster, things settled into a routine. By the end of the day, the Rockers were soaked through but ecstatic about raising $750.

Peter Ferguson

This Lot Rocks!

A week later, the team gathered at the lot, carrying tools purchased with their earnings. Staring at the **fallow** field of dirt, rubble, and weeds Mariana thought, "This bears no **resemblance** to the soccer field in my dream." But she kicked into action with the others, scooping up debris and depositing it in a rented dumpster.

Then Mariana bent down to pick up a rock. She grunted when it wouldn't budge. Jamil helped her shovel around it until they saw it was a huge boulder. Mr. Sanchez studied it. *"Esta roca es enorme.* We need a bigger tool." All were awed when he returned a while later with a backhoe.

After the boulder had been extracted, they all looked into the gaping hole. "Let's haul in dirt from the perimeter," Jamil proposed. It took a while, but with everyone working together they moved enough soil from the field's edges to fill the hole. In the next few weeks, the Rockers even enlisted neighbors to donate materials for a drainage system, sod for grass, and bleachers.

Opening day attracted a huge crowd of soccer fans, all **enthralled** by the new field. Before the game, the Rockers huddled together. "We did it. Together we turned an **unseemly** lot into our 'field of dreams,'" Mr. Boyd said. "Now let's get out there!"

Later, as the clock was running out on the 0-0 score, Mariana kicked the ball hard. When she saw it slip through the opposing goalie's hands, she realized that her dream had actually come true!

Make Connections

Tell how sharing ideas helps build the soccer field. **ESSENTIAL QUESTION**

When has working with others helped you accomplish a goal? **TEXT TO SELF**

Make Predictions

Sometimes the narrator or the characters in a story provide clues to what will happen later in the plot. You can use these clues to make predictions. As you continue reading, **confirm** or **revise** your predictions.

 Find Text Evidence

You may have made a prediction about what will happen at the Town Council meeting after you read the first three paragraphs on page 167 of "The Rockers Build a Soccer Field."

---

page 167

"I slept very well, Papa. I had a dream that I scored the winning goal on a brand new soccer field!"

Mr. Sanchez smiled and said, "Your dream could be a sign that River Edge will finally get a **regulation** soccer field. Maybe you have special **insight** into what will happen at tonight's Town Council meeting. Remember, we must get the whole team there to convince them we need a better field."

That night, Mariana and her father arrived at the meeting hall to find it filled to **capacity**. They sat with the other River Edge Rockers, their community soccer team. Councilwoman Maloof opened the discussion, and Mr. Boyd, the Rockers' manager, spoke first. "Our team currently practices in a tiny school yard, and only when it's not already booked." The team nodded briskly.

Mr. Sanchez says Mariana's "dream could be a sign" about what will happen at the Town Council meeting. From this, I predicted the Council will play a role in building a new soccer field.

Your Turn

Explain how you confirmed or revised your prediction about the town council's role in building the field. Identify the passages in the story that support your answer.

Theme

The theme of a story is the overall idea or message the author wants to convey. It is usually not stated directly. To determine a story's theme, consider what the characters do and experience as the events in the plot unfold.

 Find Text Evidence

When I reread "The Rockers Build a Soccer Field," I see that Mariana is the main character. To help me decide what the theme of the story is, I can ask myself what Mariana's experience was as she and her team worked together to build the soccer field.

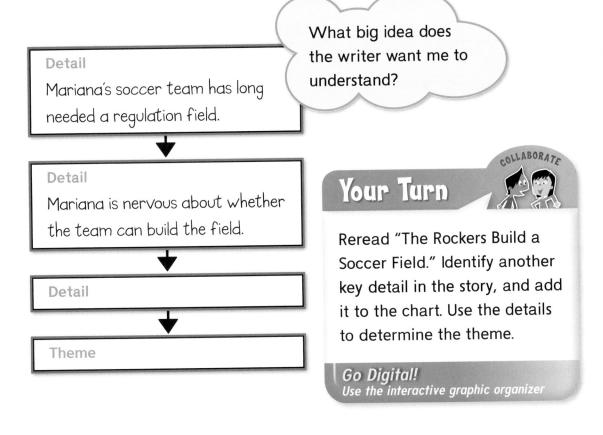

What big idea does the writer want me to understand?

Detail

Mariana's soccer team has long needed a regulation field.

Detail

Mariana is nervous about whether the team can build the field.

Detail

Theme

COLLABORATE

Your Turn

Reread "The Rockers Build a Soccer Field." Identify another key detail in the story, and add it to the chart. Use the details to determine the theme.

Go Digital!
Use the interactive graphic organizer

Realistic Fiction

"The Rockers Build a Soccer Field" is fiction that has realistic characters, setting, and plot.

Realistic fiction:
- May include foreign language dialogue
- May contain foreshadowing to hint at later events

Find Text Evidence

"The Rockers Build a Soccer Field" has a realistic setting and plot. Mr. Sanchez's dialogue in Spanish tells us about his background. Mariana's dream foreshadows what may happen later.

---

page 167

A Dream to Share

"Buenos días, Mariana," Mr. Sanchez greeted his daughter at the breakfast table. *"¿Dormiste bien?"*

"I slept very well, Papa. I had a dream that I scored the winning goal on a brand new soccer field!"

Mr. Sanchez smiled and said, "Your dream could be a sign that River Edge will finally get a **regulation** soccer field. Maybe you have special **insight** into what will happen at tonight's Town Council meeting. Remember, we must get the whole team there to convince them we need a better field."

That night, Mariana and her father arrived at the meeting hall to find it filled to **capacity**. They sat with the other River Edge Rockers, their community soccer team. Councilwoman Maloof opened the discussion, and Mr. Boyd, the Rockers' manager, spoke first. "Our team currently practices in a tiny school yard, and only when it's not already booked." The team nodded briskly.

Mrs. Yamagata, owner of Something Sushi, walked to the podium. "I believe the town owns an empty lot next to my restaurant," she said. "Couldn't that be a soccer field?" The Rockers applauded.

"A soccer field would be a good use for that lot," Councilwoman Maloof said. "But the town simply doesn't have the money to build and maintain one."

"The Rockers can do it!" Jamil spoke up.

"Jamil's right," Mr. Sanchez said. He began to **negotiate** with the Council. "If the town lets the Rockers use the vacant lot, *we* will turn it into a soccer field."

After some discussion, the Council reached a decision. "We hereby approve using the vacant lot adjacent to Something Sushi for a community soccer field!" Mariana looked nervously at her cheering teammates, then at her father. Mr. Sanchez winked at her, as if to say, "Didn't you have a dream?"

167

Foreign Language Dialogue Dialogue in a foreign language reveals characters' cultural backgrounds.

Foreshadowing Foreshadowing gives the reader a hint at later plot events.

Your Turn

COLLABORATE

Use context clues in "The Rockers Build a Soccer Field" to decide what two examples of foreign language dialogue probably mean. Identify two events that lead to the ending foreshadowed in Mariana's dream.

Context Clues

When you read an unfamiliar word in a story, use what you know about the other words in the same sentence to help you figure out its meaning. Use the order of the words to identify the part of speech of the unfamiliar word. The structure of the sentence may help you determine the word's meaning.

 Find Text Evidence

I wasn't sure what the word convince *means in the sentence below. I saw that it comes before the pronoun* them, *so I think* convince *is a verb. The team needs help to get a better soccer field. The phrase* to convince them *must mean "to get them to agree."*

> "Remember, we must get the whole team there to *convince* them we need a better field."

Your Turn

Use context clues and what you know about word order and sentence structure to help you figure out the meanings of the following words in "The Rockers Build a Soccer Field."

debris, *page 169*
extracted, *page 169*
perimeter, *page 169*

Write About the Text

Pages 166–169

Michael

I responded to the prompt: *Add a scene to the story in which Mariana asks a neighbor to donate some paint for the bleachers. Use details from the story.*

Student Model: *Narrative Text*

One Friday after school, Mariana

spotted Mrs. Lopez, her next-door

neighbor, working in her flower garden.

"Hi, Mrs. Lopez," Mariana said. "I'm

sorry to bother you, but I wanted to

ask if you might help out our soccer

team. We've been working to clear

the vacant lot next to Something

Transitions

I included the phrase "One Friday after school" to let the reader know when the event took place.

Relevant Details

I used text evidence to explain the reason for Mariana's request.

Sushi and turn it into a soccer field.

We're almost finished, but we will paint

the bleachers soon. Would you be able

to donate some paint?"

"Oh, Mariana, I am happy to help! I

think it's wonderful you kids took the

initiative to tackle a project like this!"

Mrs. Lopez answered.

Grammar

The word *paint* is an **action verb**. *Bleachers* is the **direct object**.

Grammar Handbook See page 457.

Dialogue

I developed the scene by adding a conversation between Mariana and Mrs. Lopez.

Your Turn

Add a scene to the end of the story in which you use foreshadowing. Use details from the story.

Go Digital!
Write your response online.
Use your editing checklist.

Weekly Concept Transformations

Essential Question

What kinds of challenges transform people?

Go Digital!

176

Challenges
That Transform Us

I'd often thought about giving rock climbing a try. It seemed like a challenge I'd enjoy. But it wasn't until my best friend suggested we take lessons that I finally got started.

▶ Sometimes it was slow going. There was more to learn than either of us had imagined. But he and I always motivate each other.

▶ Each time I mastered a climbing skill, it was like solving another dilemma. It felt great.

So, after months of persistent practice, here I am! It's been a truly transforming experience.

Talk About It

Write words you have learned about transforming experiences. Then talk with a partner about a time when you were motivated to meet a challenge.

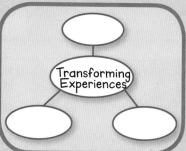

Transforming Experiences

Vocabulary

Use the picture and the sentences to talk with a partner about each word.

dilemma

Joe found himself in a **dilemma** when he couldn't decide which puppy to choose.

Describe a dilemma you have faced.

feebly

The weak, newborn pony **feebly** tried to stand.

When might a person do something feebly?

persistent

The baby's parents could not stop her **persistent** crying.

What persistent noises are heard in a city?

recoiled

Hudson **recoiled** from the needle when it was time to get her booster shot.

Describe a time when you recoiled from something.

roused

The alarm clock **roused** the girl from a deep sleep.

How are you roused from sleep in the morning?

skewed

To avoid the horse-drawn wagon, the car **skewed** to the side of the road.

How are the meanings of skewed and swerved related?

summon

Jon was able to **summon** a burst of energy and win the race.

When might you need to summon a burst of energy?

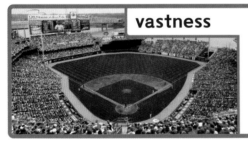

vastness

The **vastness** of the crowd made it hard for me to find my friends.

What is a synonym for vastness?

Your Turn

COLLABORATE

Pick three words. Write three questions for your partner to answer.

Go Digital! *Use the online visual glossary*

Facing the STORM

Essential Question

What kinds of challenges transform people?

Read how a severe weather threat transforms a shy and timid girl.

Isabel Moreno sat carefully inserting papers into a folder. She had been at the Gateway Nature Center's office all morning and was weary of filing. She wanted desperately to work with the animals, especially the injured birds that the center rehabilitated. But her mom, who was the assistant director of the center, said Isabel was too young and there was no time to supervise her.

"I've been a weekend volunteer this whole school year," Isabel thought. "I know more about birds than almost anyone here," she said to herself with conviction, recalling as evidence the extensive research she had done reading books and web sites on natural history. Then she sighed. She had never been good at speaking up for herself, and who would listen to a shy seventh grader anyway?

Suddenly, the quiet was shattered by Amy Jensen bursting in and letting the door slam. Isabel felt herself shrink. Amy, who had been a volunteer a bit longer than Isabel, was 16 and strutted around like she owned the place. "Hey, Isabel, I've got a job for you," she barked, planting a hand on Isabel's shoulder.

Isabel **recoiled** from Amy's touch, but she willed herself to remain still. "Don't make trouble," she reminded herself, though she would have loved to brush Amy's hand off. "I have to finish this filing," she squeaked **feebly**.

Just then, Isabel's mother rushed into the room with Mr. Garza, the custodian. "The hurricane forecast for Miami has **skewed** to the south and is entering the Gulf," Mrs. Moreno reported. "We should be okay up here in the inlet, but we'll likely get some fierce and **persistent** winds. I've sent the other volunteers home, but I need you girls to help Mr. Garza get the storm shutters down in here and in the aviary. Then I'll take you home." Isabel leaped to her feet, excited to have an opportunity to help the birds.

Mrs. Moreno's cell phone jangled, and she answered it at once, listening intently. "Change of plans," she announced as she hung up. "The winds are worse than expected along the coastline, so the Gulf Shore Preserve needs help preparing for the storm. I've got to go down there with the staff. We'll take the inlet bridge, so we shouldn't be gone long. Stay inside with Mr. Garza after you get the storm shutters down. And call me on my cell if there are any problems," she directed as she dashed out.

Amy crowed that she was now "in charge." Isabel groaned inwardly, but said nothing. Mr. Garza and the girls worked quickly and were soon back inside, listening to the wind batter and rattle the shutters. When Mr. Garza found an emergency weather report on the computer, a worried expression crossed his face. "A storm surge is heading our way, right up the inlet," he announced. "We're in for some flooding."

Authoritative as ever, Amy called Isabel's mother to tell her the news, but she sounded flustered when she hung up. "The surge has flooded the bridge, and they're stuck there!" she gasped. "What do we do?"

Isabel was unnerved that both Mr. Garza and Amy seemed so panicked, but after silently considering the **dilemma** for a few seconds, she **roused** herself and said calmly, "We should move the birds to the reptile house. It's on higher ground." As she strode out of the building with Mr. Garza and Amy following, she caught a glimpse of the satellite image on the computer. The **vastness** of the storm nearly filled the entire Gulf now.

Once inside the aviary, Isabel watched Amy lunge from cage

to cage, agitating the birds. "Don't jump around so much!" Isabel instructed. "They're scared enough as it is, and your sudden movements aren't helping." Amy meekly calmed down, but she was shaking.

"Just think about the birds," Isabel said as they carried each cage up to the reptile house. The hawks screeched and beat their wings when they felt the wind. Isabel spoke soothingly to them, and they soon grew calmer. Amy watched in awe and tried to mimic Isabel's tone. Just as the water in the bird house had risen to their shins, they finished relocating the birds and waited inside the reptile house for the storm to subside.

After several hours, the water had receded, and Mrs. Moreno was able to return to the center. She expressed concern that she'd left them alone for so long, but Mr. Garza reassured her that Isabel's foresight and cool thinking had saved the birds.

Mrs. Moreno gazed at her daughter admiringly. "How did you **summon** such confidence and courage?" she asked Isabel.

"I'm not sure," Isabel admitted. "All I could think about was how scared the birds must have felt in their cages, and I just took charge."

"I'm proud of you, Isabel," said Mrs. Moreno.

Isabel paused a second. "I guess I'm proud of myself, Mom!"

Make Connections

Talk about how Isabel was transformed during the hurricane. ESSENTIAL QUESTION

Describe a time when you showed unexpected courage. TEXT TO SELF

Make Predictions

When reading realistic fiction, use what you know about the ways the characters act to predict what they might do next. Then use text evidence to **confirm** or **revise** your predictions.

 ## Find Text Evidence

After you read the first page of "Facing the Storm," you may have used what you know about the characters to predict how Isabel and Amy would react to the approaching storm. Reread page 182 to confirm or revise your prediction.

page 182

Amy crowed that she was now "in charge." Isabel groaned inwardly, but said nothing. Mr. Garza and the girls worked quickly and were soon back inside, listening to the wind batter and rattle the shutters. When Mr. Garza found an emergency weather report on the computer, a worried expression crossed his face. "A storm surge is heading our way, right up the inlet," he announced. "We're in for some flooding."

Authoritative as ever, Amy called Isabel's mother to tell her the news, but she sounded flustered when she hung up. "The surge has flooded the bridge, and they're stuck there!" she gasped. "What do we do?"

On page 181, Amy tells Isabel "I've got a job for you." So I predicted she would give Amy orders during the storm. <u>But then I read that Amy was "flustered" when she heard Mrs. Moreno was stuck on the bridge.</u> So I revised my prediction.

Your Turn

COLLABORATE

What prediction did you make about what would happen after Amy became flustered? Tell how you confirmed or revised that prediction. Identify the passages in the story that support your answer.

Theme

To identify a story's theme, use what you learn about the characters and events in the plot to consider what message or idea the author is trying to convey. Often, authors use a central plot event to focus the reader's attention on a message.

 Find Text Evidence

As I reread "Facing the Storm," I see that each of the characters is affected in a significant way by the hurricane. Thinking about how the characters react and change as a result of this central event will help me identify the theme of the story.

Detail
Shy Isabel feels frustrated that she doesn't get to work with the birds at the nature center.

⬇

Detail
Normally bossy Amy is flustered as the storm approaches.

⬇

Detail

⬇

Theme

Your Turn COLLABORATE

Reread "Facing the Storm." Identify another key detail about a character or the plot, and add it to the chart. Use the details to determine the theme.

Go Digital!
Use the interactive graphic organizer

Realistic Fiction

The adventure story "Facing the Storm" is realistic fiction.

Realistic Fiction:
- May have third-person narration with a point of view limited mostly to one character's perspective
- Often includes strong, vivid verbs to describe events

Find Text Evidence

Phrases such as "desperately wanted" and "felt herself shrink" indicate that "Facing the Storm" is told mostly from Isabel's perspective. The author's use of vivid verbs, such as shattered, bursting, *and* strutted, *help me visualize the characters' actions.*

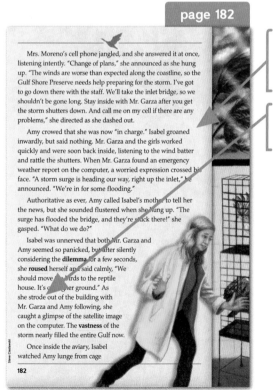

page 182

Mrs. Moreno's cell phone jangled, and she answered it at once, listening intently. "Change of plans," she announced as she hung up. "The winds are worse than expected along the coastline, so the Gulf Shore Preserve needs help preparing for the storm. I've got to go down there with the staff. We'll take the inlet bridge, so we shouldn't be gone long. Stay inside with Mr. Garza after you get the storm shutters down. And call me on my cell if there are any problems," she directed as she dashed out.

Amy crowed that she was now "in charge." Isabel groaned inwardly, but said nothing. Mr. Garza and the girls worked quickly and were soon back inside, listening to the wind batter and rattle the shutters. When Mr. Garza found an emergency weather report on the computer, a worried expression crossed his face. "A storm surge is heading our way, right up the inlet," he announced. "We're in for some flooding."

Authoritative as ever, Amy called Isabel's mother to tell her the news, but she sounded flustered when she hung up. "The surge has flooded the bridge, and they're stuck there!" she gasped. "What do we do?"

Isabel was unnerved that both Mr. Garza and Amy seemed so panicked, but after silently considering the **dilemma** for a few seconds, she **roused** herself and said calmly, "We should move the birds to the reptile house. It's on higher ground." As she strode out of the building with Mr. Garza and Amy following, she caught a glimpse of the satellite image on the computer. The **vastness** of the storm nearly filled the entire Gulf now.

Once inside the aviary, Isabel watched Amy lunge from cage

182

Third-Person Limited Point of View A third-person narrator presents events mainly through one character's point of view.

Strong, Vivid Verbs Strong verbs give the reader a more vivid picture of the events.

COLLABORATE

Your Turn

Identify two sentences from "Facing the Storm" that show the story is told mainly from Isabel's point of view. Then identify three vivid verbs that help you visualize the action.

Paragraph Clues

As you read a story, you may come across a word that has more than one possible meaning. To figure out which meaning is correct in the story, look for context clues within the paragraph that contains the multiple-meaning word.

 Find Text Evidence

I see the word filing *in the first paragraph of "Facing the Storm" on page 181.* Filing *can mean "smoothing and shaping with a tool" or "putting papers away." Other information in the paragraph tells me that Isabel is "inserting papers into a folder" and working in an office, so I know the second meaning of* filing *is the correct one.*

> Isabel Moreno sat carefully inserting papers into a folder. She had been at the Gateway Nature Center's office all morning and was weary of filing.

Your Turn

Use paragraph clues to determine the correct meaning of these words as they are used in "Facing the Storm":

bursting, *page 181*
batter, *page 182*
instructed, *page 183*
tone, *page 183*

Write About the Text

Pages 180–183

Evelyn

I responded to the prompt: *Add descriptive details and dialogue to the scene when Isabel's mother arrives after the storm. Include details from the story.*

Student Model: *Narrative Text*

Suddenly, Isabel realized this was her big *chance*. "I think I've proven something, too, Mom," Isabel added. "I've shown that I'm *not* too young to work with the birds. During this emergency, I stayed *calm* and made the birds' safety our number-one priority. I was the one who realized we needed

Dialogue

I developed the scene by considering earlier events to extend the conversation.

Grammar

Past-tense verbs show actions that took place in the past.

Grammar Handbook See page 458.

Details

I included text evidence to make Isabel's argument stronger.

Kali Nine LLC/iStock/360/Getty Images

188

to move the birds to higher ground, so

I've earned the right to work with the

injured birds. I want to be trained."

Isabel's mom wrinkled her forehead.

"Well, you've certainly learned to stand

up for yourself! You're right, Isabel. It's

time I trained you to rehabilitate

the birds."

Strong Conclusion
My final sentence brings a resolution to Isabel's problem.

Your Turn

Add a scene to the end of the story in which Amy and Mr. Garza explain Isabel's actions to her mother. Include details from the story.

Go Digital!
Write your response online.
Use your editing checklist.

Essential Question

What can people accomplish by working together?

Go Digital!

INSPIRED WORK

Helping to build homes for people who can't afford them on their own is a time-honored tradition.

▶ Working side-by-side with other volunteers increases morale and productivity.

▶ We rely on everyone's ingenuity to help solve problems and get the job done right.

Whenever I'm asked to volunteer for this program, I don't have to think twice!

Talk About It

Write words you have learned about working together for the common good. Then talk with a partner about a time you were inspired to lend a hand in helping others.

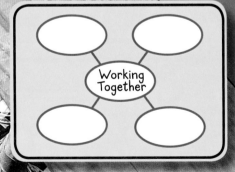

Working Together

Vocabulary

Use the picture and the sentences to talk with a partner about each word.

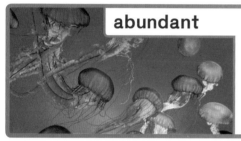

abundant

We saw many jellyfish, as they are **abundant** in warm ocean waters.

What else is abundant in the ocean?

impoverished

People in the **impoverished** town lived in poorly constructed huts.

What is a synonym for impoverished?

ingenuity

The unique design of the dome shows great **ingenuity**.

How might an inventor show ingenuity?

productivity

Because **productivity** was high, the company had many cars to sell.

What happens when productivity is low?

sharecropper

The **sharecropper** is required to give half the crop to the owner of the farmland.

Why is it important that a sharecropper have a good crop?

solitude

Josie found a quiet, empty spot for reading her book in **solitude**.

What other activities are more easily done in solitude?

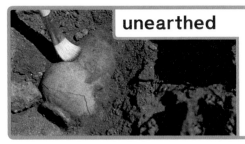

unearthed

The scientist **unearthed** an ancient vase that had been buried for centuries.

What is an antonym of unearthed?

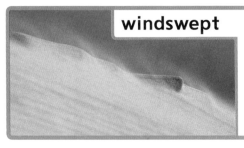

windswept

Sand blew across the **windswept** desert.

Describe what you might see in a windswept field.

COLLABORATE

Your Turn

Pick three words. Write three questions for your partner to answer.

Go Digital! *Use the online visual glossary*

Jewels from the Sea

Essential Question

What can people accomplish by working together?

Read about the way one group of women improved their lives and their community.

A Life by the Sea

On their **windswept** island off the coast of eastern Africa, the women of Zanzibar were living much as their ancestors had. They cared for their children and cultivated their gardens. They farmed seaweed from the ocean and gathered shells to sell to tourists who visited their beautiful homeland. Some of the women worked long hours breaking rocks into gravel. Life on the Fumba Peninsula had often been hard for them. They made very little money, and some would say the women were **impoverished**. But they had always managed to feed their families. The ocean had provided for them, supplying **abundant** fish and oysters for food, and colorful shells to sell.

The lustrous interior of an oyster shell.

However, gifts from the ocean were not limitless. In the early 2000s, the women began to notice that oysters were not as plentiful as they once had been. In fact, Zanzibar's oysters were being harvested faster than they could replenish themselves. In ten short years, the number of oysters had declined dramatically. The women worried about the uncertain future.

A Fresh Approach

The women began to look beyond the **solitude** of their isolated coastal villages for help. To start, they welcomed the interest of scientists who were studying marine life in the waters surrounding Zanzibar. With guidance from the scientists, the women would work together to manage the way oysters were harvested. They soon discovered they had the power to bring oyster populations back to healthy levels.

The women's search for solutions also **unearthed** another new idea. The women had always discarded the oysters' shells after removing the flesh. But visiting experts, who help communities sustain their resources, pointed out that the shells could be valuable, too. They offered to teach the women the skills needed for polishing the shells and turning them into jewelry. Before long, local residents and tourists were buying earrings, necklaces, and bracelets that the women made from shells. The income the women earned from selling jewelry was more than they had ever made before. It occurred to them that, with a little **ingenuity**, they had actually become businesswomen.

Building on Their Success

The women believed they could do even more. They wanted to have control of their business, not to be like a **sharecropper** who owns no land and so

keeps only a part of the harvest. It was suggested that they join forces to cultivate *mabe* (MAH-bay) pearls, also known as "half-pearls." These pearls are created when a bead or other irritant is placed inside a living oyster. The oyster coats the irritation with layers of a shiny substance called *nacre* (NAY-ker). The nacre later hardens into a shimmering pearl, perfectly suited for jewelry.

This new project would also work well with the plans to restore the oyster beds. Four "no-take" zones were soon established for the oysters that would produce mabe pearls. There was only one problem. The pearls had to be cultivated underwater. Even though the women had lived all their lives by the sea, they did not know how to swim! So the next step for these strong-willed women was to learn to swim.

Others in the village were impressed by the women's determination. Many joined

The women harvesting oysters.

them to help see the project through. The first harvest of mabe pearls in 2008 was so successful that professional jewelers quickly bought up the gleaming harvest to make expensive jewelry.

Toward New Horizons

The women wanted to learn still more ways to improve their business. To do so, they would have to travel thousands of miles across the ocean. Just as learning to swim had been a first, leaving Zanzibar would be a new experience. But together they would go. In 2009, a small group flew to Newport, Rhode Island, in the U.S. to learn about designing and marketing jewelry. They met a master jeweler, who taught them how to wrap strands of fine silver wire into delicate designs around the mabe pearls. They also met people who shared tips on expanding small businesses into large ones. The women

One of the women polishes a *mabe* shell.

absorbed all this and brought it home with them.

The women of Zanzibar still live on their beautiful island. But today there is a difference. By working together, the women have become powerful caretakers of local natural resources and created prosperity in their community. Their hard-earned **productivity** will continue when they teach the next generation of young women how to accomplish great things.

Make Connections

Explain the steps that the women of Zanzibar took together to accomplish their goal. ESSENTIAL QUESTION

Talk about a time when you worked together with others to accomplish a common goal. TEXT TO SELF

(i) Klaus Hartung

Summarize

A nonfiction narrative may include ideas that are new to you. As you read "Jewels from the Sea," summarizing ideas in your own words will help you understand them. Pause after reading each section to identify the main idea for each set of related details.

 Find Text Evidence

You may not be sure how to summarize the section "A Life by the Sea" on page 195 of "Jewels from the Sea." Reread the section to decide what the important details have in common.

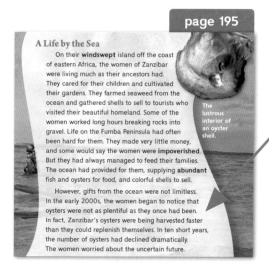

page 195

A Life by the Sea

On their **windswept** island off the coast of eastern Africa, the women of Zanzibar were living much as their ancestors had. They cared for their children and cultivated their gardens. They farmed seaweed from the ocean and gathered shells to sell to tourists who visited their beautiful homeland. Some of the women worked long hours breaking rocks into gravel. Life on the Fumba Peninsula had often been hard for them. They made very little money, and some would say the women were **impoverished**. But they had always managed to feed their families. The ocean had provided for them, supplying **abundant** fish and oysters for food, and colorful shells to sell.

However, gifts from the ocean were not limitless. In the early 2000s, the women began to notice that oysters were not as plentiful as they once had been. In fact, Zanzibar's oysters were being harvested faster than they could replenish themselves. In ten short years, the number of oysters had declined dramatically. The women worried about the uncertain future.

The lustrous interior of an oyster shell.

I read details about what the women had done for many years and about how "the number of oysters had declined." I can summarize by saying a problem may have developed as a result of unchanging habits.

Your Turn

COLLABORATE

Reread the rest of "Jewels from the Sea." Use key details to identify the main ideas in each section. Then summarize the ideas in your own words.

Sequence

The author of a nonfiction narrative may organize the text by explaining a sequence of steps taken over time. Identifying the steps in the sequence can help you understand how the outcome was achieved and what the author's message is.

 Find Text Evidence

When I reread the first two sections of "Jewels from the Sea," I can look for steps the women took to identify and solve their economic problem. As I read on, I can consider all the steps to determine how the women increased their prosperity.

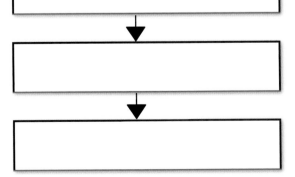

> Event
> The women realize they have a problem with harvesting oysters.

↓

> The women ask for help. They learn how to replenish the oysters and make jewelry from the shells.

↓

> [ ]

↓

> [ ]

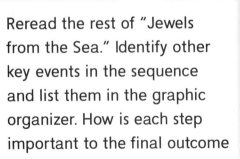

Your Turn COLLABORATE

Reread the rest of "Jewels from the Sea." Identify other key events in the sequence and list them in the graphic organizer. How is each step important to the final outcome that the author describes?

Go Digital!
Use the interactive graphic organizer

Narrative Nonfiction

"Jewels from the Sea" is narrative nonfiction.

Narrative nonfiction:

- Provides factual information in "story" form
- May express the author's point of view through a particular voice or tone

Find Text Evidence

"Jewels from the Sea" explains how a group of women in Zanzibar worked together to improve the economic well-being of their community. The author's tone is kind and understanding. I can tell that, in his point of view, the women are worthy of our respect.

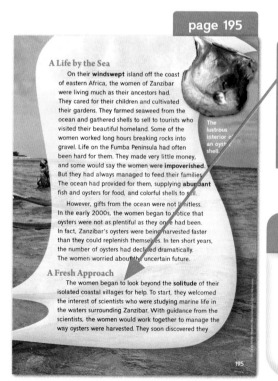

page 195

A Life by the Sea

On their **windswept** island off the coast of eastern Africa, the women of Zanzibar were living much as their ancestors had. They cared for their children and cultivated their gardens. They farmed seaweed from the ocean and gathered shells to sell to tourists who visited their beautiful homeland. Some of the women worked long hours breaking rocks into gravel. Life on the Fumba Peninsula had often been hard for them. They made very little money, and some would say the women were **impoverished**. But they had always managed to feed their families. The ocean had provided for them, supplying **abundant** fish and oysters for food, and colorful shells to sell.

However, gifts from the ocean were not limitless. In the early 2000s, the women began to notice that oysters were not as plentiful as they once had been. In fact, Zanzibar's oysters were being harvested faster than they could replenish themselves. In ten short years, the number of oysters had declined dramatically. The women worried about the uncertain future.

A Fresh Approach

The women began to look beyond the **solitude** of their isolated coastal villages for help. To start, they welcomed the interest of scientists who were studying marine life in the waters surrounding Zanzibar. With guidance from the scientists, the women would work together to manage the way oysters were harvested. They soon discovered they

The lustrous interior of an oyster shell.

195

Text Feature

Author's Voice/Tone The author's voice and tone show how he or she feels about the topic. The tone may be expressed in headings as well as in the main text.

COLLABORATE

Your Turn

Find three passages in "Jewels from the Sea" that express the author's point of view. Tell your partner what the tone of each passage is.

Prefixes and Suffixes

Knowing the meaning of common prefixes and suffixes can help you figure out the meaning of an unfamiliar word. The chart below shows the meanings of some prefixes and suffixes.

Prefix	Meaning	Suffix	Meaning
re-	back; again	*-ity, -ty*	quality of; state of
un-	not; opposite of	*-ful*	full of; characterized by

 Find Text Evidence

I'm not sure what the meaning of the word prosperity *is on page 197. I know that the suffix -ity, means "quality or state of." So* prosperity *must mean "the quality or state of prospering or living well."*

> The women have become powerful caretakers of local natural resources and created prosper|ity| in their community.

Your Turn

Use the prefixes and suffixes in the chart above to help you figure out the meanings of the following words in "Jewels from the Sea."

replenish, *page 195*

uncertain, *page 195*

successful, *page 197*

Write About the Text

Pages 194–197

Dena

I answered the question: *How was each step the women of Zanzibar took important to the final outcome? Use text evidence.*

Student Model: *Informative Text*

The women of Zanzibar took many steps to use their local natural resource, oysters, to ensure their community's prosperity. First, and most importantly, the women discovered how to manage the oyster harvest so that the oyster population had replenished itself. Later, experts explained to the women how oysters could provide income in multiple ways.

Introduce a Topic

My first sentence contains my thesis statement.

Grammar

This is an example of a **helping verb** followed by a **past participle**.

Grammar Handbook See page 459.

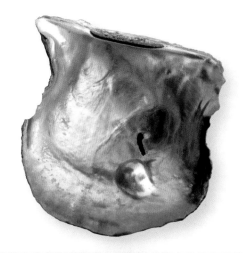

This new idea is why the women learned how to cultivate pearls and to create jewelry from oyster shells. After mastering these skills, the women traveled to the United States to learn about designing and marketing pearl jewelry. The steps they took helped develop a local, natural resource into a steady, growing source of income for years to come.

Relevant Evidence
I included details to explain how each step advanced the outcome.

Strong Conclusion
My final sentence summarizes how the steps led to the outcome.

Your Turn

Explain how creating a jewelry business also helps the women increase the oyster population. Include text evidence.

Go Digital!
Write your response online.
Use your editing checklist.

Essential Question

How can one person affect the opinions of others?

Go Digital!

Being the First

We may see nothing unusual in this photograph today. But in 1983, a woman on the crew of the space shuttle Challenger was big news.

▶ Sally Ride was the first American woman—and the youngest American till then—to enter space. She was a true trailblazer.

▶ In all, Sally spent 343 hours in space. Her perseverance in attaining her goals inspired a generation of young women.

As a physicist and teacher, Sally has worked to help girls interested in science establish milestones of their own.

Talk About It

Write words you have learned about reaching milestones. Then talk with a partner about a trailblazer whom you admire.

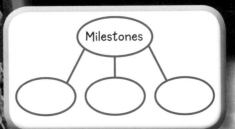

Milestones

205

Vocabulary

Use the picture and the sentences to talk with a
partner about each word.

adept

Terry is an **adept** gardener who grows
prize-winning flowers.

Describe an activity at which you are
adept.

aristocracy

Members of the **aristocracy** in France
often lived in palaces.

How are the meanings of aristocracy
and wealthy related?

collective

A **collective** cheer rang out as all the
fans began to yell at once.

What is an antonym for collective?

perseverance

Although he struggled at first, Ty
showed **perseverance** and succeeded.

Describe a time when perseverance
helped you succeed.

prevail

Despite his injury, Gustavo was able to **prevail** during the rest of the season.

Describe a time when you were able to prevail after a setback.

prominent

Albert Einstein was an important, **prominent** scientist of the 20th century.

Name someone who is considered a prominent athlete.

spectators

The **spectators** watched players at the tournament with interest.

Where else might you find spectators?

trailblazer

Neil Armstrong, the first person to walk on the moon, is a **trailblazer** who is admired by many people.

Identify a trailblazer whom you admire.

Your Turn

COLLABORATE

Pick three words. Write three questions for your partner to answer.

Go Digital! *Use the online visual glossary*

MARIAN ANDERSON

STRUGGLES and TRIUMPHS

Essential Question

How can one person affect the opinions of others?

Read how the artistry of Marian Anderson changed people's minds about where African-American singers could perform.

A Voice of Great Promise

On February 27, 1897, a baby girl came into the world, crying with all her might. No one knew then that this voice would one day move mountains. It was not easy for an African American born at the turn of the twentieth century to follow her dream. But Marian Anderson would become one of the greatest singers of her time.

There were many opportunities for young Marian to explore her musical talent in her Philadelphia, Pennsylvania, neighborhood. She began singing in her local church choir at the age of six, but because she was such an **adept** singer, she was soon invited to perform outside of church. The Philadelphia Choral Society even awarded her $500 to take singing lessons. With such advantages, Marian was shocked by her first experience of racism.

Racism and Rejection

After graduating high school, Marian went to the admissions office of a local music school. "I want to study music here," she told the young clerk. When the clerk told her that African-American students were not accepted at the school, Marian was stunned, but she didn't argue. She wondered, "How can someone surrounded by the beauty of music be so full of hatred?"

The rejection did not stop the singer. Marian's church donated money for her to study with Giuseppe Boghetti, a famous voice teacher. In 1925, Boghetti entered Marian in a voice contest in which she competed against 300 others to win the honor of singing with the New York Philharmonic orchestra.

Unfortunately, her next big performance in New York City was not so successful. Because she was black, very few people came to hear her. Some critics found her performance to be "lacking." As a result, fewer people asked her to sing concerts.

It seemed that Marian's career was over. The discrimination she encountered at the music school could be found nearly everywhere in the United States. Many white audiences refused to hear African-American performers, and many concert halls would not allow black singers to perform. "If I cannot sing in America," Marian told herself, "I will go to Europe." She left in 1930, hoping that audiences overseas would give her a chance.

To Europe — And Back Again

In Europe, **prominent** composers and conductors praised Marian. Audiences flocked to hear her. To them, she was musical **aristocracy**, one of the most gifted singers ever. A man named Sol Hurok, who saw Marian perform in Paris, became her manager. Soon he had a request. "Come back to America to sing again," he pleaded.

"Will they ever respect me in America the way they do here?" Marian wondered. She decided to find out. She returned to the same concert hall where her career had nearly ended a decade before. This time, the performance was a success.

The singer's popularity grew, and Hurok began to book more recitals in the U.S. Still, like other African Americans at the time, Marian was not allowed to eat in many restaurants or stay in many hotels when she traveled— and no opera house would invite an African American to sing. But it was an act of prejudice in 1939 that gained Marian the greatest fame.

Change Did Not Come Easily

Hurok tried to arrange for Marian to sing at Constitution Hall, owned by the Daughters of the American Revolution (DAR). Though the DAR told Hurok no dates were available, they continued to book white performers. Outraged, First Lady Eleanor Roosevelt resigned from the DAR in protest.

Marian's supporters breathed a **collective** sigh of relief when a federal official offered her use of the Lincoln Memorial for a concert on Easter Sunday, 1939.

Marian was not sure what to do. The dignified woman was troubled by the drama of the situation. The prejudice barring her from Constitution Hall existed well beyond the concert hall's walls. Besides, the whole idea could backfire, and American audiences might once again reject her. On the other hand, Marian understood that the concert was not just about her; it was about helping all African Americans. Should she lend her voice so that others could **prevail** against injustice?

Marian decided to take the chance. The concert drew nationwide attention, and Marian was stunned when nearly 75,000 **spectators** attended. Millions more listened to the live radio broadcast.

Fifteen long years would pass before New York's Metropolitan Opera invited Marian to sing, but she was the first African American ever to receive such acknowledgment. On opening night, even before she sang a single note, the audience applauded for five full minutes. Her performance established Marian once more as a **trailblazer** who opened up opportunities for black Americans.

The celebrated conductor Arturo Toscanini said that a voice such as Marian's was "heard once in 100 years." Indeed, Marian Anderson's glorious singing, combined with her **perseverance** in the face of prejudice, shattered racial barriers and enriched the lives of countless people.

Time & Life Pictures/Getty Images

Make Connections

Talk about the way that Marian Anderson's singing changed the way Americans thought about African-American performers. **ESSENTIAL QUESTION**

Describe how a person you know or have read about helped changed your beliefs about something. **TEXT TO SELF**

Summarize

When you read a biography, summarizing key events can help you understand which information is most important about the person's life. As you read "Marian Anderson: Struggles and Triumphs," identify the most important events in Anderson's life, and use them to summarize her accomplishments in your own words.

 ## Find Text Evidence

You may not know how to summarize Anderson's early life. Reread the section "A Voice of Great Promise" on page 209 of "Marian Anderson: Struggles and Triumphs."

page 209

A Voice of Great Promise

On February 27, 1897, a baby girl came into the world, crying with all her might. No one knew then that this voice would one day move mountains. It was not easy for an African American born at the turn of the twentieth century to follow her dream. But Marian Anderson would become one of the greatest singers of her time.

There were many opportunities for young Marian to explore her musical talent in her Philadelphia, Pennsylvania, neighborhood. She began singing in her local church choir at the age of six, but because she was such an **adept** singer, she was soon invited to perform outside of church. The Philadelphia Choral Society even awarded her $500 to take singing lessons. With such advantages, Marian was shocked by her first experience of racism.

I read that Marian Anderson "began singing in her local church choir at the age of six" and that she received an award to take singing lessons. I can summarize this section by saying that Marian's talent as a singer was recognized very early in her life.

 COLLABORATE

Your Turn

Reread the section "Racism and Rejection." Identify the key events and tell what they have in common. Then summarize the main ideas in the section.

Cause and Effect

Authors of informational texts sometimes organize their ideas by describing cause-and-effect relationships. A biography often explains how certain events during a person's lifetime had an effect on later events.

 ## Find Text Evidence

When I reread "Marian Anderson: Struggles and Triumphs," I can look for cause-and-effect relationships among events in Anderson's life. Signal words and phrases, such as because *and* as a result, *can help me identify which events influenced others.*

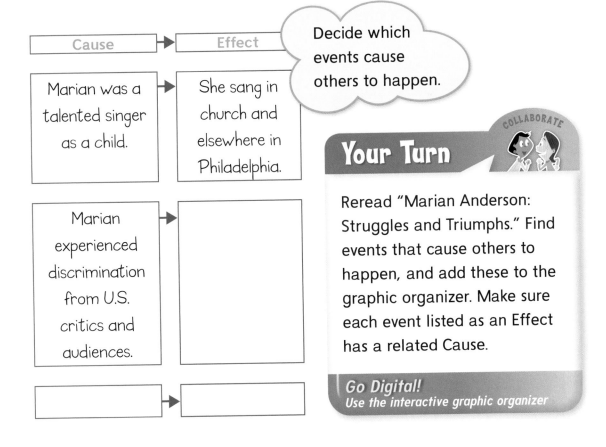

Cause	→	Effect

Marian was a talented singer as a child. → She sang in church and elsewhere in Philadelphia.

Decide which events cause others to happen.

Marian experienced discrimination from U.S. critics and audiences. →

Your Turn COLLABORATE

Reread "Marian Anderson: Struggles and Triumphs." Find events that cause others to happen, and add these to the graphic organizer. Make sure each event listed as an Effect has a related Cause.

Go Digital!
Use the interactive graphic organizer

Biography

The selection "Marian Anderson: Struggles and Triumphs" is a biography. A biography provides information about the life of a person, who is referred to as the **subject** of the biography.

A **Biography**:
- May suppose what the subject thought or said
- May use suspense to describe an event in the subject's life

 Find Text Evidence

"Marian Anderson: Struggles and Triumphs" is a biography because it gives factual information about Anderson's life. Reading what she might have thought helps me understand her feelings. Suspenseful descriptions of events help make them vivid.

page 209

A Voice of Great Promise

On February 27, 1897, a baby girl came into the world, crying with all her might. No one knew then that this voice would one day move mountains. It was not easy for an African American born at the turn of the twentieth century to follow her dream. But Marian Anderson would become one of the greatest singers of her time.

There were many opportunities for young Marian to explore her musical talent in her Philadelphia, Pennsylvania, neighborhood. She began singing in her local church choir at the age of six, but because she was such an **adept** singer, she was soon invited to perform outside of church. The Philadelphia Choral Society even awarded her $500 to take singing lessons. With such advantages, Marian was shocked by her first experience of racism.

Racism and Rejection

After graduating high school, Marian went to the admission office of a local music school. "I want to study music here," she told the young clerk. When the clerk told her that African American students were not accepted at the school, Marian was stunned, but she didn't argue. She wondered, "How can someone surrounded by the beauty of music be so full of hatred?"

The rejection did not stop the singer. Marian's church donated money for her to study with Giuseppe Boghetti, a famous voice teacher. In 1925, Boghetti entered Marian in a voice contest in which she competed against 300 others to win the honor of singing with the New York Philharmonic orchestra.

Unfortunately, her next big performance in New York City was not so successful. Because she was black, very few people came to hear her. Some critics found her performance to be "lacking." As a result, fewer people asked her to sing concerts.

209

Text Features

Fictionalized Elements Supposing what the subject thought brings her to life.

Suspense Using suspense helps the reader understand how the subject experienced a challenging event.

Your Turn

Find an example of what Anderson may have thought. Find an example of suspense. Tell your partner what you learned from each example.

214

Paragraph Clues

When you are unsure of the meaning of a word in an informational text, you can use clues in nearby sentences to verify the meaning. When possible, use several clues to help you determine the most likely meaning of the word.

 Find Text Evidence

I'm not completely sure what the word advantages *means in the sentence below. The previous sentence says she was awarded $500. Receiving awards is valuable and helpful. So I think that* advantages *must mean "valuable help." When I replace* advantages *with* valuable help, *the sentence makes sense.*

> The Philadelphia Choral Society even awarded her $500 to take singing lessons. With such **advantages**, she was shocked by her first experience of racism.

Your Turn

Use context clues to determine the meanings of the following words from "Marian Anderson: Struggles and Triumphs."

admissions, *page 209*
discrimination, *page 210*
prejudice, *page 210*

Write About the Text

Pages 208–211

Daniel

I answered the question: *How does the author feel about Marian Anderson? Use text evidence.*

Student Model: *Informative Text*

Strong Introduction
My topic sentence clearly addresses the focus of my writing.

Grammar

The word *was* is an example of a **linking verb**.

Grammar Handbook
See page 460.

The author feels tremendous respect for Marian Anderson, both for her singing talent and for her personal qualities. The author praises Anderson by saying she was "one of the greatest singers of her time," a "dignified woman," and "a trailblazer who opened up opportunities for black Americans." The strongest praise appears at the

Develop a Topic
I included quotations to support the main idea of my text.

Style and Tone
I used formal language throughout my writing.

end of the article, where the author says her "glorious singing, combined with her perseverance in the face of prejudice, shattered racial barriers and enriched the lives of countless people." The author clearly admires Anderson as much for her strong will and courage as for her beautiful voice.

Your Turn

What effect did racism have on Anderson's career choices? Include text evidence.

Go Digital!
Write your response online.
Use your editing checklist.

Weekly Concept A Greener Future

Essential Question

What steps can people take to promote a healthier environment?

Go Digital!

Henglein and Steets/Cultura/Getty Images

218

GREEN MEANS CLEAN

It used to be that a discussion about farming would focus on crops, plowing, rainfall, and fertilizer. But these days, *farming* could just as easily mean harvesting energy from the Sun and from wind.

▶ Unlike generators that burn fossil fuels, solar farms and wind farms produce electricity without harmful emissions.

▶ These farms are built where the terrain provides optimal conditions for gathering energy. Solar farms can be built on top of parking lots. Some wind turbines are even built out in the ocean.

Advocates for farming energy from renewable sources say the benefits of generating clean electricity far outweigh any disadvantages.

Talk About It

Write words you have learned about promoting clean energy sources. Then talk with a partner about how people's understanding of energy production is changing.

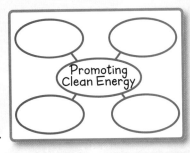

Promoting Clean Energy

Vocabulary

Use the picture and the sentences to talk with a
partner about each word.

advocates

Advocates for safe neighborhoods
fought to save their local firehouses.

What cause have student advocates
worked for in your school?

commonplace

It is **commonplace** for kids to play
kickball during their free time.

What is a commonplace homework
assignment that you receive?

designate

Before starting the game, we need to **designate**
which teammate plays each position.

How does your school designate which
students will be hall monitors?

initial

She suddenly realized that her **initial**
response was incorrect.

What is an antonym of initial?

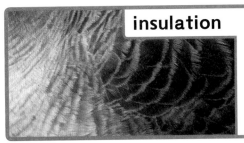

insulation

Many birds have layers of soft inner feathers that provide natural **insulation**.

What are some places where insulation is used in your home?

invasive

Certain vines from foreign countries are considered **invasive** because they grow too quickly and cover up native plants.

How might noise feel invasive?

irrational

Many people have an **irrational** fear of the number 13, believing without proof that it brings bad luck.

What is a synonym for irrational?

optimal

Often, the **optimal** time for fishing is early in the morning.

Describe a time when you experienced optimal conditions for a favorite activity.

COLLABORATE

Your Turn

Pick three words. Write three questions for your partner to answer.

Go Digital! **Use the online visual glossary**

(t) Jacqui Hurst/Garden Picture Library/Getty Images;
(b) Ingram Publishing

Essential Question

What steps can people take to promote a healthier environment?

Read about different "green" solutions in the city of the future.

The roof of a barge in London, England, is insulated by several kinds of plants growing on it.

IS YOUR CITY GREEN?

These days, people are trying to be better stewards, or caretakers, of Earth by living in a "green" way. **Advocates** of living in greener communities believe the advantages far outweigh any drawbacks. They think it is **irrational** to delay solving environmental problems. They say we can use ideas and technologies available right now to create the city of the future today.

Buildings with Green Roofs

Modern buildings in the green city of the future are designed to save water and energy. Outdated buildings of the past were not. Rooftops covered with grass and other living plants provide **insulation** that keeps buildings cooler. These roofs can also collect, filter, and reuse rainwater that would otherwise be wasted.

Turbines harvest the wind's energy.

Clean Energy

It is **commonplace** in the green city to use sources of energy that are renewable and cause no pollution. Solar panels convert the Sun's energy into electric power. Huge turbines generate electricity by harvesting the wind's energy on nearby wind farms. Even rivers are harnessed to produce electricity, and geothermal energy from deep within Earth is used to heat homes.

What you won't find in this city are gas stations on every corner. Tax breaks encourage people to use clean energy. And government agencies impose fees on the sale of fossil fuels to discourage their use.

Moving Right Along

Most people in the green city of the future **designate** mass transit as their preferred method of travel. Since passengers who have chosen to ride trains are not driving their cars, less fuel is burned. Any private cars still in use are hybrid or plug-in electric vehicles. Hybrid cars run on both fuel and batteries. Some electric cars do not use gas at all. Instead, owners plug their cars into standard electrical outlets to charge the batteries.

In the green city, many cars, trucks, and buses burn fuels made from renewable sources rather than oil. For example, a biofuel called ethanol is made from corn and sugar cane crops. Biodiesel is made from soybean oil, animal fat, or even cooking grease!

Open Spaces

Citizens of the green city understand that protecting native species is key to conserving natural spaces. Because native plants are original to the ecosystem, they provide the **optimal** habitat for local insects, birds, and other animals. Native plants that are well adapted to the local climate also require less water. Alien, or imported, plants are quickly identified and removed. Otherwise, they may become **invasive** and overwhelm local species.

Residents recognize that a process called *composting* helps reduce the amount of solid waste that is sent to landfills. It also increases the richness of local soil. People mix food scraps and yard waste with water and air in large bins. Helpful bacteria and fungi then break down this pile of "garbage" into an eco-friendly and economical fertilizer that improves the health of city parks and backyards.

An electric car is plugged into a recharging station.

HOW TO MAKE COMPOST

Cooking up some rich compost is easy when you follow these steps.

"Green" (Wet) Material (nitrogen-rich)

- grass; garden trimmings
- food scraps: fruits and vegetables (no meat, bones, dairy products, or grease)
- coffee grounds and filters; tea bags
- egg shells

"Brown" (Dry) Material (carbon-rich)

- autumn leaves
- straw
- sawdust
- shredded newspapers

  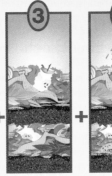 

① layer of brown material and layer of green material

+ ② water

+ ③ brown and green

+ ④ water

+ ⑤ after 2-4 weeks, turn/stir pile

repeat steps 1 through 5 for 2 more months

COMPOST

Karen Minot

POINT COUNTERPOINT

Your House Should Be More Passive!

I believe that all new houses should be "passive" homes. This means they would be built with materials and systems that reduce energy use. Most people think it's too expensive to do this. Actually, the savings over several years on the cost of electricity and carbon-based heating fuels soon exceed the higher **initial** cost of the energy-saving features. Some families are concerned that "thermal mass" floors used to retain heat in winter are too unattractive. Or they may think that keeping plants alive on the roof is too difficult. But these objections don't take into account a growing number of flooring styles and easy-to-maintain "green" roofing systems. The combined benefits of lower energy costs and less pollution from fossil fuels are reason enough to build more passive homes.

Make Connections

Talk about the "green" solutions that people can put into practice today. ESSENTIAL QUESTION

Describe some of the steps you currently take to protect the environment. TEXT TO SELF

Ask and Answer Questions

When you reread an expository text, you can ask yourself questions about sections that were unclear to you the first time you read them. Looking in the text for the answers to your questions can help you understand the information.

 ## Find Text Evidence

When you first read the section "Buildings with Green Roofs," on page 223 of "Is Your City Green?" it may not have been clear to you why buildings should have green roofs.

page 223

Buildings with Green Roofs

Modern buildings in the green city of the future are designed to save water and energy. Outdated buildings of the past were not. Rooftops covered with grass and other living plants provide **insulation** that keeps buildings cooler. These roofs can also collect, filter, and reuse rainwater that would otherwise be wasted.

Wh...
are gas...
Tax bre...
use cle...
agencie...
fossil f...

I asked myself why people would want a green roof. <u>I read that a green roof saves water and energy by keeping "buildings cooler" and reusing rainwater.</u> I can infer from this that green roofs save money and protect the environment.

Your Turn

What does the author mean by "clean energy?" Reread the section "Clean Energy" on page 223. Tell how you used details from the section to answer the question. As you read, remember to use the strategy Ask and Answer Questions.

Main Idea and Key Details

The main idea is the most important point the author makes about a topic, but it may not be stated directly. If no sentence in the text states the idea that ties all the key details together, use what the details have in common to identify the main idea.

 Find Text Evidence

When I reread "Moving Right Along" on page 224 of "Is Your City Green?" I can think about how the key details are connected.

> What idea ties all the key details together?

Main Idea
Many choices reduce fuel use for transportation in the green city.
Detail
Most people in the green city prefer to use mass transit.
Detail
Private vehicles are hybrid fuel-electric or electric.
Detail
Vehicles burn renewable fuels.

COLLABORATE

Your Turn

Reread the section "Open Spaces" on page 224 of "Is Your City Green?" Identify key details and use what they have in common to determine the main idea of the section.

Go Digital!
Use the interactive graphic organizer

Expository

"Is Your City Green?" is an informational article. It provides facts about a topic and gives reasons why people have made certain choices. Expository articles often include graphic illustrations, such as flowcharts, and some may feature a sidebar to expand on one aspect of the topic.

 Find Text Evidence

"Is Your City Green?" explains how some people are choosing to take better care of the environment. The flowchart helps me understand in more detail one of the processes mentioned in the article. The sidebar expresses an opinion about one subject in the text.

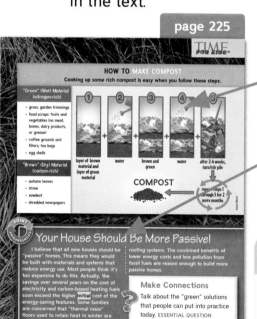

page 225

Text Features

Flowcharts Flowcharts are diagrams that show the steps in a process. They usually include captions.

Sidebars A sidebar may make a claim and provide reasons and evidence to support it.

COLLABORATE

Your Turn

Find and list two text features in "Is Your City Green?" Tell your partner how each increases your understanding of the topic.

Synonyms and Antonyms

Synonyms are words that have the same or similar meanings. Words are **antonyms** when they have opposite meanings. You can use the relationships between synonyms and antonyms in the same sentence or paragraph to help you understand the meaning of one or both words.

 Find Text Evidence

I wasn't sure what the word *drawbacks* means in the second sentence of "Is Your City Green?" If advantages far outweigh drawbacks, drawbacks must be different from advantages. So I think *drawbacks* is an antonym of *advantages*. Words that mean the opposite of *advantages* include *difficulties* or *problems*.

> Advocates of living in greener communities believe the advantages far outweigh any drawbacks.

COLLABORATE

Your Turn

Find a synonym or antonym in the same sentence or nearby sentences for each of the following words in "Is Your City Green?" Explain how you determined whether the meanings are similar or opposite.

modern, *page 223*
harvesting, *page 223*
alien, *page 224*

229

Write About the Text

Pages 222-225

Fatimah

I answered the question: *Does the author successfully support her argument for building a green city? Use text evidence to support your answer.*

Student Model: *Argument*

Introduce a Claim
I stated my opinion in the first sentence.

Relevant Evidence
I supported my claim with facts from the text.

The author of "Is Your City Green?" presents a strong argument for building a green city. The author points out the many advantages of green cities. For example, green cities save water and energy, use renewable sources of energy, preserve natural spaces, and reduce waste through composting. However, the author does

not mention that some renewable sources of energy cause environmental problems, too. For example, the damming of a river to produce electricity may harm the river's ecosystem. The author should have thought about such opposing claims and addressed them.

Counterarguments
I presented and supported an opposing claim to one of the author's claims.

Grammar

Irregular verbs, such as *thought,* do not follow the same spelling rules as those of other verbs.

Grammar Handbook See page 461.

Your Turn

Does the author successfully support her argument for building energy-efficient houses? Use text evidence to support your answer.

Go Digital!
Write your response online.
Use your editing checklist.

Brand X Pictures

Challenges

First, I believe that this nation should commit itself to achieving the goal, before this decade is out, of landing a man on the moon and returning him safely to the earth. No single space project in this period will be more impressive to mankind, or more important for the long-range exploration of space; and none will be so difficult or expensive to accomplish.

—President John F. Kennedy
from a special address to Congress,
May 25, 1961

the Big Idea

How do people meet challenges and solve problems?

Neil Armstrong was the first person to walk on the moon.

233

Essential Question

How do people meet environmental challenges?

Go Digital!

RESPONDING TO DISASTER

Rescuing this baby tern from the dangers of an oil spill is no simple matter.

▶ Terns are small shore birds that lay their eggs in the sand, so crews cleaning the beach must be told to walk with extra care.

▶ Though tern chicks leave their nests just a few days after hatching, they are still quite vulnerable. Rescuers must know a lot about them to care for them properly.

The tenacity of human effort in response to an environmental calamity offers shore animals a better chance of survival.

Talk About It

Write words you have learned about challenges to the environment. Then talk with a partner about the difficulties that bird rescuers face.

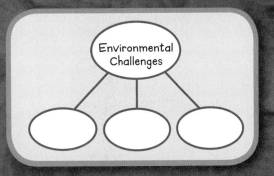

Environmental Challenges

Liu Jin/AFP/Getty Images

235

Vocabulary

Use the picture and the sentences to talk with a
partner about each word.

alignment

Proper **alignment** of a car's wheels
keeps the ride safe and steady.

How are the meanings of the words
alignment and position related?

calamity

The oil spill was a **calamity** because it
damaged so many natural habitats.

What is a synonym for calamity?

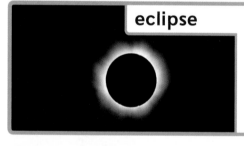

eclipse

During a solar **eclipse**, the moon blocks
the sun's light.

What do you think a partial solar
eclipse is?

generated

The electrical storm **generated**
dangerous cloud-to-ground lightning.

What is a synonym for generated?

inconvenience

The heavy traffic was an **inconvenience** to drivers.

Describe an inconvenience that has slowed your trip to school.

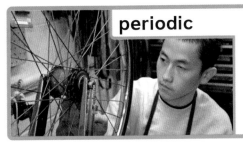

periodic

Twice a year, Kyung-su takes his bike to the shop for a **periodic** tune-up.

What is an antonym of periodic?

prolonged

Prolonged delays at the airport made our departure late.

When has a prolonged activity made you late?

tenacity

Hans showed **tenacity** when he completed the entire bike ride.

When have you showed tenacity?

Your Turn

COLLABORATE

Pick three words. Write three questions for your partner to answer.

Go Digital! **Use the online visual glossary**

(t to b) Jon Hicks/Photographer's Choice/Getty Images; Steve Skjold/Alamy; M. Scott Brauer/Demotix/Demotix/Corbis; Horst Friedrichs/Workbook Stock/Getty Images

The Day the Dam
BROKE

Essential Question
How do people meet environmental challenges?

Read how one of the greatest natural disasters of the 1800s hit a Pennsylvania town.

Johnstown, 1889

Down in the Valley

Johnstown, Pennsylvania, lies in a beautiful valley in the Appalachian Mountains. Two rivers flank the town, so in the early 1800s people began using the water power to run grist mills for grinding flour.

By 1834, Johnstown had become a key junction on the Pennsylvania Canal System. Many new businesses were **generated**. The new prosperity was enough to offset any hardships caused by **periodic** flooding when the rivers swelled with snow melt and heavy spring rains. For Johnstown's residents, moving to higher ground until the water receded was an **inconvenience** they could tolerate.

The Stage Is Set

To supply water to the Canal System during dry seasons, the state built a rock-and-earth dam 14 miles upstream from Johnstown on the Conemaugh River. At the dam's base, a drain fed water into the canal. But excess water from the lake behind the dam could also run off a spillway.

By 1852, both canal and dam were abandoned when the Pennsylvania Railroad completed a line between Johnstown and Pittsburgh. In 1875,

a man named Benjamin Ruff bought the property around the lake to build an exclusive resort called the South Fork Fishing and Hunting Club.

Ruff repaired the dam and stocked the lake with fish. But valves and pipes previously laid in careful **alignment** to control the water flow were removed, and the drain beneath the dam was filled in. The dam's lip was lowered by two feet when the road on top was widened, and the spillway was screened in from a bridge above to keep fish from escaping. Unknowingly, Ruff had set the stage for disaster.

A Tremendous Roar

On May 30, 1889, the worst storm ever recorded in Johnstown's history hit the area. Nearly 10 inches of rain fell in just 24 hours. The next morning, the rivers around Johnstown swelled into roaring torrents. As they had so many times before, residents moved to higher ground to wait out the flood.

Upriver, South Fork Club members feared the dam would fail if the lake rose any higher. Workers frantically tried to strengthen the dam. Men were sent to Johnstown to warn people. But the townspeople had heard too many such alarms over the years and they ignored the warnings.

Just after 3:00 P.M., the dam collapsed. Club members watched in horror as a 40-foot wave, about 20 million tons of water a half-mile wide, crashed down the river valley. Within minutes, the flood devoured four small towns. In less than an hour, it roared into Johnstown. Most people saw nothing. They heard only a thunderous rumble. But then the water was upon them.

Those not instantly killed were swept away by the angry surge. A jumbled mass of water, houses, trees, train cars, animals, and people smashed into the stone arches of the

Johnstown after the 1936 flood

railroad bridge downriver. Anyone still alive at that point met with **prolonged** torment when the debris caught fire. Many more died. That evening, a telegraph message arrived in Pittsburgh from Robert Pitcairn, railroad superintendent and a member of the South Fork Club. It said simply, "Johnstown is annihilated."

After the Flood

Response was swift as news spread. People around the world sent money, food, and clothing. The recently created Red Cross arrived to help survivors. Down, but not defeated, the people of Johnstown showed great **tenacity**. They set up tents and began to rebuild.

The 1889 flood is among the worst disasters in American history. Many blamed the South Fork Club for causing the **calamity** with its mishandling of the dam. The people of Johnstown sued. But the

Primary Sources

Sources of information are considered primary if they come from people living at the time of the event described. Examples include letters, eye-witness accounts, photographs, newspaper articles, and government documents.

There are many first-hand accounts by survivors of the 1889 Johnstown flood. Gertrude Quinn Slattery, for example, was only six years old at the time, but she later recalled being swept away on a "raft with a muddy mattress and bedding." Like others, she remembered "holding on for dear life . . ." Thankfully, she lived to tell her story.

Johnstown today

courts ruled the flood an accident and awarded no money. Some club members contributed to relief efforts. Andrew Carnegie donated $10,000 and rebuilt the town's library. Other members remained silent.

When another flood hit Johnstown in 1936, the federal government paid to have the rivers re-routed. Johnstown residents rebuilt once again, believing there would be no more floods. But on July 20, 1977, nearly 12 inches of rain fell in 10 hours. Six dams burst, pouring 128 million gallons of water into Johnstown.

This time, many people moved, and businesses closed for good. Like an **eclipse** darkening the sky, the 1977 flood dimmed Johnstown's future.

Today, key activities help reduce the danger to Johnstown. The National Weather Service sponsors a flood watchers program, and studies are done to identify weaknesses in the flood protection systems. But there is also an emergency plan, just in case the waters overrun Johnstown again.

Ilene MacDonald/Alamy

Make Connections

How did the people of Johnstown respond to the challenges of flooding? ESSENTIAL QUESTION

Talk about a disaster you have heard or read about. Tell how people responded to the challenges they faced from the environment. TEXT TO SELF

Reread

When you read a historical account like "The Day the Dam Broke," pause often to reread detailed information. If you are not sure why an event happened, reread the details provided by the author to make sure you understand them.

 ## Find Text Evidence

It may not be clear to you why Benjamin Ruff made changes to the dam and unknowingly "set the stage for disaster." Reread "The Stage is Set" on page 239 of "The Day the Dam Broke."

page 239

Ruff repaired the dam and stocked the lake with fish. But valves and pipes previously laid in careful **alignment** to control the water flow were removed, and the drain beneath the dam was filled in. The dam's lip was lowered by two feet when the road on top was widened, and the spillway was screened in from a bridge above to keep fish from escaping. Unknowingly, Ruff had set the stage for disaster.

A Tremendous Roar

On May 30, 1889, the worst storm ever recorded in Johnstown's history hit the area. Nearly 10 inches

I read Ruff's changes meant that water flow valves were removed, the drain "was filled in," and the "lip was lowered." From this, I can infer that the changes helped keep fish in the lake but made the dam unsafe.

Your Turn

Why did railroad superintendent Robert Pitcairn report that Johnstown had been "annihilated?" Reread the section "A Tremendous Roar" on pages 239–240 to answer the question. As you read, remember to use the strategy Reread.

Author's Point of View

Historical accounts are often written to be objective, to tell all sides of a story from an unbiased point of view. But authors may reveal their attitudes. Readers must separate unsupported statements from those backed by evidence.

Find Text Evidence

When I reread "The Day the Dam Broke," I can ask myself whether the author has a particular point of view about the Johnstown flood. I can look for details that let me know whether the author is objective in presenting supported claims or shows some bias.

Details	Author's Point of View
Facts about the rivers, periodic flooding, and changes to the dam provide background information.	
Vivid descriptions of the flood are followed by facts about the survivors receiving help.	

Your Turn

Reread "The Day the Dam Broke." On the graphic organizer, list more details about how the information is presented. Then identify the author's overall point of view.

Go Digital!
Use the interactive graphic organizer

Expository

"The Day the Dam Broke" is an expository text about a historical event. It was written by someone who did not witness the events as they happened, so it is a secondary source.

An **Expository** text:
- May provide facts about people and events in the past
- May draw upon evidence from primary sources

 Find Text Evidence

"The Day the Dam Broke" provides an overview of Johnstown's problem with flooding. It also gives me a vivid description of the 1889 disaster. The photographs and details from the time of the flood help me visualize the events.

page 240

heard too many such alarms over the years and they ignored the warnings.

Just after 3:00 P.M., the dam collapsed. Club members watched in horror as a 40-foot wave, about 20 million tons of water a half-mile wide, crashed down the river valley. Within minutes, the flood devoured four small towns. In less than an hour, it roared into Johnstown. Most people saw nothing. They heard only a thunderous rumble. But then the water was upon them.

Those not instantly killed were swept away by the angry surge. A jumbled mass of water, houses, trees, train cars, animals, and people smashed into the stone arches of the

Johnstown after the 1936 flood

Primary Sources

Sources of information are considered primary if they come from people living at the time of the event described. Examples include letters, eye-witness accounts, photographs, newspaper articles, and government documents. There are many first-hand accounts by survivors of the 1889 Johnstown flood. Gertrude Quinn Slattery, for example, was only six years old at the time, but she later recalled being swept away on a "raft with a muddy mattress and bedding." Like others, she remembered "holding on for dear life . . ." Thankfully, she lived to tell her story.

railroad bridge downriver. Anyone still alive at that point met with **prolonged** torment when the debris caught fire. Many more died. That evening, a telegraph message arrived in Pittsburgh from Robert Pitcairn, railroad superintendent and a member of the South Fork Club. It said simply, "Johnstown is annihilated."

After the Flood
Response was swift as news spread. People around the world sent money, food, and clothing. The recently created Red Cross arrived to help survivors. Down, but not defeated, the people of Johnstown showed great **tenacity**. They set up tents and began to rebuild.

The 1889 flood is among the worst disasters in American history. Many blamed the South Fork Club for causing the **calamity** with its mishandling of the dam. The people of Johnstown sued. But the

240

Text Feature

Primary Sources Primary sources include eyewitness accounts, government documents, and photographs taken when the events occurred.

COLLABORATE

Your Turn

Identify two examples of primary source information in "The Day the Dam Broke." Tell what you learned about the flood from each example.

Paragraph Clues

Sometimes the sentence containing an unfamiliar or multiple-meaning word provides no context clues to the word's meaning. When that is true, reread the entire paragraph to look for clues that help you find or verify the word's meaning.

 ## Find Text Evidence

I'm not sure what the word torrents *means on page 239 of "The Day the Dam Broke." In the same paragraph, I read that "nearly 10 inches of rain fell" in Johnstown on May 30, 1889, and that the "residents moved to higher ground to wait out the flood." I think* roaring torrents *must mean "huge amounts of rushing water."*

> On May 30, 1889, the worst storm ever recorded in Johnstown's history hit the area. Nearly 10 inches of rain fell in just 24 hours. The next morning, the rivers around Johnstown swelled into roaring torrents. As they had so many times before, residents moved to higher ground to wait out the flood.

Your Turn

Use paragraph clues to find or verify the meanings of the following words in "The Day the Dam Broke":

prosperity, *page 239*
frantically, *page 239*
annihilated, *page 240*

Write About the Text

Pages 238–241

Ben

I answered the question: *Should the South Fork Club have been held more responsible for the 1889 Johnstown Flood?*

Student Model: *Argument*

The South Fork Club should have been held more responsible for the 1889 Johnstown Flood. Benjamin Ruff was only concerned with the members of his club. When Mr. Ruff repaired the dam and stocked it with fish, he removed the valves, pipes, and drains that controlled the flow of water. He was

Introduce a Claim
My opening sentence clearly states my argument.

Grammar

This sentence contains a **pronoun,** *he,* and its **antecedent,** "Mr. Ruff."

Grammar Handbook See page 462.

Radius Images/Alamy

246

more worried about fish escaping from the lake than about protecting people in the towns from floods. Then the worst storm in Johnstown's history hit. The dam collapsed, and water flooded and destroyed Johnstown. This tragedy might not have happened if Benjamin Ruff had properly repaired the dam.

Sequence

I used the word *then* to help the reader understand the order of events.

Strong Conclusion

My concluding statement supports my argument and follows from the evidence I presented.

Your Turn

Should Johnstown remain a populated city? Provide evidence to support your response.

Go Digital!
Write your response online.
Use your editing checklist.

Essential Question

How do people meet personal challenges?

Go Digital!

RISING TO THE CHALLENGE

The paintings of Huang Guofu, a native of Chongqing, China, are assessed highly by art dealers and collectors from around the world.

► When Huang was just 4 years old, he lost his arms in an accident. At age 12, he began to paint using his right foot to hold the brush. He also paints with his mouth.

► Huang practiced a long time before he felt his paintings showed what he intended.

Huang is quick to tell young people that there are no obstacles to doing anything they truly want to do.

Talk About It COLLABORATE

Write words you have learned about overcoming challenges. Then talk with a partner about how Huang Guofu met a personal challenge.

Overcoming Challenges

Vocabulary

Use the picture and the sentences to talk with a
partner about each word.

assess

Tests help teachers **assess** how well
students are learning.

How do sports fans assess how well an
athlete is performing?

compensate

On hot days, a fan can help **compensate**
for the lack of a breeze.

How are the meanings of the words
compensate and replace related?

deteriorated

The paint had **deteriorated** after years
of exposure to weather.

What is a synonym for deteriorated?

devastating

The **devastating** fire destroyed many
trees.

What other natural occurrences have
devastating effects?

implement

My school plans to **implement** a program that promotes eating healthy foods.

What program do you think your school should implement?

peripheral

The wide brim of her hat blocked some of her **peripheral** vision.

Why might peripheral vision be important?

potential

The dark clouds indicate the **potential** for a rain storm.

When is the potential for snow the greatest?

summit

The climbers finally reached the **summit** of the mountain.

What is an antonym of summit?

Your Turn

COLLABORATE

Pick three words. Write three questions for your partner to answer.

Go Digital! *Use the online visual glossary*

She Had to
WALK
Before She Could
RUN

Essential Question

How do people meet personal challenges?

Read how a young woman overcame physical challenges to become an Olympic athlete.

Wilma Rudolph at the
1960 Summer Olympics

In a crowded Olympic stadium, the gun sounded and Wilma Rudolph took off like a bolt of lightning. As this amazing athlete ran confidently around the track, she never lost her cool. Sprinting toward the finish line, Wilma used her **peripheral** vision to ensure that her competitors would not catch up. The crowd roared with elation as "the fastest woman in the world" finished more than three yards ahead of the other athletes.

Against All Odds

Though Wilma Rudolph inspired many during that 1960 Summer Olympics in Rome, Italy, her childhood had been riddled with hardships. Wilma was one of 22 children born to an impoverished Tennessee family. While she was a toddler, her health **deteriorated** because of life-threatening illnesses.

When she was four years old, Wilma contracted polio, a severe disease that causes paralysis. As a result, Wilma lost the use of her left leg. Having polio could have been **devastating** for Wilma. Instead, she faced this physical challenge with a positive attitude and never lost sight of her goal.

Wilma's mother taught her very early to believe she could achieve any goal, and the first was to walk without leg braces. Once a week, she drove Wilma 90 miles round-trip to Nashville for physical therapy. Her mother also instructed Wilma's siblings on how to massage their sister's legs. Done several times a day, this monotonous routine continued for several years.

An Inspiring Comeback

Wilma's doctors had little hope that she would ever be able to walk again. When she was nine years old, they decided to **assess** her progress. After the doctors removed the braces, they were amazed to see that Wilma could walk on her own. They were stunned by what this young girl could do despite having contracted a crippling disease for which there was no cure.

From then on, Wilma never looked back. To **compensate** for the years she had been in braces, Wilma became extremely active. As proof of her determination, she ran everyday. She decided never to give up, no matter what happened.

Wilma's brothers set up a basketball hoop in the backyard, and she and her siblings played all day. Wilma became an avid basketball player at school, too. A track coach named Ed Temple from Tennessee State University spotted Wilma at a basketball tournament and was extremely impressed by her athletic ability and **potential**. He invited her to attend a sports camp. Once again, Wilma's life changed dramatically, this time for the better.

An Olympic Champion

The minute Wilma ran on a track, she loved it. When she was just sixteen years old, she qualified for the 1956 Summer Olympic Games in Melbourne, Australia. And Wilma came home wearing the bronze medal she had won in the relay race.

After high school, Wilma was awarded a full scholarship to major in education at Tennessee State University. But once again, Wilma had to overcome challenges. In 1958, having put her shoulder to the wheel both in class and during track-and-field events, she became too ill to run. After she had a tonsillectomy, however, she felt better and started to run again. Unfortunately, Wilma pulled a muscle at a track meet in 1959, and Coach Temple had to **implement** a plan for her recovery. Wilma recovered just in time to qualify for the 1960 Summer Olympics in Rome.

Wilma displays her gold medals (above); at the 1960 games

(t) Bettmann/Corbis; (b) Mark Kauffman/Time Life Pictures/Getty Images

Wilma Rudolph's Olympics Statistics

Date	Event	Time	Medal
1956	200 Meters	Not in finals	None
1956	4 x 100 Meters Relay	44.9 seconds	Bronze
1960	100 Meters	11.0 seconds	Gold
1960	200 Meters	24.0 seconds	Gold
1960	4 x 100 Meters Relay	44.5 seconds	Gold

In her individual sprints, Wilma outshone her competition and won two gold medals with ease. During the relay event, however, the team comprised of four athletes from Tennessee State found themselves in hot water. After a poor baton pass, Wilma had to pick up her pace and run like the wind to complete the last leg of the race. She successfully overtook Germany's last runner to win the race. Wilma became the first American woman in track and field to win three gold medals. Of her feeling of accomplishment, she said she knew it was something "nobody could ever take away from me, ever."

Giving Back

The **summit** of Wilma's career might have been her achievements as an Olympic athlete. Instead, she went on to accomplish much more. After graduating from college, she taught school and coached track. Soon Wilma was traveling the country, giving speeches to school audiences.

To inspire others to do their best in spite of all challenges, she would note that "the triumph can't be had without the struggle." Wilma achieved her dreams and, ever after, helped others to reach theirs.

Make Connections

Talk about how Wilma met personal challenges to become a successful athlete. ESSENTIAL QUESTIONS

Describe a time when someone you know had a personal challenge and overcame it. TEXT TO SELF

Reread

When you read a biography, you may need to clarify what the author thinks is important about each of the events in the subject's life. As you read "She Had to Walk Before She Could Run," you can pause to reread difficult sections to make sure you understand the points the author is making in them.

 Find Text Evidence

You may need to reread the section "Against All Odds" on page 253 to make sure you understand the significance of what happened to Rudolph when she was a young child.

page 253

Against All Odds

Though Wilma Rudolph inspired many during that 1960 Summer Olympics in Rome, Italy, her childhood had been riddled with hardships. Wilma was one of 22 children born to an impoverished Tennessee family. While she was a toddler, her health **deteriorated** because of life-threatening illnesses.

When she was four years old, Wilma contracted polio, a severe disease that causes paralysis. As a result, Wilma lost the use of her left leg. Having polio could have been **devastating** for Wilma. Instead, she faced this physical challenge with a positive attitude and never lost sight of her goal.

I read that Rudolph had poor health as a toddler and contracted polio at age four. That tells me that Rudolph's greatest challenges arose when she was still very young.

Your Turn

COLLABORATE

How does the author show Rudolph's determination once her leg braces were removed? Reread "An Inspiring Comeback" on page 253–254 to answer the question. As you read, remember to use the strategy Reread.

Author's Point of View

The author of a biography usually expresses a personal point of view about the subject. As you read a biography, identifying this point of view can help you determine whether the author's assertions are backed by evidence or are unsupported.

 ## Find Text Evidence

As I reread "She Had to Walk Before She Could Run," I can look for details that reveal the author's attitude toward Wilma Rudolph. Then I can decide when statements about Rudolph are supported.

Details
The author refers to Rudolph as an "amazing athlete" at the Olympics.
Rudolph faced the challenges of her illness with a "positive attitude."

Author's Point of View

Your Turn

COLLABORATE

Reread "She Had to Walk Before She Could Run." Identify more details that show the author's attitude toward Rudolph. Then explain how this point of view is, or is not, supported by evidence.

Go Digital!
Use the interactive graphic organizer

Biography

"She Had to Walk Before She Could Run" is a biography.

A **Biography**:

- Often focuses on a certain time period or important aspect of the subject's life
- May include text features that provide specific details

Find Text Evidence

This biography of Wilma Rudolph focuses on the ways she dealt with the difficult challenges she faced. The information in the table gives me specific details about her accomplishments.

page 255

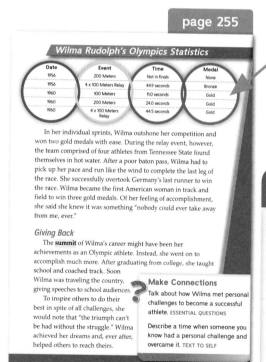

Wilma Rudolph's Olympics Statistics

Date	Event	Time	Medal
1956	200 Meters	Not in finals	None
1956	4 x 100 Meters Relay	44.9 seconds	Bronze
1960	100 Meters	11.0 seconds	Gold
1960	200 Meters	24.0 seconds	Gold
1960	4 x 100 Meters Relay	44.5 seconds	Gold

In her individual sprints, Wilma outshone her competition and won two gold medals with ease. During the relay event, however, the team comprised of four athletes from Tennessee State found themselves in hot water. After a poor baton pass, Wilma had to pick up her pace and run like the wind to complete the last leg of the race. She successfully overtook Germany's last runner to win the race. Wilma became the first American woman in track and field to win three gold medals. Of her feeling of accomplishment, she said she knew it was something "nobody could ever take away from me, ever."

Giving Back

The **summit** of Wilma's career might have been her achievements as an Olympic athlete. Instead, she went on to accomplish much more. After graduating from college, she taught school and coached track. Soon Wilma was traveling the country, giving speeches to school audiences.

To inspire others to do their best in spite of all challenges, she would note that "the triumph can't be had without the struggle." Wilma achieved her dreams and, ever after, helped others to reach theirs.

Make Connections

Talk about how Wilma met personal challenges to become a successful athlete. ESSENTIAL QUESTIONS

Describe a time when someone you know had a personal challenge and overcame it. TEXT TO SELF

255

Text Features

Tables Tables show detailed information in an organized way.

Photographs Photographs show the subject at the time described.

Your Turn

COLLABORATE

Identify a challenge that Rudolph faced after recovering from polio. How does this information reflect the author's focus in this biography? Tell why the author chose to separate the information in the table from the main text.

Idioms

The expression *it's raining cats and dogs* is an idiom. As a whole, the expression has a meaning that goes beyond the individual definitions of the words. If you read an expression that does not make sense in "She Had to Walk Before She Could Run," consider whether the phrase might be an idiom. Look for context clues to help you understand it or verify what you think it means.

 Find Text Evidence

The phrase put her shoulder to the wheel *confuses me. It doesn't make sense that Rudolph would place her shoulder against a wheel in school or on the track. But the sentence also says that Wilma became too ill to run. I think the expression is an idiom that means "Wilma worked extremely hard."*

> In 1958, having put her shoulder to the wheel both in class and during track-and-field events, she became too ill to run.

Your Turn

Use context clues to determine the meaning of each of the following idioms in "She Had to Walk Before She Could Run."

she never lost her cool, *page 253*

Wilma never looked back, *page 254*

found themselves in hot water, *page 255*

Write About the Text

Pages 252–255

Maria

I answered the question: *Whom do you think was the most powerful influence in Wilma's life?*

Student Model: *Argument*

Wilma Rudolph's family was the

most powerful influence in her life.

When she had polio, Wilma's mother

drove her 90 miles round-trip every

week for physical therapy. Her siblings

massaged her legs several times a day.

Then she got the braces off her leg

and began playing basketball with her

Grammar

This sentence includes both a **subject pronoun** and an **object pronoun**.

Grammar Handbook See page 462.

Supporting Details

I supported my argument with evidence from the text.

siblings. As a result of this exercise, Wilma became physically fit soon after she began walking. By the time Wilma was a teenager, people noticed that she was a great athlete. This success couldn't have happened unless her family helped with her therapy and then with getting her in shape.

Transitions
I used the phrase "By the time Wilma was a teenager" to signal a shift in the subject matter.

Strong Conclusion
My conclusion sums up the argument I presented.

Your Turn

What qualities are the most important to become a successful athlete? Defend your argument with evidence from the text.

Go Digital!
Write your response online.
Use your editing checklist.

Bettmann/Corbis

Essential Question

When are decisions hard to make?

Go Digital!

Making the Right Choice

We were given several options for our spring project. Each will entail getting out and talking to people in our community. Now my problem is deciding which one to do!

▶ Choosing a topic I feel comfortable with will make it easier to interview people.

▶ But maybe that's *too* easy. What would happen if I chose a topic I don't have much empathy for?

You know what? Something tells me I'll be glad I chose something unfamiliar.

Talk About It

Write words you have learned about making a difficult decision. Then talk with a partner about a time you were glad you made the right choice.

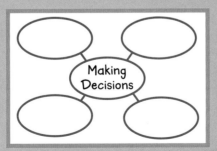

Making Decisions

Vocabulary

Use the picture and the sentences to talk with a
partner about each word.

benefactor

A wealthy **benefactor** gave the museum
a large donation.

Why might a benefactor choose to
help others?

empathy

My dog died last year, so I have
empathy for Deb's loss of her cat.

How are the meanings of empathy and
understanding related?

endeavor

Jackie loves adventure, so her next
endeavor will be climbing a mountain.

What new endeavor would you like
to try?

entail

Swimming the 200-meter race in less than
two minutes would **entail** a lot of training.

What preparation does getting good
grades entail?

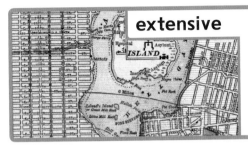

extensive

The map shows the city's **extensive** network of streets.

How else might you see how extensive a streetscape is?

indecision

My **indecision** about what to wear makes me late some mornings.

Describe a time that indecision delayed you.

multitude

They saw a **multitude** of birds nearly covering the beach.

What is a synonym for multitude?

tentatively

In case the water was too cold, she tested it **tentatively** with her toes.

What else might a person do tentatively?

COLLABORATE

Your Turn

Pick three words. Write three questions for your partner to answer.

Go Digital! *Use the online visual glossary*

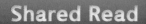
Treasure in the Attic

Cast of Characters

LIZ, a 12-year-old girl
EMMA, Liz's cousin, age 11
MR. SNOW, a shopkeeper
YARD SALE CUSTOMER

? Essential Question

When are decisions hard to make?

Read about a decision that two cousins need to make when they discover a long-lost family heirloom.

266

SCENE 1 *The attic of Liz's house; Liz and Emma are kneeling.*

Emma *(looking through a box)*: We'll never get through all this stuff!

Liz: We have to. I need twenty-five more dollars for that new bike. My dad says we can sell at a yard sale anything we find up here. You can keep half of whatever we make.

Emma *(coughing)*: I know. I just didn't realize it would entail breathing in so much dust.

Liz *(with enthusiasm)*: I don't think anyone has looked at Grandpa's and Grandma's stuff since they moved to Florida. There's a multitude of treasures up here.

Emma: Be on the lookout for a pair of pearl earrings. Grandma says Great-Grandma forgot what she did with them. You're supposed to inherit them, since you're the oldest heir among the grandkids.

Liz: Wow. I hope they're worth a lot of money!

Emma: If I had something of Great-Grandma's, I'd never sell it.

Liz *(finding an old diary, flipping pages)*: Wow, a diary! Listen to this: (reading) "October 7, 1936. I feel such empathy for Anna Snow and her family. They may have to leave us to find work elsewhere. This terrible Depression has bred such suffering for our neighbors. We are fortunate that Albert's income is not solely dependent on local business. My new endeavor is to be Anna's benefactor. If I gave her my pearl earrings, Anna could sell them to pay debts. She'd surely do the same for me. But can I? Albert would never approve if I gave away his wedding gift to me. Yet I must do it! It will be our secret—Anna's and mine...."

Emma *(excitedly)*: So that's what happened to Great-Grandma's earrings! Anna Snow must have been a wonderful friend. Could hers be the same family that owns Snow's General Store?

Liz: Let's go find out.

SCENE 2 *Snow's General Store; enter Liz and Emma.*

Mr. Snow: Good morning. May I help you young ladies?

Emma *(tentatively)*: Um... Mr. Snow, we were wondering if you might be related to Anna Snow.

Mr. Snow: Yes, I'm her grandson. Why do you ask?

Liz: We're trying to solve a mystery. Our great-grandmother, Flossie Howard, was a good friend of your grandmother's. She wrote about her in a diary she kept. *(She shows the diary to Mr. Snow.)*

Mr. Snow: Flossie Howard, you say? That name rings a bell, but I can't quite place it. There were lots of Howards in town in those days.

Liz *(with disappointment)*: Well...thanks anyway.

Mr. Snow: I do hope you solve your mystery.

SCENE 3 *Liz's yard, a few days later; the girls are setting items out for the yard sale as neighbors arrive.*

Tristan Elwell

Emma: Look, Liz. Isn't that Mr. Snow from the store? I wonder what he's doing here.

Mr. Snow: Hello, girls. I think this might belong to you. *(He hands Liz a small yellowed envelope.)*

Liz *(reading)*: "For Flossie."

Mr. Snow: I knew I'd heard that name somewhere. After you left, I found that envelope tucked away in the back of the store safe.

Liz *(opens the envelope, finds a note and the pearl earrings; reading)*: "Dearest Flossie, I can't tell you how

268

much I appreciate the gesture. But I can't accept this kindest of offers. The earrings are yours and too lovely to part with."

Mr. Snow: Her brother Bert took charge of the store when she and Granddad left. In all the hubbub, I guess she forgot she'd stowed the earrings in the safe. And she never did come back.

Liz: Even so, they've been secure all these years. Thanks very much, Mr. Snow.

Yard Sale Customer: Those earrings are lovely. Would you take twenty-five dollars for them?

Liz: Twenty-five dollars? I could get my new bike.

Emma: But the earrings are family heirlooms! And we don't even know what they're worth.

Liz (*to herself, seized by indecision*): I'd really like the money for the bike. But... maybe Emma's right. They *are* Great-Grandma's earrings. (*to Yard Sale Customer*) Sorry, ma'am, they're not for sale. (*to Emma*) We should each keep one. I'll earn money for the bike some other way. Hey, I'll bet the *basement* could use an extensive cleaning out!

Make Connections

Talk about the decisions that the characters, both past and present, find difficult to make. **ESSENTIAL QUESTION**

Talk about what you had to consider at a time when you made a difficult decision. **TEXT TO SELF**

Summarize

Just as you would for a story, you can summarize a play to help you understand and remember the most important events in the plot. Pause after reading each of the three scenes in "Treasure in the Attic" to review key plot events.

 Find Text Evidence

Reread Scene 1 on page 267. Identify key details and use them to retell in your own words what is most important in this scene.

---

page 267

SCENE 1 *The attic of Liz's house; Liz and Emma are kneeling.*

Emma *(looking through a box)*: We'll never get through all this stuff!

Liz: We have to. I need twenty-five more dollars for that new bike. My dad says we can sell at a yard sale anything we find up here. You can keep half of whatever we make.

Emma *(coughing)*: I know. I just didn't realize it would entail breathing in so much dust.

Liz *(with enthusiasm)*: I don't think anyone has looked at Grandpa's and Grandma's stuff since they moved to Florida. There's a multitude of treasures up here.

Emma: Be on the lookout for a pair of pearl earrings. Grandma says Great-Grandma forgot what she did with them. You're supposed to inherit them, since you're the oldest heir among the grandkids.

Liz: Wow. I hope they're worth a lot of money!

I read that two cousins are looking in the attic for things to "sell at a yard sale." Liz finds their great-grandmother's diary, and they read about earrings they know have been missing. I can summarize this scene by saying that, while busy trying to earn money, Liz and Emma stumble upon a mystery they want to solve.

Your Turn

COLLABORATE

Reread Scenes 2 and 3. Use the most important events to summarize each scene. As you read, remember to use the strategy Summarize.

Theme

To determine the theme, or central message, of a play, pay attention to the dialogue and stage directions. Think about what causes the characters to say what they say. Also consider how the characters may have changed by the end of the play.

 Find Text Evidence

When I reread Scene 1 of "Treasure in the Attic," I think about what effect Liz's hopes for buying a new bike may have on her decisions later in the play. The girls' reactions to reading their great-grandmother's diary also help me understand the characters.

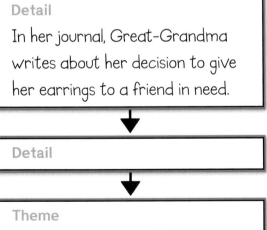

Detail
The reason Liz seeks items to sell is that she wants to buy a bike.

Use the characters' words and actions as clues to the theme.

Detail
In her journal, Great-Grandma writes about her decision to give her earrings to a friend in need.

Detail

Theme

COLLABORATE

Your Turn

Reread "Treasure in the Attic." Identify other important details about a main character or plot event, and add them to the graphic organizer. Then use all the details to determine the theme of the play.

Go Digital!
Use the interactive graphic organizer

Drama

"Treasure in the Attic" is a play, a work to perform on a stage.

A **Play**:

- Is written as lines of dialogue to be spoken by actors
- Has stage directions to indicate setting and action
- May have long sections, *acts,* and short sections, *scenes*

Find Text Evidence

"Treasure in the Attic" is a play in three scenes. Stage directions in italics tell where each scene takes place and how characters speak.

page 267

SCENE 1 *The attic of Liz's house; Liz and Emma are kneeling.*

Emma *(looking through a box)*: We'll never get through all this stuff!

Liz: We have to. I need twenty-five more dollars for that new bike. My dad says we can sell at a yard sale anything we find up here. You can keep half of whatever we make.

Emma *(coughing)*: I know. I just didn't realize it would **entail** breathing in so much dust.

Liz *(with enthusiasm)*: I don't think anyone has looked at Grandpa's and Grandma's stuff since they moved to Florida. There's a **multitude** of treasures up here.

Emma: Be on the lookout for a pair of pearl earrings. Grandma says Great-Grandma forgot what she did with them. You're supposed to inherit them, since you're the oldest heir among the grandkids.

Liz: Wow. I hope they're worth a lot of money!

Emma: If I had something of Great-Grandma's, I'd never sell it.

Liz *(finding an old diary, flipping pages)*: Wow, a diary! Listen to this: (reading) "October 7, 1936. I feel such **empathy** for Anna Snow and her family. They may have to leave us to find work elsewhere. This terrible Depression has bred such suffering for our neighbors. We are fortunate that Albert's income is not solely dependent on local business. My new **endeavor** is to be Anna's **benefactor.** If I gave her my pearl earrings, Anna could sell them to pay debts. She'd surely do the same for me. But can I? Albert would never approve if I gave away his wedding gift to me. Yet I must do it! It will be our secret—Anna's and mine...."

Emma *(excitedly)*: So that's what happened to Great-Grandma's earrings! Anna Snow must have been a wonderful friend. Could hers be the same family that owns Snow's General Store?

Liz: Let's go find out.

Scenes A scene consists of dialogue and action in one particular time and setting.

Stage Directions Stage directions describe the setting and characters' actions. They are not spoken by the actors.

Your Turn

COLLABORATE

Tell your partner why the action in "Treasure in the Attic" is divided into three scenes. Then find two stage directions that identify a setting and two that describe a character's action. Tell how these stage directions help you visualize the plot of the play.

Homophones

Homophones are words that sound the same when spoken but have different meanings and are often spelled differently. When you read a word that sounds like another word, use context clues to help you choose the correct meaning.

 Find Text Evidence

When the dialogue in "Treasure in the Attic" is spoken aloud, audiences might confuse the word pair *on page 267 with its homophone* pear. *Emma's dialogue refers to earrings, however, so I know that the meaning of* pair *in this context is "two of something," not "a kind of fruit."*

> Be on the lookout for a <u>pair</u> of pearl earrings.

Your Turn

COLLABORATE

Use context clues to find the meaning of each of these words in "Treasure in the Attic." Then tell why the meaning of its homophone is not the correct one.

sale, *page 267,* and **sail**
heir, *page 267,* and **air**
bred, *page 267,* and **bread**

Write About the Text

Pages 266–269

Naomi

I responded to the prompt: *Imagine it is October of 1936. Write a flashback scene between Great-Grandma and Anna.*

Student Model: *Narrative Text*

Anna: Flossie, I cannot let you help me like this. Times are hard for all of us. I can't let you make that sacrifice for my family.

Flossie: It would be so sad if you left. Please let me do something. I can sell some of my jewelry or give it to you to sell.

Develop Characters

I used dialogue to help the reader understand the types of people Anna and Flossie were.

Grammar

This phrase contains the **possessive pronoun,** *my*.

Grammar Handbook
See page 463.

274

Anna: Thank you so much for your concern, Flossie. I will miss you so much.

Flossie: Then let me help you and your family. Let's say no more about it. I'll do something for you, and we don't ever have to speak of it again.

Inferences
I used details from the play to decide what else the characters might say to each other.

Point of View
I concluded the scene by identifying Flossie's point of view.

Your Turn

Imagine that the girls discover that Anna is still alive. Write a dialogue among the three of them.

Go Digital!
Write your response online.
Use your editing checklist.

Essential Question

How do people uncover
what they have in common?

Go Digital!

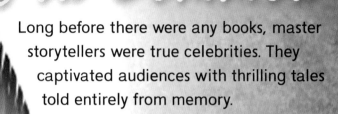
A Lot in Common

Long before there were any books, master storytellers were true celebrities. They captivated audiences with thrilling tales told entirely from memory.

▶ Storytelling is very much alive today. This man draws listeners in with a tale of the Acjachemen people, a Native American tribe in California.

▶ The best stories usually feature suspenseful plots and characters that most everyone can relate to.

Sharing the excitement of a good story can bring people of all backgrounds and ages together.

Talk About It

Write words you have learned about how people find out what they have in common. Then talk with a partner about why certain stories appeal to so many people.

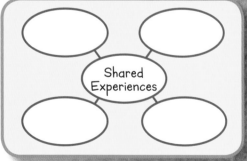

Shared Experiences

McGraw-Hill Companies, Inc.

Vocabulary

Use the picture and the sentences to talk with a partner about each word.

adjustment

Starting at a new school in the middle of the year was a big **adjustment** for me.

Describe a big adjustment you have had to make.

chattering

Some audience members were still **chattering** after the movie had started.

When else might chattering annoy people?

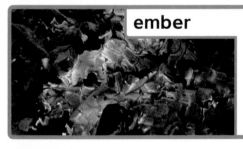

ember

Risa made sure to put out the last **ember** before leaving the campfire.

How can you tell if an ember is still burning?

mentor

Young volunteers often need a **mentor** who can guide them.

How are the meanings of mentor and teacher related?

nomadic

The **nomadic** people of Mongolia still move their camps several times a year.

What is a synonym for nomadic?

rapport

The supportive coach had a great **rapport** with members of his team.

Describe someone you have a good rapport with.

reunites

Our family **reunites** each summer with a special picnic.

What event reunites your family members?

sturdy

Juan wore **sturdy** shoes to go hiking.

What is an antonym of sturdy?

COLLABORATE

Your Turn

Pick three words. Write three questions for your partner to answer.

Go Digital! **Use the online visual glossary**

My Visit to Arizona

Essential Question

How do people uncover what they have in common?

Read how a girl from Argentina meets the challenges of making new friends in a foreign country.

Silvina and her parents have traveled from their ranch in Argentina to one in Arizona. The trip reunites Silvina's father with his college friend, Mr. Gomez. While her parents share ideas about raising cattle, Silvina spends her days with the Gomez boys, Mike and Carl, and their grandfather.

Shocking

—*Short Sharp Shocks. Try to say it three times fast.*

My English tutor at home taught me that tongue twister. How perfectly it describes my arrival in Arizona!

Shock 1: We are staying on the hot, dusty Gomez Ranch. My family travels so much, I think we are **nomadic**. But usually we sleep in nice, air-conditioned hotels.

Shock 2: People here think I can ride horses. Do I tell them the only saddle I have used is on a bicycle? And that I am more inclined to read *books* about horses?

Shock 3: English lessons do not automatically prepare you to understand the way people speak in Arizona.

—*Pull up a chair and get comfy*, says Grampa G.

But the chairs are too big for me to lift. And who is *Comfy*? Must everyone here talk so fast?

Nodding and Smiling

—*Our ranch covers 150 acres*, Grampa G says. *Permit me to show you around.*

I am thinking, Show me a round *what*? but there is no time to ask, because he is pushing me toward an army of cattle.

—*Here's the finest herd in the Southwest, 'bout 200 strong.*

I think Grampa G would make an excellent **mentor**, if only I understood half of all he is **chattering** about.

I nod and smile and pretend I understand.

Siede Preis/Photodisc/Getty Images

I lift my camera to take a photo of him with a big steer.

At least I am not the only one nodding and smiling now.

—*Here's a **sturdy** fellow*, says Grampa G. *The strongest horse for miles.*

He leads the biggest, blackest horse I have ever seen right up to me.

—*Silvina, let me present Stormy to you.*

I stare in disbelief. Is he giving me a horse?

Say something, Silvina. Say something, quick!

—*Thank you, but I cannot accept such a big present*, I sputter.

Grampa G laughs and laughs.

Finally, he stops laughing and tells me what is so funny.

Apparently, *PRES*ent and pre*SENT* are two different words.

I will never learn English!

Riding and Reading

It has happened: Mike discovered I never rode a horse.

Now he and Carl want me to ride that beast Stormy.

—*Riding's a cinch*, says Mike. *Easy as falling out of bed.*

Or off a cliff, I think. But I do not say that.

—*He looks like the wild horse from* The Black Stallion, I say.

—*I love that book!* shouts Carl.

I tell him how I read it in English class, and he forgets all
    about putting me on Stormy and we talk about books instead.

What a relief! I am content for the first time in days.

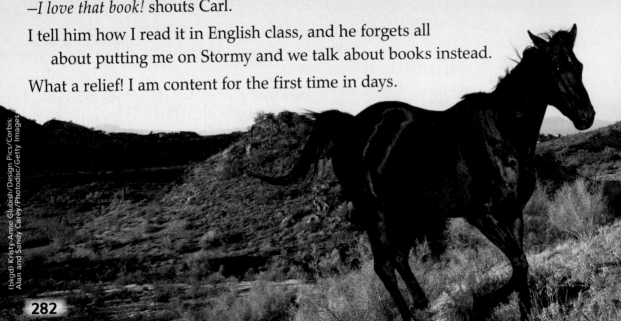

—*So, Silvina, you ready to ride Stormy?* interrupts Mike.

Goodbye, contentment. Can my camera save me again?

I point it at the brothers standing next to the black colossus.

Suddenly Carl runs to the house and brings out a camera.

—*Hey, can you show me how to work this thing?* he asks. *I got it
    last month and never figured it out.*

At last, something I can do!

Six weeks later, we are all sitting around a campfire, each
    roasting a marshmallow on a glowing **ember**.

—*These would go well with* dulce de leche, I say.

For once, Mike and Carl look confused instead of me.

—*A very delicious caramel,* I explain. *It is good on anything.*

Carl uses his camera to take a panoramic shot of the desert.

Then he takes one of this international group of friends,
    who are laughing and talking with an easy **rapport**.

I will place those photos in a digital scrapbook with
    the one of me riding Stormy.

I still prefer reading to riding, but I am glad I can do both.

My **adjustment** to Arizona was
    slow, but I learned so much!

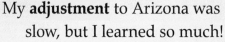

(bl) BMD/Flickr/Getty Images; (i) Jack Kurtz/ZUMA Press/Newscom

Make Connections

Talk about how Silvina
discovers what she has in
common with the Gomez
family. **ESSENTIAL QUESTION**

Describe a time when
you learned how to adjust
to new people or a new
place. **TEXT TO SELF**

Summarize

Even when a story is told in verse form, you can summarize the most important events to help you understand the plot.

Find Text Evidence

To help you understand the plot of the section "Shocking" on page 281of "My Visit to Arizona," you can summarize the key events by restating what happens in your own words.

> page 281

Shocking
—Short Sharp Shocks. Try to say it three times fast.

My English tutor at home taught me that tongue twister. How perfectly it describes my arrival in Arizona!

Shock 1: We are staying on the hot, dusty Gomez Ranch. My family travels so much, I think we are **nomadic**. But usually we sleep in nice, air-conditioned hotels.

Shock 2: People here think I can ride horses. Do I tell them the only saddle I have used is on a bicycle? And that I am more inclined to read *books* about horses?

Shock 3: English lessons do not automatically prepare you to understand the way people speak in Arizona.

—Pull up a chair and get comfy, says Grampa G.

But the chairs are too big for me to lift. And who is *Comfy?* Must everyone here talk so fast?

<u>Silvina says her arrival in Arizona can be described as three "Short Sharp Shocks."</u> I can summarize her experience by saying that she is surprised her family is not staying in a hotel; that people think she knows how to ride horses; and that she doesn't understand English as well as she expected to.

Your Turn

Reread the rest of the story. Use the most important events to summarize each section of "My Visit to Arizona." As you read, remember to use the strategy Summarize.

Theme

When you read fiction, use details in the text to help you identify how a character feels. Understanding what causes a character to feel a certain way can help you determine the theme, or central message, that the author wants to convey.

 Find Text Evidence

When I reread "My Visit to Arizona," I can look for details that tell me how Silvina feels during different events in the plot. Then I can think about how the details fit together and express a central message.

Detail

It is a "shock" to Silvina that people think she can ride a horse and that they "talk so fast."

↓

Detail

↓

Detail

↓

Theme

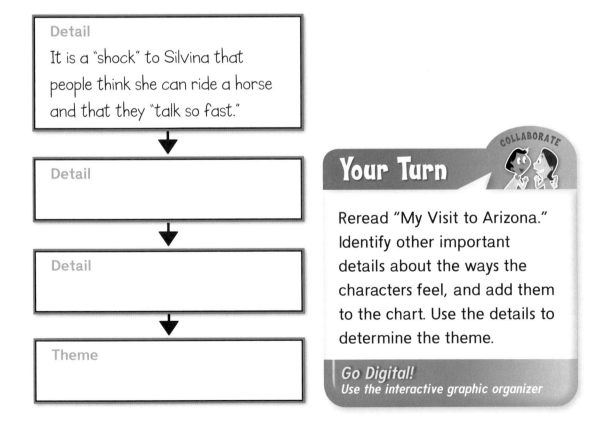

COLLABORATE

Your Turn

Reread "My Visit to Arizona." Identify other important details about the ways the characters feel, and add them to the chart. Use the details to determine the theme.

Go Digital!
Use the interactive graphic organizer

Free-Verse Fiction

"My Visit to Arizona" is a story written in free verse. The text is organized into lines and stanzas, but it has no rhyme or meter.

Free-Verse Fiction:
- May use an *interior monologue,* the narrator's "thoughts"
- May show dialogue without using quotation marks

Find Text Evidence

In "My Visit to Arizona," I learn about Silvina's experience through her inner thoughts, or interior monologue. The characters' dialogue is shown using dashes, not the usual quotation marks.

---

page 281

Silvina and her parents have traveled from their ranch in Argentina to one in Arizona. The trip reunites Silvina's father with his college friend, Mr. Gomez. While her parents share ideas about raising cattle, Silvina spends her days with the Gomez boys, Mike and Carl, and their grandfather.

Shocking

—*Short Sharp Shocks. Try to say it three times fast.*
My English tutor at home taught me that tongue twister.
How perfectly it describes my arrival in Arizona!

Shock 1: We are staying on the hot, dusty Gomez Ranch.
My family travels so much, I think we are **nomadic**.
But usually we sleep in nice, air-conditioned hotels.

Shock 2: People here think I can ride horses.
Do I tell them the only saddle I have used is on a bicycle?
And that I am more inclined to read books about horses?

Shock 3: English lessons do not automatically prepare
you to understand the way people speak in Arizona.

—*Pull up a chair and get comfy, says Grampa G.*
But the chairs are too big for me to lift. And who is *Comfy*?
Must everyone here talk so fast?

Nodding and Smiling

—*Our ranch covers 150 acres, Grampa G says. Permit me to show you around.*
I am thinking, Show me a round *what*? but there is no time to ask, because he is pushing me toward an army of cattle.
—*Here's the finest herd in the Southwest, 'bout 200 strong.*
I think Grampa G would make an excellent **mentor**, if only I understood half of all he is **chattering** about.
I nod and smile and pretend I understand.

281

Interior Monologue The story is told in the main character's "voice," as if we are reading her thoughts.

Dialogue Shown Differently The exact words the characters speak are printed in a different style, without quotation marks.

Your Turn

COLLABORATE

Find two passages in "My Visit to Arizona" that are examples of Silvina's interior monologue. Then identify an example of dialogue in the poem.

Homographs

Homographs are two words that are spelled the same way but have different meanings and may be pronounced differently. Use context clues to help you choose the correct meanings and pronunciations of homographs.

 Find Text Evidence

I'm not sure which meaning the homograph content *has on page 282 in "My Visit to Arizona." I know it can be a noun pronounced* CON-tent, *which means "topics treated" or "what is contained." But it can also be an adjective pronounced* con-TENT, *which means "satisfied." The context clue of Silvina's exclamation* What a relief! *tells me that the second meaning is correct.*

> What a relief! I am <u>content</u> for the first time in days.

Your Turn

Use context clues to determine the correct meaning and pronunciation of each of these homographs in "My Visit to Arizona."
   inclined, *page 281*
   steer, *page 282*
   shot, *page 283*

Write About the Text

Pages 280–283

Leah

I responded to the prompt: *Write a diary entry from Silvina's perspective describing how she taught Carl to use his camera.*

Student Model: *Narrative Text*

Today I taught Carl how to use

his new digital camera. It wasn't hard.

His camera has more features than

mine, but I figured it out pretty quickly.

I showed him how to use the zoom

feature and how to turn the automatic

flash on and off. Carl didn't even know

Grammar

The **verb** *taught* and the **pronoun** *I* in this sentence are in **agreement**.

Grammar Handbook See page 464.

Sequence

I inferred what the character would teach Carl and the order in which she would do it.

that his camera could take panoramic

photos or shoot video! I liked showing

him how it worked. It made me feel

smart! Believe it or not, it actually made

me feel a little more confident about

riding Stormy!

Ideas
Based on details from the text, I identified Silvina's perspective and used it in my paragraph.

Strong Conclusion
My concluding statement followed from the narrative events and connected my paragraph to the story.

Your Turn

Write a diary entry from Silvina's perspective describing her experience of riding a horse for the first time.

Go Digital!
Write your response online.
Use your editing checklist.

Essential Question

How can we take responsibility?

Go Digital!

Steve Bronstein/Stone+/Getty Images

290

Owning UP
It all happened so fast!

▶ First there was that glorious *thwack!* when I smacked the ball and sent it soaring toward left field.

▶ But then there was that awful *crash!* when my home-run hit smashed through our neighbor's window.

I wished I could just celebrate my amazing hit. But I knew I had to go accept my obligation to pay for the window. It wasn't fun, but it was the right thing to do.

Talk About It

Write words you have learned about being answerable to others for one's actions. Then talk with a partner about a situation in which you took responsibility for something you had done.

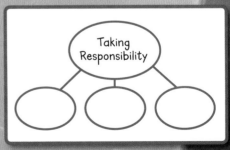

Taking Responsibility

Vocabulary

Use the picture and the sentences to talk with
a partner about each word.

answerable

The soccer players are **answerable** to
the coach for their actions during the
game.

To whom are you answerable at school?

lounge

The family waited in the airport **lounge**
before their flight.

Where else might you wait in a lounge?

obligation

I have an **obligation** to make sure my
dog is walked and fed.

What is a synonym for obligation?

proportion

The dinosaur's head was small in
proportion to its bulky body.

How would you describe a puppy's paws
in proportion to its legs?

Poetry Terms

free verse

Free verse poems don't rhyme and often sound like normal speech.

How is a free verse poem different from a sonnet?

narrative poem

In a **narrative poem**, the author tells a story in verse form.

What elements beside a plot would you expect to find in a narrative poem?

alliteration

A poem that includes **alliteration** groups together words that begin with the same sound.

Give an example of alliteration.

assonance

Assonance is the repetition of a vowel sound in words that are near one another in a poem.

Why might a poet use assonance?

Your Turn

COLLABORATE

Pick three words or poetry terms, and write a question about each for your partner to answer.

Go Digital! **Use the online visual glossary**

Hey, Nilda,

By now you're wondering, worrying
Why I've seemed so weird this week
   —not calling you, not texting,
Slipping silently past you in the hall
   at school,
Pretending to listen to music or
   checking my watch.

Outside, with classes over,
I've made a beeline for the bus,
Other kids, eager to leave,
Hustle and rush,
Feeling free and gleeful.
   But not me.
   I hide behind my hair.

Essential Question

How can we take responsibility?

Read a poet's view of being responsible in a friendship.

Here at home, my secret doesn't sit so well.
Once you know what I did,
You'll see red.
I know I'm answerable to you,
I have an obligation to make it right.
So here's what happened:
You think someone stole your camera . . .
No, I borrowed it without asking—
  Just to try it out, but
  Then I lost it.

I looked, looked, looked
In the laugh-loud cafeteria, the echo-hollow gym,
The bottom of my crammed and
  messy locker,
The plastic couches in the teachers' lounge,
And the shush-quiet aisles of the library—
Every place I could think of.
And it's gone.
My fault.
I'll give you my allowance for
  the next few months.
But I wonder—can money
  mend a friendship?

Rachel

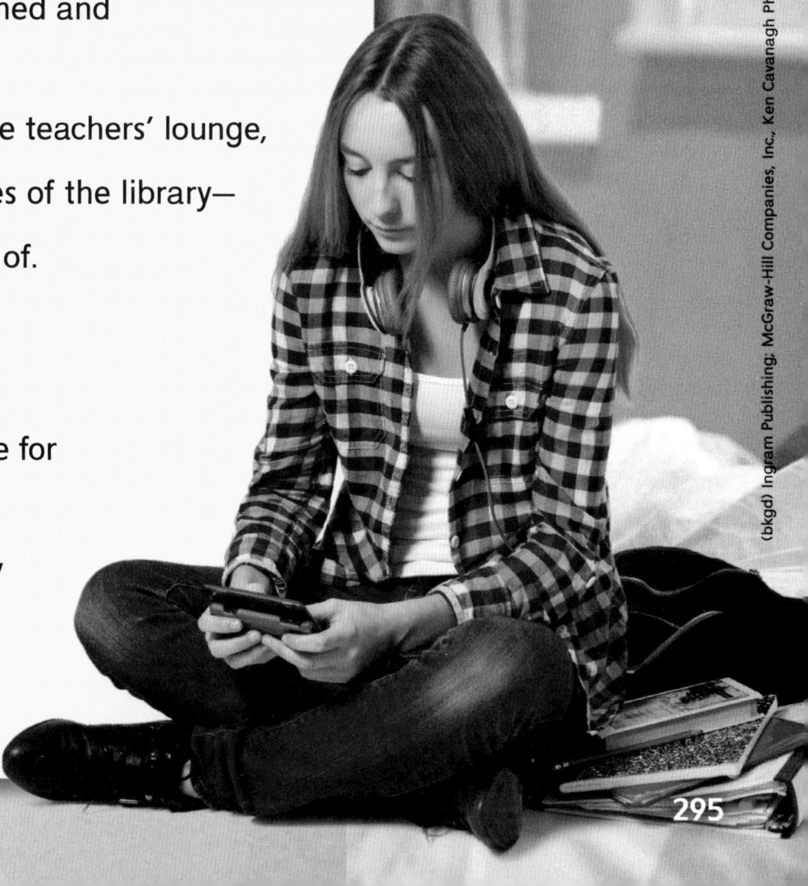

(bkgd) Ingram Publishing; McGraw-Hill Companies, Inc., Ken Cavanagh Photography

Hi Rachel,

Yep, you're right.

I wondered why you were walking around

Like you were scared or angry or

As if you'd been crying or trying to hide,

—Or all of the above.

Good thing I wasn't holding anything breakable

When I read your message,

Because I might have dropped it

—Or flung it across the room.

Instead, I dropped down into our rickety recliner

And clenched my teeth tight,

My body shaking as hard

As if I were outside

Wearing shorts in the freezing rain.

I mean, come on!

You borrowed my new camera

   without asking?

Then let me think it was stolen?

I thought I could trust you.

And I thought you would trust me enough

To tell me the truth.

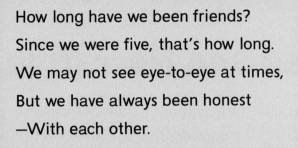

How long have we been friends?
Since we were five, that's how long.
We may not see eye-to-eye at times,
But we have always been honest
—With each other.

Just so you know:
I found my camera yesterday,
Stuck in a big box with some
　　socks in the lost and found.

Let's not blow this out of
　　proportion,
Maybe just treat it as water
　　under the bridge.
Start again, okay?
Still friends?
I hope so.
I've got two tickets to Friday's
　　concert, and
I don't want to go by myself.

Nilda

—Lareine Interne

Make Connections

Talk about the ways that Rachel and Nilda
express their views on taking responsibility.
ESSENTIAL QUESTION

Describe a time when you took responsibility
for your actions in a friendship. TEXT TO SELF

Free Verse and Narrative

Free verse is poetry that does not make use of rhyme or a regular meter. It may contain imagery and descriptive language. **Narrative** poetry tells a story in verse form. Like a story, it has characters, a setting, and a plot.

Find Text Evidence

I can tell that "Hey Nilda" is free verse because it doesn't contain a pattern of rhyming words or stressed syllables. It sounds similar to regular speech. It is also a narrative poem, because it tells a story. The poet's word choice helps me visualize events in the plot.

page 294

By now you're wondering, worrying
Why I've seemed so weird this week
—not calling you, not texting,
Slipping silently past you in the hall
    at school,
Pretending to listen to music or
    checking my watch.

Outside, with classes over,
I've made a beeline for the bus,
Other kids, eager to leave,

"Hey Nilda" is a free-verse narrative poem. It tells a story with language that people use in real life.

COLLABORATE

Your Turn

Reread "Hi Rachel" on pages 296–297. Decide if it is free verse, narrative poetry, or both. Explain your choice.

Point of View

In a narrative poem, as in fiction, the story may be told by one of the characters. That character is known as the **speaker** of the poem. The poet uses the first-person point of view of the speaker to express a particular feeling or idea.

Find Text Evidence

As I reread "Hey Nilda," I notice that the speaker, Rachel, uses the first-person pronouns I, me, and my. From this, I can tell that the events in this narrative poem will be described from her perspective.

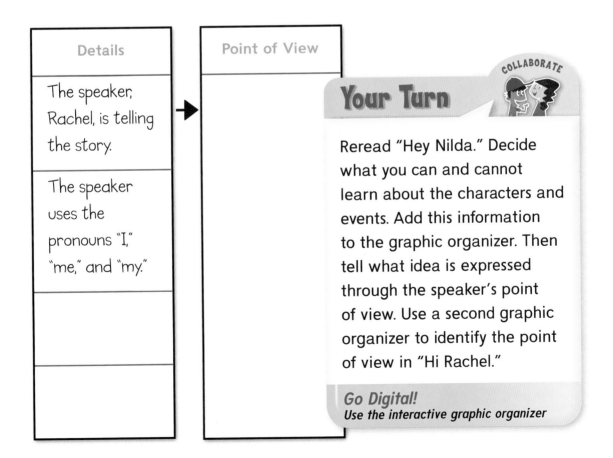

Details	Point of View
The speaker, Rachel, is telling the story.	
The speaker uses the pronouns "I," "me," and "my."	

COLLABORATE

Your Turn

Reread "Hey Nilda." Decide what you can and cannot learn about the characters and events. Add this information to the graphic organizer. Then tell what idea is expressed through the speaker's point of view. Use a second graphic organizer to identify the point of view in "Hi Rachel."

Go Digital!
Use the interactive graphic organizer

Alliteration and Assonance

Alliteration is the repetition of a consonant sound at the beginnings of words that are near one another. **Assonance** is the repetition of a vowel sound within a group of words. Poets use both devices to add a song-like quality to a poem and to draw attention to feelings or ideas expressed in certain passages.

 ## Find Text Evidence

Reread "Hey Nilda" on page 294. Look for examples of alliteration and assonance. Think about what the poet's use of the two devices tells you about Rachel's state of mind.

page 294

Shared Read · Genre · Poetry

Hey Nilda

By now you're wondering, worrying
Why I've seemed so weird this week
 —not calling you, not texting,
Slipping silently past you in the hall
 at school,
Pretending to listen to music or
 checking my watch.

Outside, with classes over,
I've made a beeline for the bus,
Other kids, eager to leave,
Hustle and rush,
Feeling free and gleeful.
 But not me.
 I hide behind my hair.

Essential Question
How can we take responsibility?

Read a poet's view of being responsible in a friendship.

294

Repeating the w *sound at the beginnings of words and the long* e *sound within words hints at the tension and worry that Rachel is feeling about what has happened.*

 COLLABORATE

Your Turn

Reread the first stanza of "Hi Rachel." Identify examples of alliteration and assonance in it.

Figurative Language

The meaning of an **idiomatic expression** is different from the literal meanings of individual words in the expression. Poets may use idiomatic expressions, such as "talks a mile a minute," to make the speaker's words sound like everyday speech. Look for context clues in a poem to help you determine the meanings of idiomatic expressions.

 Find Text Evidence

In "Hey Nilda," I know the phrase *made a beeline* doesn't refer to actual bees or lines. The nearby phrase *hustle and rush* tells me that people are moving about quickly. I think *made a beeline* means that the speaker "walked quickly and directly" to the bus.

> Outside, with classes over,
>
> I've <u>made a beeline</u> for the bus,
>
> Other kids, eager to leave,
>
> Hustle and rush,
>
> Feeling free and gleeful.

Your Turn

COLLABORATE

Find another idiomatic expression in "Hey Nilda" and two in "Hi Rachel." Identify the meaning of each.

Write About the Text

Pages 294–297

Alfredo

I responded to the prompt: *Write a free-verse poem about a problem you've recently had.*

Student Model: *Narrative Text*

I am reluctant to admit

I lost the retainer that my mom said

Is very expensive—already—

The third time this year.

And Mom threatened to hang mine

From my neck by a string if

I lost it again!

Imagine my cringing anxiety

At the image of a retainer necklace!

If only she knew how hard it is

Grammar

That is a **relative pronoun.**

Grammar Handbook See page 464.

Sensory Language

I used the strong, descriptive words *cringing anxiety* to show the intensity of embarrassment.

Point of View

I expressed my point of view by stating my feelings outright.

To keep that blue box from slipping

Off the table at lunch,

Or out of my backpack as we

Change classes all day.

Maybe I should just ask for two

replacements right off—next time...

Jon, my ally, says not to sweat it—

Just keep in touch with the

Orthodontist on the sly.

Strong Conclusion

The last lines of my poem show a solution to the problem based on the narrative events.

Your Turn

Write a free-verse poem about a problem you recently resolved.

Go Digital!
Write your response online.
Use your editing checklist.

Discoveries

The Big Idea

How can discoveries open new possibilities?

A Journey of Discovery

The expedition of Messrs. Lewis and Clark . . . has had all the success which could have been expected. They have traced the Missouri nearly to its source, descended the Columbia [River] to the Pacific Ocean, ascertained with accuracy the geography of that interesting communication across our continent, learned the character of the country, of its commerce, and inhabitants; and it is but just to say that Messrs. Lewis and Clark, and their brave companions, have by this arduous service deserved well of their country.

—Thomas Jefferson
from an address to Congress, December 2, 1806

Essential Question

Why do people tell and retell myths?

Go Digital!

TELLING and RETELLING Myths

This performer from the Beijing Opera is portraying a celebrated Chinese general. Audiences never tire of witnessing the larger-than-life exploits of this beloved hero.

▶ The general's fabled honor and courage are symbolized by the actor's red face paint and the long black beard made of yak hair.

▶ Because he is depicted this way in books and paintings, too, the audience knows exactly who he is the moment he steps on the stage.

The fact that the general's story is such a favorite only adds to people's enjoyment of each performance.

Talk About It

Write words you have learned about retelling the stories of famous heroes. Then talk with a partner about how the heroic character shown here is portrayed.

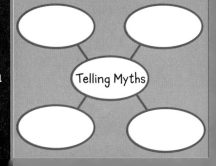

Telling Myths

Vocabulary

Use the picture and the sentences to talk with a
partner about each word.

audacity

People who are brave enough to sail on
the open sea show great **audacity**.

Describe a time when someone you know
showed audacity.

deception

Those tags must be a **deception**, because
the "sale" price is no lower than the price
for those items at other stores.

What is a synonym for deception?

desolate

No one has lived in that neglected,
desolate region for many years.

Describe what might make a place
look desolate.

exploits

Sharon's athletic **exploits** have earned
her many trophies.

Describe the exploits of someone whose
skills you admire.

oblivious

Damon relished the oatmeal, **oblivious** to the fact that it was good for him.

When have you been oblivious to something?

somber

Watching the serious documentary put Donna in a **somber** mood.

What puts you in a somber mood?

steadfast

Steadfast in her desire to play piano, Karina practiced every day.

What skill have you pursued in a steadfast way?

valiant

The **valiant** firefighter carried the child away from the burning building.

What is an antonym of valiant?

Your Turn

COLLABORATE

Pick three words. Write three questions for your partner to answer.

Go Digital! **Use the online visual glossary**

THUNDER HELPER

Jago

Essential Question

Why do people tell and retell myths?

Read about a Creek boy who gains
the ability to help his people.

The Creek are Native Americans who come from what are now Florida, Alabama, and Georgia. Their myths, passed down from generation to generation, are often about the relationship between people and the natural world.

A long time ago, a boy and his three uncles set out from their village to go hunting. As always, the boy looked for ways to be useful to his people, so he set about catching fish in a nearby stream and gathering firewood while his uncles tracked deer. When his uncles returned, he would prepare *sofki*, a corn soup, and add the deer meat to make a mouth-watering stew.

One morning, the boy was walking toward the stream, dreaming of the tasty fish he would catch and listening to the chittering of the birds. All at once, he heard a loud roaring sound. Quickly, and as sly as a fox, he crouched, set an arrow against his bow, and readied himself for whatever might happen.

The boy crept slowly toward the eerie rumbling, until he reached the stream. There, towering above the rushing water, he saw two unearthly creatures locked in a terrifying struggle. One was dark and formless, yet seemed to be the source of the booming roar. The other, a long, wiry monster, was tightly coiled around the first.

The boy watched, his mouth agape with wonder. "The giant serpent must be the dreaded Tie-Snake!" he thought, remembering stories his elders told about the trickster that fooled people and drew them down into the murky and **desolate** underworld. "But who is the shapeless one? Could it be Thunder himself?" the boy wondered. In a **valiant** move, he raised his loaded bow and shouted to Tie-Snake, "Let go of him!"

Tie-Snake hissed back, "Boy, if you kill the evil Thunder, I will protect you

311

always and share all the mysteries of the underworld with you!"

Thunder bellowed his response. "Listen to me, boy. Tie-Snake speaks only lies. Strike him with your arrow, and I shall grant you the power to be a strong, brave, and wise warrior for your people."

Without listening to more of Tie-Snake's **deception**, the boy took aim and let his arrow fly at the serpent. Tie-Snake fell into the stream and disappeared beneath the waters. A moment later, Thunder spoke again. "Be warned. You must tell no one the source of your new power, or it will leave you."

"I promise," said the boy solemnly, and Thunder evaporated into thin air.

The boy's uncles returned to camp that evening. Despite their questions about his time alone in the forest, the boy kept his promise, and his uncles remained **oblivious** of the power that Thunder had given him. But the boy was eager to employ his new abilities for worthy causes, and he worked hard to hone his hunting skills once he returned home. In just a few short months, to the surprise of the elders, the boy had become one of the best hunters in the village. His **steadfast** efforts in pursuit of food were soon recognized by all the people.

It was not long after when the Creek elders learned one of their most fearsome enemies was threatening to attack them. The boy took this opportunity to request a meeting with the village leaders. "Respected elders," the boy said boldly. "Though I am only a boy, I have

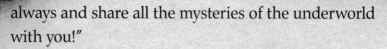

Jago

the courage and cunning to fight the enemy. Will you let me perform this deed to save our people?"

The boy's **audacity** impressed the elders. They conferred among themselves and soon nodded their heads in agreement. The chief declared, "You have proven your strength and bravery with your hunting. Now, as you go alone to fight the enemy, you must demonstrate your wisdom." With determination, the boy said, "I will not disappoint my people."

That very evening, the boy set off through the forest to face the enemy. The villagers gathered to await his return, and as the hours passed with no word the Creek fell into a **somber** mood. Then suddenly, a deafening roar of thunder made the villagers cover their ears. Their eyes shot upward as flashes of lightning streaked the sky. Moments later, smoke filtered out through the trees, and the people sensed that the boy had been victorious. They rejoiced that the enemy would no longer threaten their village.

When the boy made his way out of the forest, there was much celebration in honor of his **exploits**. The elders called him *Menewa*, meaning "great warrior." And from that day on, whenever the Creek heard Thunder, they knew that Menewa, his helper, was at work to keep their people safe.

Make Connections

Talk about why the characters and plot of "Thunder Helper" would appeal to listeners generation after generation. **ESSENTIAL QUESTION**

Tell why a myth or story you know has special meaning to you. **TEXT TO SELF**

Make Predictions

As you read a myth like "Thunder Helper," pause periodically to make predictions about what will happen next. Then use evidence in the text to **confirm** or **revise** your predictions.

Find Text Evidence

After reading about the boy's encounter with Thunder, you may have made a prediction about how he would use his new "power to be a strong, brave, and wise warrior" for his people.

> **page 312**
>
> power, or it will leave you."
>
> "I promise," said the boy solemnly, and Thunder evaporated into thin air.
>
> The boy's uncles returned to camp that evening. Despite their questions about his time alone in the forest, the boy kept his promise, and his uncles remained **oblivious** of the power that Thunder had given him. But the boy was eager to employ his new abilities for worthy causes, and he worked hard to hone his hunting skills once he returned home. In just a few short months, to the surprise of the elders, the boy had become one of the best hunters in the village. His **steadfast** efforts in pursuit of food were soon recognized by all the people.

I predicted that the boy would use his new power to become a hunter like his uncles. I confirmed this when I read how he became "one of the best hunters in the village."

Your Turn

What prediction did you make after reading about the boy's meeting with the elders? Identify the passages you used to make or confirm your prediction.

Problem and Solution

In a myth, the **characters** may include people, animals, and personified forces of nature, such as Rain or Wind. The **plot** often describes how the main character solves a problem.

 Find Text Evidence

On page 311 of "Thunder Helper," I read that the boy always "looked for ways to be useful to his people." I can infer that this overall goal of being useful was a factor in deciding which creature, Tie-Snake or Thunder, to help during their battle.

The main character solves his problem in stages.

Character
a Creek boy, his uncles, Tie-Snake, Thunder, the elders
Setting
the forest, the boy's village
Problem
The boy wants the ability to be useful.
Event
The boy helps Thunder, who rewards him with special power.
Solution

COLLABORATE

Your Turn

Reread the rest of "Thunder Helper." On the graphic organizer, record other key events. Use the events to determine whether the boy finds a solution to his problem.

Go Digital!
Use the interactive graphic organizer

Myth

"Thunder Helper" is a myth, a kind of story that is often told to explain the unknown or to teach what is important in a culture.

Myths:

- Often include non-human characters
- May offer explanations for natural occurrences

 Find Text Evidence

The myth "Thunder Helper" includes one monster-like character, Tie-Snake, and one representing a natural occurrence, Thunder. It also suggests the respect that the Creek people had for nature.

page 311

The Creek are Native Americans who come from what are now Florida, Alabama, and Georgia. Their myths, passed down from generation to generation, are often about the relationship between people and the natural world.

A long time ago, a boy and his three uncles set out from their village to go hunting. As always, the boy looked for ways to be useful to his people, so he set about catching fish in a nearby stream and gathering firewood while his uncles tracked deer. When his uncles returned, he would prepare *sofki*, a corn soup, and add the deer meat to make a mouth-watering stew.

One morning, the boy was walking toward the stream, dreaming of the tasty fish he would catch and listening to the chittering of the birds. All at once, he heard a loud roaring sound. Quickly, and as sly as a fox, he crouched, set an arrow against his bow, and readied himself for whatever might happen.

The boy crept slowly toward the eerie rumbling, until he reached the stream. There, towering above the rushing water, he saw two unearthly creatures locked in a terrifying struggle. One was dark and formless, yet seemed to be the source of the booming roar. The other, a long wiry monster, was tightly coiled around the first.

The boy watched, his mouth agape with wonder. "The giant serpent must be the dreaded Tie-Snake!" he thought, remembering stories his elders told about the trickster that fooled people and drew them down into the murky and **desolate** underworld. "But who is the shapeless one? Could it be Thunder himself?" the boy wondered. In a **valiant** move, he raised his loaded bow and shouted to Tie-Snake, "Let go of him!"

Tie-Snake hissed back, "Boy, if you kill the evil Thunder, I will protect you

311

Non-human Characters Characters with non-human powers give myths their larger-than-life quality.

Explanations for Natural Occurrences Myths are often told to help make nature more understandable.

COLLABORATE

Your Turn

Find passages in "Thunder Helper" that describe the non-human characters. Tell your partner how these descriptions help to give the myth a larger-than-life quality.

Word Origins

Modern English words usually have origins in other languages or in an older form of English. Recognizing that an unfamiliar word has a common origin with one you know can help you figure out its meaning. Here are some word origins and their meanings:

evaporatus – Latin, "turn into vapor"

ieldra – Old English, "of earlier birth"

han – Old English, "sharpening stone"

sollemnis – Latin, "official"

 Find Text Evidence

When I read the word elders *on page 312 of "Thunder Helper," I notice that it sounds like* older. *Both words have similar origins, so in this context I think* elders *means "older people."*

In just a few short months, to the surprise of the elders, the boy had become one of the best hunters in the village.

Your Turn

Use the word origins above and context clues to verify the meaning of these words from "Thunder Helper."

evaporated, *page 312*

solemnly, *page 312*

hone, *page 312*

Write About the Text

Pages 310–313

Erin

I responded to the prompt: *Continue the discussion between the boy and Tie-Snake before Thunder bellows his response.*

Student Model: *Narrative Text*

Develop Character
I used dialogue to help develop Tie-Snake's character.

Supporting Details
I included a descriptive detail to show how the boy felt about Tie-Snake.

> The boy cried, "I hear you, Tie-Snake, but I do not believe you!"
>
> Tie-Snake hissed as he struggled with his opponent, "Boy, if you kill Thunder, I will grant you wonderful things! You shall have the softest blankets, the sturdiest shoes, the sharpest arrows, and the most powerful bows ever known!"
>
> Angrily, the boy shook his head.
> "I hear you, Tie-Snake, but you are

a clever trickster! Why should I

believe you?"

    Tie-Snake tried to tighten his long,

scaly body as it coiled around Thunder.

Then he called to the boy once more.

"If you kill Thunder, I will grant you a

life longer than any human has

ever lived! Surely that is fair

reward for killing Thunder!"

Grammar

The word *clever* is an **adjective** that describes the noun *trickster*.

Grammar Handbook See page 465.

Transitions

I used the word *then* to show how one event led to another.

Your Turn

Create additional conversation between the boy and the elders before they decide to let the boy fight the enemy alone.

Go Digital!
Write your response online.
Use your editing checklist.

Essential Question

How do people show inner strength?

Go Digital!

Relying on Inner Strength

I can't believe my piano recital is tomorrow night! I've been practicing for weeks now, but I still feel kind of nervous.

- ▶ I know really well all the pieces I'm going to play, but I've never performed them in front of lots of people before.

- ▶ My teacher is helping me with some last-minute pointers. He says he believes I have the fortitude to give a great performance.

Whatever happens, I know it will all be up to me once I put my fingers down on the keys!

Talk About It COLLABORATE

Write words you have learned about ways people draw on inner strength. Then talk with a partner about a time when you needed strength to accomplish something.

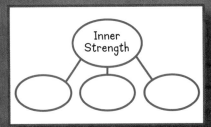

Inner Strength

Vocabulary

Use the picture and the sentences to talk with a partner about each word.

disposed

Becka is often **disposed** to eat pizza, since it is one of her favorite foods.

Name a food you are disposed to eat.

eavesdropping

Shayna learned about her surprise party by **eavesdropping** on her colleagues.

Why might someone be eavesdropping?

fortitude

It takes great **fortitude** to do the work of rebuilding after a disaster.

What other tasks does it take fortitude to accomplish?

infinite

There seems to be an **infinite** number of stars in the sky tonight.

What is a synonym for infinite?

retaliation

Even though Ryan had poked me with his elbow, my teacher says it was not right to tap him with my pencil in **retaliation**.

How is retaliation related to revenge?

rigors

The **rigors** of soccer practice left Peter exhausted.

How would you describe the rigors that athletes face?

stoop

Audra and her friend sat together on the front **stoop** of her house.

What is the purpose of a stoop?

undaunted

Kevin was **undaunted** by the snow and rode his bicycle all the way to work.

When have you felt undaunted?

COLLABORATE

Your Turn

Pick three words. Write three questions for your partner to answer.

Go Digital! *Use the online visual glossary*

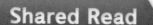

JOURNEY TO Freedom

Essential Question

How do people show inner strength?

Read about a girl who discovers her inner strength when she is called upon to help people escaping slavery.

London Ladd

324

*It is early summer 1851, and 12-year-old Abigail Parker
is still finding her way after the death of her mother
the previous winter. Her father has recently made their
Massachusetts farm a station on the Underground Railroad,
and the two nervously await their first "delivery" of people
on their way to Canada to escape slavery.*

I could not sit for being so fretful, so I paced and sometimes paused to peer out the window. Mother often said, "Patience is bitter, but its fruit is sweet." If only I were possessed of her calm.

"I see no sign of our four guests," Papa announced as he returned from checking outdoors, fueling my fears that they had met with misfortune. Just then, a sudden knock sounded, and my heart took to pounding as Papa opened the door to two weary women on the **stoop**. He assisted the older one, who appeared to be about 60, to a chair by the hearth. Her companion was maybe 14. Papa directed me to poke up the fire and fetch food and drink.

When the women got back their breath, Papa asked, "What of the others? Did they not accompany you?"

"Just Nellis and me," the girl declared, and the older woman presented a letter.

Papa handed the crumpled paper to me, saying, "If you would, Abby. My eyes fail me in dim light."

I brought the letter close by a candle and commenced reading: *"Dear Jonathan, I send you Nellis and Emma, separate from their two companions, who have fallen ill with fever, one seriously. We have insufficient room to hide four until they recover, so I hope you are **disposed** to shelter them until further transport can be arranged. Respectfully, Jacob."*

Papa nodded and said, "We must see to their safety and comfort." I guided them to the attic hiding place and wished them a peaceful night.

Come morning, afore I entered the attic, I couldn't help **eavesdropping** on the sound of choked coughing. Once inside, I shuddered when I saw Nellis's gaunt face—so ill she looked. "I fear it's the fever," she gasped.

I summoned Papa, pleading, "She needs a doctor!"

325

"Think of the risk," he scolded. "The new law allows slave catchers to come all this way north, and if we're found harboring Nellis and Emma—well, **retaliation** could be grave. We must tend to this ourselves."

"But I lack Mother's know-how for curing," I whispered.

"Back in Virginia, Nellis told me 'bout some fever herbs," Emma spoke up.

"You daren't go out, Emma," Papa cautioned, "but Abby can procure what you need." I felt near fainting, but he was resolved. "Remember," he said to me, "the fields have eyes, and the woods have ears. Take care how you act and speak, so as not to arouse suspicion."

I left in haste with my basket, rehearsing Emma's words about the needed herb. "Grows on edges of clearings, by streams or marshes . . . has dull white flowers,

wrinkled leaves, and stout stem." My search seemed endless, but finally I spied some flowers seeming to match Emma's description. I plucked the plant and some familiar mint that I knew for sure by its smell.

As I hurried home, I met our neighbor Mr. Carrington coming opposite. "Where to in such a hurry, Miss Abigail?"

Undaunted, I spun a tale about hunting up mint for Mother's special cake recipe, and my voice was wondrous calm as I presented a sprig ". . . for the Missus." Once he'd nodded thanks and continued on, I commenced to breathe again.

At home, Emma praised my harvest as she sorted through the leaves in the basket, handing me several and bidding me to mince them fine. Then she smiled. "Mint—that's good. We'll add some to mend the taste of the fever tea."

London Ladd

326

After Nellis drank the tea, she reclined in a comfortable doze. Emma and I watched over her, and before long we fell into voicing our worries. My own desperation from missing Mother was deeply felt and true, but I could barely fathom Emma's **fortitude** in facing the **rigors** of slavery as she tell'd them. I confessed my doubt of ever being able to bear such hardships as those.

"It's why folks come together. Problems shared be problems halved," said Emma smiling. "You'll soon enough have the strength of a grown lady like your mama."

Nellis's fever broke that night. As she and Emma prepared to continue their journey, they pledged **infinite** gratitude to Papa and me. Tho' sad to see them go, I wished them safe passage, and I thanked Emma for aiding me so in my own journey.

Make Connections

Talk about how Abigail showed inner strength in finding the healing herb on her own. ESSENTIAL QUESTION

Describe a time when you discovered a personal strength within you that helped you to do a difficult or demanding task. TEXT TO SELF

Make Predictions

When you read historical fiction, you may not be sure how to predict what a character living in the past would do. Use clues in the text, and knowledge you have gathered from other reading, to make logical guesses. As you read further, **confirm** or **revise** your predictions using evidence from the text.

 ## Find Text Evidence

You may not have been sure how Abby would react when Papa asks her to find the herb on page 326 of "Journey to Freedom."

page 326

ourselves."

"But I lack Mother's know-how for curing," I whispered.

"Back in Virginia, Nellis told me 'bout some fever herbs," Emma spoke up.

"You daren't go out, Emma," Papa cautioned, "but Abby can procure what you need." I felt near fainting, but he was resolved. "Remember," he said to me, "the fields have eyes, and the woods have ears. Take care how you act and speak, so as not to arouse suspicion."

I left in haste with my basket, rehearsing Emma's words about the needed herb. "Grows on edges of clearings, by streams or marshes . . . has dull white flowers,

As I hurried home, I met our neighbor Mr. Carrington coming opposite. "Where to in such a hurry, Miss Abigail?"

Undaunted, I spun a tale about hunting up mint for Mother's special cake recipe, and my voice was wondrous calm as I presented a sprig ". . . for the Missus." Once he'd nodded thanks and continued on, I commenced to breathe again.

At home, Emma praised my harvest as she sorted through the leaves in the basket, handing me several and bidding me to mince them fine. Then she smiled. "Mint—that's good. We'll add some to mend the taste of the fever tea."

> *I predicted that Abby would do her best to find the herb, even though she felt unsure. I confirmed my prediction when I read that she rehearsed "Emma's words about the needed herb" and that she used them to select a plant "seeming to match Emma's description."*

 ## Your Turn

COLLABORATE

What did you predict Abby would do when, on her way home, she met her neighbor? What passages in the text did you use to revise or confirm your prediction?

Cause and Effect

When reading fiction, you learn about the **characters** from their responses to key events in the **plot**. As you read a story, pay attention to how each event causes a reaction in one or more of the characters.

 Find Text Evidence

As I reread the beginning of "Journey to Freedom," I note that the knock at the door causes Abigail's heart to start pounding. I can infer from this reaction that, in addition to feeling "fretful" and impatient while waiting for the guests' arrival, she is also nervous.

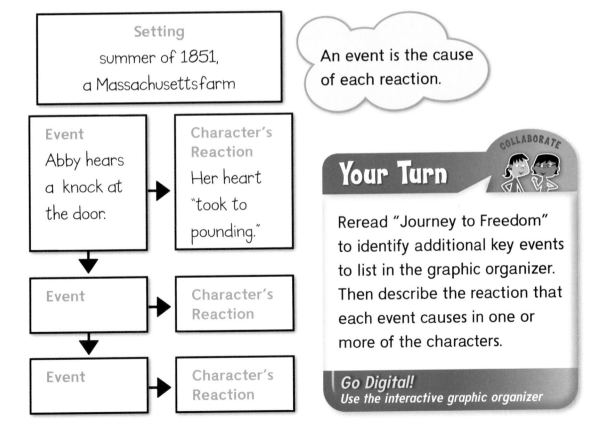

Setting
summer of 1851, a Massachusetts farm

An event is the cause of each reaction.

Event		Character's Reaction
Abby hears a knock at the door.	→	Her heart "took to pounding."
Event	→	Character's Reaction
Event	→	Character's Reaction

COLLABORATE

Your Turn

Reread "Journey to Freedom" to identify additional key events to list in the graphic organizer. Then describe the reaction that each event causes in one or more of the characters.

Go Digital!
Use the interactive graphic organizer

329

Historical Fiction

"Journey to Freedom" is historical fiction set in an actual place. The characters face problems that real people faced in the past.

Historical Fiction:

- May use dialect, a way people spoke in a certain region
- May use characters' letters to develop the plot

 Find Text Evidence

"Journey to Freedom" has a realistic setting from history. The dialect Abby uses in narrating the story and in her dialogue helps me to imagine a real Massachusetts girl in 1851. The letter that Abby reads provides information that is important to the plot.

page 325

It is early summer 1851, and 12-year-old Abigail Parker is still finding her way after the death of her mother the previous winter. Her father has recently made their Massachusetts farm a station on the Underground Railroad, and the two nervously await their first "delivery" of people on their way to Canada to escape slavery.

I could not sit for being so fretful, so I paced and sometimes paused to peer out the window. Mother often said, "Patience is bitter, but its fruit is sweet." If only I were possessed of her calm.

"I see no sign of our four guests," Papa announced as he returned from checking outdoors, fueling my fears that they had met with misfortune. Just then, a sudden knock sounded, and my heart took to pounding as Papa opened the door to two weary women on the **stoop**. He assisted the older one, who appeared to be about 60, to a chair by the hearth. Her companion was maybe 14. Papa directed me to poke up the fire and fetch food and drink.

When the women got back their breath, Papa asked, "What of the others? Did they not accompany you?"

"Just Nellis and me," the girl declared, and the older woman presented a letter.

Papa handed the crumpled paper to me, saying, "If you would, Abby. My eyes fail me in dim light."

I brought the letter close by a candle and commenced reading: *"Dear Jonathan, I send you Nellis and Emma, separate from their two companions, who have fallen ill with fever, one seriously. We have insufficient room to hide four until they recover, so I hope you are **disposed** to shelter them until further transport can be arranged. Respectfully, Jacob."*

Papa nodded and said, "We must see to their safety and comfort." I guided them to the attic hiding place and wished them a peaceful night.

Come morning, afore I entered the attic, I couldn't help **eavesdropping** on the sound of choked coughing. Once inside, I shuddered when I saw Nellis's gaunt face—so ill she looked. "I fear it's the fever," she gasped.

I summoned Papa, pleading, "She needs a doctor!"

325

Text Features

Dialect A character's style of speech or narration shows the way people spoke in the historical setting.

Letters A letter from one character to another affects events in the plot.

Your Turn

COLLABORATE

Identify two examples of dialect in "Journey to Freedom." Use context clues to help you explain in your own words what the character is saying. Then tell why the letter that Abby reads is important to the plot.

Adages and Proverbs

"A penny saved is a penny earned" is an adage. Adages and proverbs are sayings that often use colorful or figurative language to express a widely accepted statement about life.

 ## Find Text Evidence

I'm not sure of the meaning of the sentence The fields have eyes, and the woods have ears, *on page 326 of "Journey to Freedom." Papa says that Abby must be careful "not to arouse suspicion," so I think he knows that personifying the fields and woods as having eyes and ears makes the warning easier for her to remember.*

> "Remember," he said to me, "the fields have eyes, and the woods have ears. Take care how you act and speak, so as not to arouse suspicion."

Your Turn

COLLABORATE

Use context clues to help you determine the meaning of each proverb or adage as it is used in "Journey to Freedom."

Patience is bitter, but its fruit is sweet. *page 325*

Problems shared be problems halved. *page 327*

Write About the Text

Pages 324–327

I responded to the prompt: *Write a letter from Jonathan to Jacob. Describe Abby's dangerous mission.*

Manuel

Student Model: *Narrative Text*

Dear Jacob,

　　Nellis and Emma arrived safely, but by the next morning Nellis was ill with fever. Emma said, "I can brew a healing tea, but I need special herbs." My brave daughter Abby went out in search of the herbs. Abby said her heart pounded so loudly she feared someone might hear it. What if Emma and Nellis

Develop Events

I included some dialogue to help develop the plot.

Strong Word Choice

I used a descriptive phrase to show Abby's fear.

Duane Osborn/Somos Images/Corbis

332

were found out? At last she found the

herbs near a stream and collected a

handful. On Abby's way home a neighbor

questioned her but she kept calm. She

told him she was going to bake a cake!

Emma brewed those herbs into a tea

for Nellis, and she is feeling better.

I am so proud of Abby!

Sincerely,

Jonathan

Sequence Words

I used a transitional phrase to indicate a shift from one time frame to another.

Grammar

This sentence contains the **demonstrative adjective** *those* and the **article** *a*.

Grammar Handbook See page 465.

Your Turn

Write a letter from Emma to the two companions left behind at Jacob's place. Describe the situation at Jonathan's.

Go Digital!
Write your response online.
Use your editing checklist.

Essential Question

How do people benefit from innovation?

Go Digital!

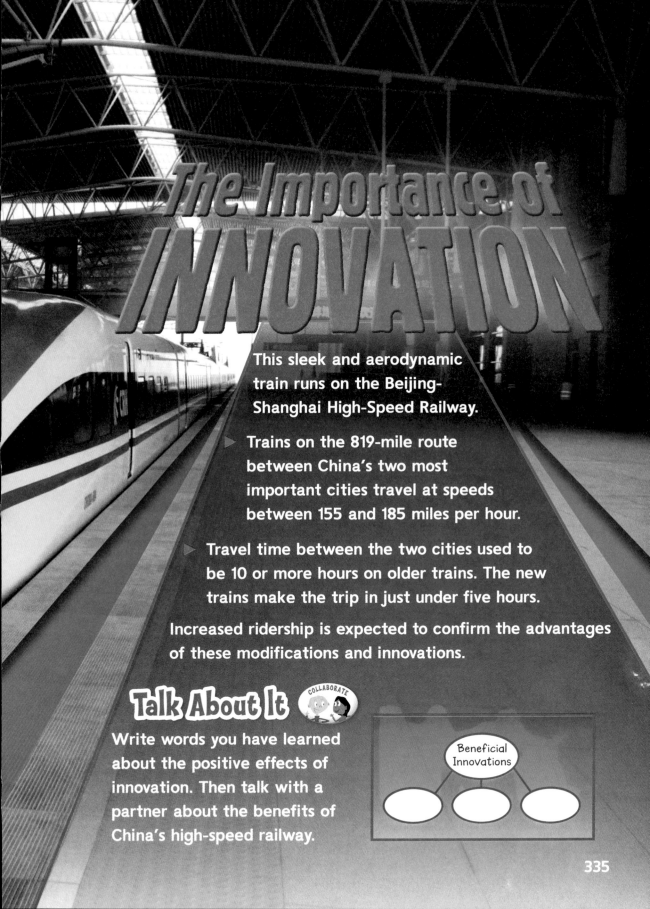

The Importance of INNOVATION

This sleek and aerodynamic train runs on the Beijing-Shanghai High-Speed Railway.

▶ Trains on the 819-mile route between China's two most important cities travel at speeds between 155 and 185 miles per hour.

▶ Travel time between the two cities used to be 10 or more hours on older trains. The new trains make the trip in just under five hours.

Increased ridership is expected to confirm the advantages of these modifications and innovations.

Talk About It COLLABORATE

Write words you have learned about the positive effects of innovation. Then talk with a partner about the benefits of China's high-speed railway.

Beneficial Innovations

Vocabulary

Use the picture and the sentences to talk with a partner about each word.

industrial

Factory smokestacks can be seen rising above the **industrial** landscape.

How is an industrial area different from farmland?

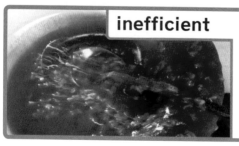

inefficient

Sitting at a table that wobbles a lot would be an **inefficient** way to eat soup.

What else is an inefficient way to eat?

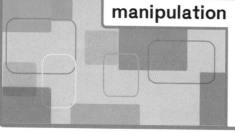

manipulation

Repeating the image across the page involved **manipulation** with computer software.

How are the meanings of manipulation and change related?

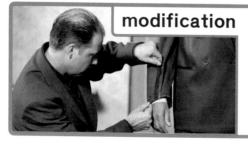

modification

The tailor's **modification** to the sleeve made the suit fit perfectly.

What is a synonym for modification?

mutated

Orchids with unusual features are often **mutated** forms of common varieties.

What is an antonym of mutated?

nutrients

Fruits and vegetables contain vitamins and other **nutrients** that keep our bodies healthy.

Name something you eat that contains important nutrients.

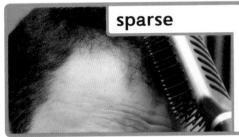

sparse

My father is balding, so his hair is becoming **sparse** in certain spots.

What things are sparse in a desert?

surplus

To avoid running out of our favorite spices, we made sure to keep a **surplus**.

Describe a time you had a surplus of something.

COLLABORATE

Your Turn

Pick three words. Write three questions for your partner to answer.

Go Digital! **Use the online visual glossary**

The Science of Silk

Essential Question

How do people benefit from innovation?

Read how innovations in silk production have made this once rare cloth available to many people.

338

Frank Greenaway/Dorling Kindersley/Getty Images; De Agostini Picture Library/De Agostini/Getty Images; Gio Barto/Photographer's Choice/Getty Images; Graphic Science/Alamy

When the silk-making process was first developed five thousand years ago in China, silk was a rare and expensive luxury. Silk would still be **sparse** today if people had not engaged in the **manipulation** of a natural process. Sericulture, the breeding of silkworms to produce silk, has improved greatly over the centuries. The technologies used in making silk thread and weaving silk fabric have also benefited from important innovations.

A Better Silkworm

The silkworm is the larva, or caterpillar, of *Bombyx mori,* the domesticated silk moth typically used in silk production. (The name *Bombyx mori* means "mulberry silk moth.") This animal's life cycle has four stages: egg; larva that makes the cocoon; pupa that changes inside the cocoon; and winged adult moth. Silk is the material that the larva naturally produces to make its cocoon.

Bombyx mori is a hybrid, the result of breeding particular species over many years. This selective **modification** of inherited traits was done to make a stronger and more productive moth. For example, a *Bombyx mori* moth lays about 500 eggs, more than other species. The eggs are hardier than other silkworm eggs. As a result, more of them survive to develop into larvae. The larvae are also healthy. They eat enough to increase 10,000 times in size in just four to six weeks.

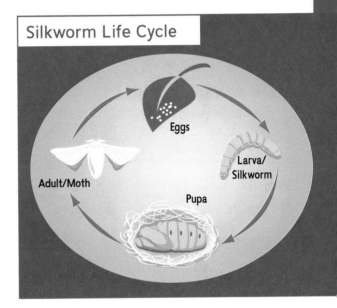

Silkworm Life Cycle

Eggs

Larva/ Silkworm

Adult/Moth

Pupa

Most moths fly during their adult stage to find mates and places with plentiful food to lay their eggs. But *Bombyx mori* is a **mutated** species of moth that is unable to fly. For this reason, it relies entirely on humans to provide its larvae with a special diet of **nutrients** from the leaves of white mulberry trees. Humans must also ensure that the eggs are kept at a temperature of 65° to 77° F until they hatch.

People go through this great effort because the silk of *Bombyx mori* is strong and breaks less often than "wild" silk. The filament from a single cocoon can be 3,000 feet long when it is unwound. *Bombyx mori* silk is whiter than wild silk, so it can absorb more dye. The filament is also round and smooth, resulting in a finer, more luminous cloth.

From Cocoon to Thread

For thousands of years, raising silkworms to make silk was an important part of Chinese culture. Women and girls were responsible for tending the worms, processing the cocoons, spinning the thread, and weaving fabric by hand. These painstaking chores produced beautiful results. They were also **inefficient**, consuming many hours per day and producing only a small amount of silk cloth.

Much of the ancient process survives in current practices. Cocoons are still harvested about eight or nine days after they form. They are placed in water so that they soften enough to be unwound without breaking the filament of raw silk. To avoid building up a **surplus** of unusable cocoons, a time-saving technique called *reeling* has been developed to unwind several cocoons at once. The cocoons are gently brushed to find the loose ends. Then the filaments are wound onto a reel.

A single raw silk filament is too thin to use for weaving. So the next common step in the process, called *throwing,* involves twisting several filaments together to form a thread. The thrown threads are then wound onto small spools called bobbins.

Silk worm spinning its cocoon (top); Weaving silk fabric in Myanmar

A secret for 3,000 years, Chinese sericulture spread to Korea about 200 B.C. , and to India, Japan, and Persia about 300 A.D.

Advances in Silk Technology

Silk moth eggs and the closely guarded secret of sericulture had to be smuggled out of China before other countries could make silk. Once the basic process was known, people sought to improve the technologies used in making silk filaments into cloth. One important invention was the French reeling machine. Its great innovation was to speed up the reeling process and reduce waste.

About 1800, the invention of the Jacquard loom enabled silk weavers to create complex designs quickly. This mechanized loom required strong threads, so even better sericulture practices were developed. More recently, **industrial** weaving machines began using air to push the thread rapidly back and forth. This meant that fewer workers were needed to oversee the looms and that costs could be lowered. As a result, fine silk products were soon available at prices that more people could afford.

Today, China remains the leading producer of silk. But the demand for fine mulberry silk products reaches far beyond China's borders. For this reason, people will continue seeking better, more economical ways to produce silk.

RedChopsticks/Getty Images

Make Connections

Talk about the role humans play in silk production. How have innovations over time benefitted people? ESSENTIAL QUESTION

What other technology have you learned about that developed through innovation over time? How has this helped you? TEXT TO SELF

Reread

Expository texts sometimes explain how parts of a process are related. You may need to reread portions of "The Science of Silk" to make sure you understand the description of a process that is new to you.

 Find Text Evidence

You may not have understood why people supply food for the larvae that are used in producing silk. Reread "A Better Silkworm" on page 339 of "The Science of Silk."

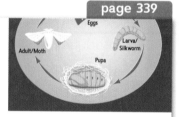

page 339

Eggs
Larva/ Silkworm
Adult/Moth
Pupa

A Better Silkworm

The silkworm is the larva, or caterpillar, of *Bombyx mori,* the domesticated silk moth typically used in silk production. (The name *Bombyx mori* means "mulberry silk moth.") This animal's life cycle has four stages: egg; larva that makes the cocoon; pupa that changes inside the cocoon; and winged adult moth. Silk is the material that the larva naturally produces to make its cocoon.

Bombyx mori is a hybrid, the result of breeding particular species over many years. This selective **modification** of inherited traits was done to make a stronger and more productive moth. For example, a

Most moths fly during their adult stage to find mates and places with plentiful food to lay their eggs. But *Bombyx mori* is a **mutated** species of moth that is unable to fly. For this reason, it relies entirely on humans to provide its larvae with a special diet of **nutrients** from the leaves of white mulberry trees. Humans must also ensure that the eggs are kept at a temperature of 65° to 77° F until they hatch.

> *I read that "most moths fly" to find places with food for their larvae, but that* Bombyx mori *is "unable to fly." I can infer from this that silk moth larvae would not survive if humans did not supply food.*

COLLABORATE

Your Turn

How must cocoons be processed in order to make silk threads for weaving? Reread "From Cocoon to Thread" on page 340. As you read, remember to use the strategy Reread.

Cause and Effect

An author may organize an expository text to show the cause-and-effect relationships among parts of a process. Explaining how various steps in a process achieve specific results helps readers understand why the process evolved the way it did.

 Find Text Evidence

When I reread the section "A Better Silkworm" on page 339 of "The Science of Silk," I can look for signal words and phrases, such as because, so, *and* as a result, *to help me identify why* Bombyx mori *was bred for use in the silk production process.*

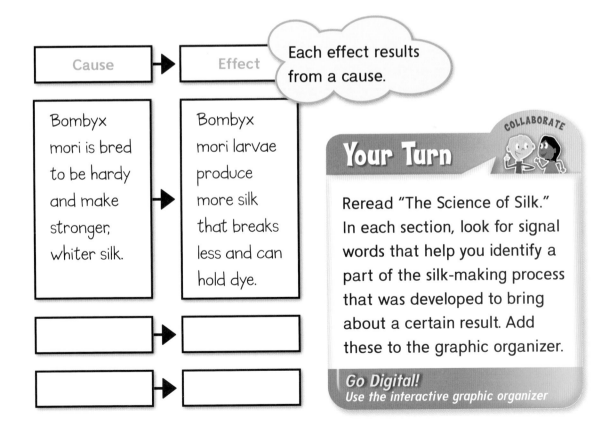

Cause		Effect

Each effect results from a cause.

Bombyx mori is bred to be hardy and make stronger, whiter silk.	→	Bombyx mori larvae produce more silk that breaks less and can hold dye.

COLLABORATE

Your Turn

Reread "The Science of Silk." In each section, look for signal words that help you identify a part of the silk-making process that was developed to bring about a certain result. Add these to the graphic organizer.

Go Digital!
Use the interactive graphic organizer

Expository

"The Science of Silk" is an expository text.

An **Expository** text:

- May provide an explanation of a scientific process and its history
- May include text features, such as photographs with captions, diagrams, and maps

 Find Text Evidence

I can tell "The Science of Silk" is an expository text because it explains how the process of making silk developed over time. The photographs illustrate topics in the text. The diagram helps me understand a natural occurrence discussed in the text. The map shows me the locations of places named in the text.

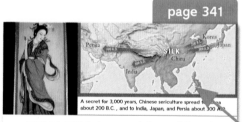

page 341

A secret for 3,000 years, Chinese sericulture spread to Korea about 200 B.C., and to India, Japan, and Persia about 300 A.D.

Advances in Silk Technology

Silk moth eggs and the closely guarded secret of sericulture had to be smuggled out of China before other countries could make silk. Once the basic process was known, people sought to improve the technologies used in making silk filaments into cloth. One important invention was the French reeling machine. Its great innovation was to speed up the reeling process and reduce waste.

About 1800, the invention of the Jacquard loom enabled silk weavers to create complex designs quickly. This mechanized loom required strong threads, so even better sericulture practices were developed. More recently, **industrial** weaving machines began using air to push the thread rapidly back and forth. This meant that fewer workers were needed to oversee the looms and that costs could be lowered. As a result, fine silk products were soon available at prices that more people could afford.

Today, China remains the leading producer of silk. But the demand for fine mulberry silk products reaches far beyond China's borders. For this reason, people will continue seeking better, more economical ways to produce silk.

Make Connections

Talk about the role humans play in silk production. How have innovations over time benefitted people? ESSENTIAL QUESTION

What other technology have you learned about that developed through innovation over time? How has this helped you? TEXT TO SELF

341

Text Features

Diagrams Diagrams illustrate concepts described in the text.

Maps Maps can show a visual representation of ideas in the text that relate to geography.

 COLLABORATE

Your Turn

Find and list three text features in "The Science of Silk." Tell your partner what you learned from each.

Context Clues

When reading an expository text, you can use context clues to find or verify the meanings of unfamiliar or multiple-meaning words. Look for clues that show cause-and-effect relationships.

 Find Text Evidence

I was unsure of the meaning of the word filament *on page 340 of "The Science of Silk." Context clues in the sentence indicate that the long filament is the result, or effect, of unwinding a single cocoon, so I think* filament *means "a very thin fiber."*

The <u>filament</u> from a single cocoon can be 3,000 feet long when it is unwound.

Your Turn

COLLABORATE

Use context clues that indicate cause-and-effect relationships to find the meanings of these words in "The Science of Silk."

hybrid, *page 339*
productive, *page 339*
oversee, *page 341*

Praweena/iStock/360/Getty Images

Write About the Text

Pages 338–341

Roshan

I answered the question: *How does the life cycle of the silk moth affect the production of silk? Provide text evidence in your answer.*

Student Model: *Informative Text*

Strong Opening
I introduced the topic in my first sentence.

Logical Order
I described the details and facts in the order in which they happened.

The *Bombyx mori* is the moth most often used to produce silk. Selective breeding has made this moth strong and productive. Like other silk moths, the *Bombyx mori* has four stages in its life cycle. These stages are the egg, larva, pupa, and adult. The larva, called a silkworm, develops from the egg. It feeds on mulberry leaves for about four weeks, and then it spins a cocoon.

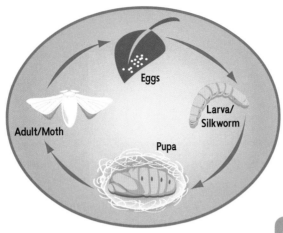

Eggs

Larva/
Silkworm

Pupa

Adult/Moth

It becomes a pupa. The pupa changes into an adult moth inside the cocoon.

Silk makers unwind the filament that makes up the cocoon. The filament from the *Bombyx mori* cocoon is smoother than that of other silk moths and makes a finer cloth. Since the filament strands are so thin, several strands are twisted together before they are woven into silk fabric.

Grammar

The **comparative adjective** *smoother* shows how two things are different.

Grammar Handbook
See page 466.

Supporting Details
I included details from the text to support my topic.

Your Turn

How has the process of creating silk changed over time? Use details from the text.

Go Digital!
Write your response online.
Use your editing checklist.

347

Essential Question

How does technology lead to discoveries?

Go Digital!

BREAKTHROUGH DISCOVERIES

This stunning photograph of the Whirlpool Galaxy was taken by the Advanced Camera for Surveys aboard NASA's Hubble Space Telescope.

▶ By studying such images, astronomers have confirmed that the galaxy's curving spiral arms are long trails of stars and gas laced with dust. They have also discovered that stars in the blue regions form as hydrogen gas is compressed in the pink regions.

Deciphering the structure of a galaxy 23 million light-years away has truly been a breakthrough.

Talk About It

Write words you have learned about the ways technology leads to breakthroughs. Then talk with a partner about why learning about the Whirlpool Galaxy is significant.

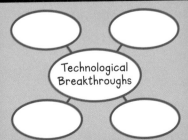

Technological Breakthroughs

Vocabulary

Use the picture and the sentences to talk with a partner about each word.

colleagues

Janell works with many **colleagues** at her company.

How are the meanings of the words colleagues and coworkers related?

conservatively

Estimating **conservatively**, this roast will serve eight people, but possibly more.

What is an antonym of conservatively?

deduction

The doctor's **deduction** is that her symptoms are just a cold.

What is a synonym for deduction?

drones

On some summer days, the sound of lawnmowers **drones** for hours.

Name something else you know that drones.

galaxy

The Milky Way **galaxy** is a system containing billions of stars.

Where is a galaxy located?

sustain

Healthy snacks will **sustain** us if we get hungry on our hike.

What else do people need to sustain themselves?

ultimately

After working hard all semester, Magda **ultimately** passed the final exam.

Describe a goal that you ultimately reached after trying for a while.

verify

There are many reasons why documents might be checked to **verify** your identity.

Who might need to verify a person's identity?

Your Turn

COLLABORATE

Pick three words. Write three questions for your partner to answer.

Go Digital! *Use the online visual glossary*

Light
Detectives

Essential Question

How does technology lead to discoveries?

Read about astronomers' use of technology
to find distant objects in our solar system.

Palomar Observatory,
California

Astronomers use a number of technologies to analyze the light that we see reflected off the most distant objects in our solar system. These scientists often serve as "light detectives" who collect celestial clues using a variety of precision tools.

Discovering Pluto

In the 1920s, astronomers noticed something strange. The outer planets seemed to be affected by an unexplained force. Was there another planet out there with gravitational pull strong enough to tug on Uranus and Neptune? To find this object, a young scientist named Clyde Tombaugh perfected an innovative method for searching the sky.

Using a new telescope at the Lowell Observatory in Arizona, Tombaugh took wide-angle photographs of slivers of the night sky. He then viewed these images in a machine called a blink comparator. This tool was a type of microscope that superimposed two images of the exact same area taken at different times, placing one on top of the other. It blinked so rapidly back and forth between the two images that Tombaugh could see whether any objects changed position from the first time period to the next. As the months passed, Tombaugh estimated he had scanned more than a million stars. His painstaking research finally paid off in February of 1930 when he discovered Pluto and its orbital movement.

Scanning the Kuiper Belt

After Tombaugh's discovery, astronomers became more interested in the outer reaches of our solar system. In 1992, they identified a disk-like region extending up to 9.3 billion miles from the sun and named it the Kuiper Belt, after Gerard Kuiper who had theorized the existence of such a region. Estimates suggested that there were about 70,000 large, icy objects in the Kuiper Belt. Were some even larger than Pluto?

To answer this question, astronomer Michael Brown and his colleagues followed a procedure similar to the method designed by Tombaugh. But they took advantage of new technology to make their search easier and more effective. Like Tombaugh, Brown's team takes repeated images using a telescope. Every three hours, a digital camera mounted on the Samuel Oschin Telescope at the Palomar Observatory in California snaps a picture of the night sky. A microwave link allows robots to control both the telescope and its camera. These robots follow a pre-programmed routine that moves the telescope and takes pictures. This automated system drones through the night while the astronomers sleep.

Oschin Telescope, Palomar Observatory

Instead of using a blink comparator, Brown's team sends the images to a bank of ten computers at the California Institute of Technology (CIT). The computers superimpose images taken at different times and identify objects that are possibly moving. Then the team analyzes the data to try to verify the movement. Most of the time, the objects identified are not breathtaking discoveries. They are simply the result of flaws in the telescope's camera. But sometimes, the computers do track down moving objects. Airplanes, satellites, and asteroids have been flagged by the system. And in 2003, the team discovered a bright shape that was moving more slowly than anything documented in our solar system. Could this be the object tugging on Uranus and Neptune?

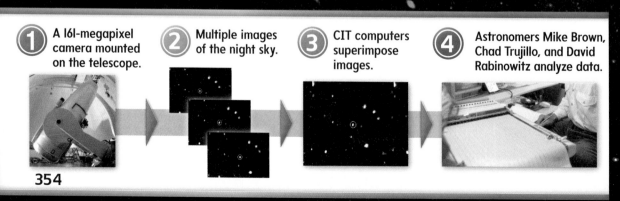

1. A 161-megapixel camera mounted on the telescope.
2. Multiple images of the night sky.
3. CIT computers superimpose images.
4. Astronomers Mike Brown, Chad Trujillo, and David Rabinowitz analyze data.

Combining New Data with Old

The super-slow speed of this object, which was eventually named Eris, posed a problem. Brown calculated that Eris takes 560 years to orbit the sun. So it would take many years to collect enough data confirming the deduction that Eris affects planetary orbits. Rather than waiting, Brown decided to check photos taken by other astronomers. Luckily, Eris appeared in photographs taken as early as 1950. By combining these images with contemporary data, the team developed a more complete view of Eris's size and movements.

The team originally estimated that Eris was 25 to 40 percent more massive than Pluto. But when they used pictures taken by the Hubble Space Telescope to confirm this hypothesis, they found out they were wrong. Eris is only slightly larger than Pluto. The overestimate was the result of Eris's extremely reflective surface. The bright, reflected light gives the impression that Eris is more substantial than it really is. Brown suggests that an atmosphere of frozen nitrogen causes Eris's high level of reflection.

As a result of Brown's discovery, astronomers reconsidered the definition of a planet. Ultimately, both Pluto and Eris were classified as "dwarf planets," rather than planets. But discoveries in the Kuiper Belt continue to sustain great interest. Conservatively, astronomers predict that new technology will allow them to identify several more dwarf planets in the Kuiper Belt. The information gained from their investigations will enrich our understanding of distant objects in other parts of the galaxy as well.

The Moon

Earth

Pluto

Eris

Relative sizes of Earth, the Moon, Pluto, and Eris

NASA

Make Connections

Talk about the technology that astronomers have used to investigate distant objects in our solar system. ESSENTIAL QUESTION

Describe a time when using a tool (a ruler, calculator, camera, etc.) to test a hypothesis helped you answer a question. TEXT TO SELF

Reread

The technical information in "Light Detectives" may be difficult to understand the first time you read it. As you reread, focus on the meanings of smaller parts of long sentences. Then think about how the ideas in those parts are connected.

 Find Text Evidence

You may not be sure how Clyde Tombaugh used photographs of the night sky to find Pluto. Reread "Discovering Pluto" on page 353.

page 353

Using a new telescope at the Lowell Observatory in Arizona, Tombaugh took wide-angle photographs of slivers of the night sky. He then viewed these images in a machine call a blink comparator. This tool was a type of microscope that superimposed two images of the exact same area taken at different times, placing one on top of the other. It blinked so rapidly back and forth between the two images that Tombaugh could see whether any objects changed position from the first time period to the next. As the months passed, Tombaugh estimated he had scanned more than a million stars. His painstaking research finally paid off in February of 1930 when he discovered Pluto and its orbital movement.

I read that Tombaugh "viewed these images in...a blink comparator." Breaking the next two sentences into parts helps me understand that this device switched images back and forth to show if an object had moved.

Your Turn

COLLABORATE

Explain why searching for dwarf planets was easier for astronomers in 2003 than it was for Clyde Tombaugh in the 1920s. As you reread "Scanning the Kuiper Belt" on pages 353-354, remember to think first about the details in smaller parts of long sentences.

Sequence

To explain how a scientific discovery came about, an author will often organize a text by describing events in sequential order. Identifying this sequence of events as you read will help you understand how the scientists reached their goal.

 Find Text Evidence

When I reread "Scanning the Kuiper Belt," I can look for a sequence of key events that led to the discovery and description of Eris.

Event
Robots controlled a telescope's camera taking pictures of the night sky.

↓

Computers analyzed the images and found a bright, moving object in 2003.

↓

↓

Your Turn COLLABORATE

Reread the last section of "Light Detectives." Identify key events in the sequence that led scientists to classify Eris as a dwarf planet. Add them to the graphic organizer. Then tell how each event helped scientists reach their conclusions.

Go Digital!
Use the interactive graphic organizer

357

Expository

"Light Detectives" is an expository text that gives an account of ways that technology is used to identify distant objects that are moving in our solar system.

An **Expository** text:

- May use technical language to explain a process
- May use photographs, diagrams, and models to illustrate scientific concepts

Find Text Evidence

In "Light Detectives," I learn how astronomers discover distant objects. The diagram illustrates a technical process described in the text. The model gives me visual information about a topic in the text.

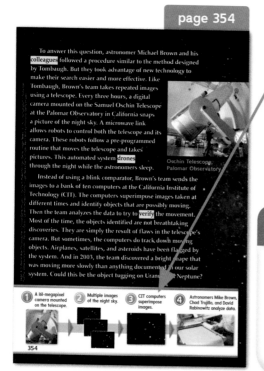

page 354

To answer this question, astronomer Michael Brown and his colleagues followed a procedure similar to the method designed by Tombaugh. But they took advantage of new technology to make their search easier and more effective. Like Tombaugh, Brown's team takes repeated images using a telescope. Every three hours, a digital camera mounted on the Samuel Oschin Telescope at the Palomar Observatory in California snaps a picture of the night sky. A microwave link allows robots to control both the telescope and its camera. These robots follow a pre-programmed routine that moves the telescope and takes pictures. This automated system drones through the night while the astronomers sleep.

Oschin Telescope, Palomar Observatory

Instead of using a blink comparator, Brown's team sends the images to a bank of ten computers at the California Institute of Technology (CIT). The computers superimpose images taken at different times and identify objects that are possibly moving. Then the team analyzes the data to try to verify the movement. Most of the time, the objects identified are not breathtaking discoveries. They are simply the result of flaws in the telescope's camera. But sometimes, the computers do track down moving objects. Airplanes, satellites, and asteroids have been flagged by the system. And in 2003, the team discovered a bright shape that was moving more slowly than anything documented in our solar system. Could this be the object tugging on Uranus and Neptune?

1. A 161-megapixel camera mounted on the telescope.
2. Multiple images of the night sky.
3. CIT computers superimpose images.
4. Astronomers Mike Brown, Chad Trujillo, and David Rabinowitz analyze data.

354

Text Features

Diagrams Diagrams help to clarify the different steps in a process.

Models Models may represent relationships among actual items.

Your Turn

COLLABORATE

Find and list three text features in "Light Detectives." Tell your partner what information you learned from each.

358

Context Clues

When you read an unfamiliar word or technical term in an expository text, use context clues in nearby sentences or paragraphs to help you figure out its meaning. You may find a passage that defines, explains, or restates the term.

 Find Text Evidence

I'm not completely sure what the phrase more massive *means on page 355 of "Light Detectives. In the same paragraph, I read the sentence,* Eris is only slightly larger than Pluto. *This restatement tells me that* more massive *means "bigger" or "larger in size."*

> The team originally estimated that Eris was 25 to 40 percent <u>more massive</u> than Pluto...
>
> Eris is only slightly larger than Pluto.

Your Turn

Use context clues that are definitions, explanations, or restatements to help you find the meanings of these terms in "Light Detectives."

blink comparator, *page 353*

superimposed, *page 353*

Kuiper Belt, *page 353*

Write About the Text

Pages 352–355

Inez

I responded to the prompt: *Describe in detail how scientists are able to detect moving objects in space.*

Student Model: *Informative Text*

Thesis Statement
I introduced the topic in my first sentence.

Strong Paragraphs
The sentences that follow the topic sentence help explain and expand the topic, strengthening the paragraph.

> Scientists use modern technology to find moving objects near the outer edges of our solar system. For example, a digital camera is set on the Samuel Oschin Telescope in California. It takes pictures of a section of space every three hours during the night. Pre-programmed robots control the camera and the telescope. The scientists don't even have to be there. They can be home in bed!

Sequence Words
I used *later* to introduce the second paragraph and to show that one step comes after another.

Later, the scientists send the pictures to computers that superimpose the images over each other. This way, the scientists can see which objects stayed still and which objects moved. The majority of things they find are not big discoveries, and some are more interesting than others. But with each new technology it will be easier to find objects far out in space.

Grammar

The word *more* in this sentence **compares** types of discoveries.

Grammar Handbook See page 466.

Your Turn

What series of events occurred that led to the discovery of Eris? Use details from the text.

Go Digital!
Write your response online.
Use your editing checklist.

Essential Question

How have tools used for exploration evolved over time?

Go Digital!

Better Ways to Explore

Though I'm only about 10 feet below the surface, being at the controls of this sub-scooter makes exploring the warm Indian Ocean waters a remarkable experience.

▶ I've always wanted to get close to sea creatures in their natural habitats, but diving and snorkeling equipment seemed so complicated and difficult.

▶ The application of simple submarine technology to a familiar scooter design lets me move around and discover at my own pace.

This new tool for shallow water exploration has opened up a whole new world to me!

Talk About It

Write words you have learned about the improvement of tools for exploration. Then talk with a partner about a technology that you know has been improved to help people make new or better discoveries.

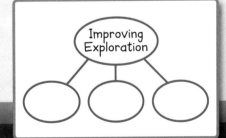

Improving Exploration

Vocabulary

Use the picture and the sentences to talk with
a partner about each word.

application

The instructions for raising a tent seemed
easy, but their **application** was difficult.

What other activities require the
application of instructions?

catastrophic

The mudslide was **catastrophic** for
many towns in the area.

What is a synonym for catastrophic?

computations

To monitor progress, they performed
computations using the data collected.

What is a tool commonly used to
perform computations?

deployed

To ensure safe conditions during the event,
the police chief **deployed** additional officers.

How are the people who take a poll
usually deployed?

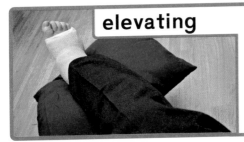

elevating

One of the doctor's recommendations was **elevating** his leg while it healed.

When might elevating a limb be recommended?

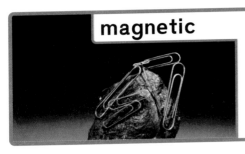

magnetic

Because of its **magnetic** properties, a certain type of ore attracts objects containing iron.

What household items often have magnetic features?

obsolete

Steam engine trains are now virtually **obsolete**.

What is an antonym of obsolete?

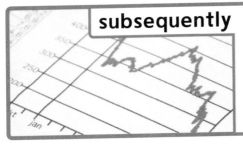

subsequently

The stock was performing poorly, so we doubted it would **subsequently** improve.

If practicing hard once helped you win, how would you subsequently prepare for games?

Your Turn

COLLABORATE

Pick three words. Write three questions for your partner to answer.

Go Digital! **Use the online visual glossary**

Essential Question

How have tools used for exploration evolved over time?

Read how advances in technology have aided exploration.

A sextant can still be used today to navigate at sea.

Thomas J. Abercrombie/National Geographic/Getty Images

Tools of the Explorer's Trade

The word *technology* sounds modern, but people have been using it for at least 300 years. Considering that one definition of *technology* is "the use of knowledge for practical purposes," we can say people have been developing new technologies since the dawn of human history. Some of them are antiquated. Others, though old, are continually improved. Stone Age axes qualify as technology, as do the wheel and the telephone. The following survey of several historical navigation techniques is one example of how technologies evolve over time.

The North Star

Sailors of early civilizations used the star Polaris, also called the North Star, to get their bearings at sea. But using the North Star for navigation had some serious drawbacks. First, it can only be seen on clear nights, so attempting to navigate through unknown waters on a cloudy night could be **catastrophic**. Second, Polaris can be seen only from the Northern Hemisphere. While navigating with the North Star was a good choice under certain circumstances, something better was needed.

The Astrolabe

The astrolabe was an advanced measuring tool invented in the Middle East. Though its primary **application** was to make **computations** about time and the positions of the Sun, Moon, planets, and stars, it was also employed as a technological aid to navigation. The astrolabe gave mariners a way to determine the latitude of their ships while at sea.

A Moorish astrolabe made in Andalusia, Spain

(l) A. Gómez/Flickr/Getty Images; (bkgd) Jeff Spielman/Photodisc/Getty Images

367

The Sextant

The sextant is another tool that used the positions of the Sun and stars to find a location on Earth. First developed in Asia Minor in the late tenth century, it was used to measure the angle between a celestial object and the horizon. When navigators considered the measurement in relation to the time of day or night it was taken, they could find their ship's location on a nautical chart. Far from **obsolete**, this technology is still used today as a backup to modern navigation technologies.

The Compass

A compass is made by balancing a **magnetic** needle above a circular dial. Earth's own strong magnetic field causes the needle to swing into a north-south position. Because a compass indicates direction in all weather and at all times of the day or night, its importance as a navigational technology was quickly recognized. Historians are unsure who invented the compass, but we do know it was in use in China as early as the eleventh century.

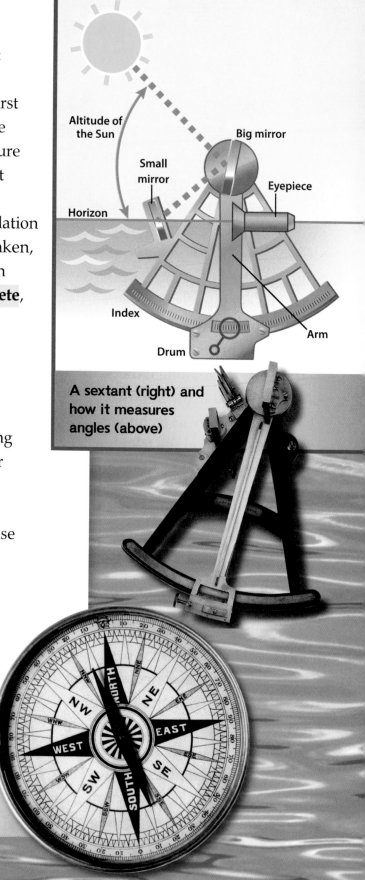

A sextant (right) and how it measures angles (above)

A compass uses Earth's magnetic field to show direction.

An Opinion: Let's Keep Looking Beyond

Many characterize the ongoing story of human exploration as one of courage and creative resourcefulness. For most of history, exploration was confined to Earth's surface. But in 1930, we began diving into the ocean's depths. By 1969, we had landed on the moon. The probes that we deployed into deep space in 1977 are still transmitting valuable data back to us across billions of miles. Subsequently, we have sent robotic vehicles to survey the surface of Mars. And we have a powerful telescope in orbit that is sending us spectacular photographs of the formation of distant stars.

Exploring the unknown has clearly fueled our inventiveness, but it also inspires our imaginations. Because we are constantly elevating our aspirations, we have been able to increase our knowledge even when expectations have been the worst. Modern technologies are providing more and better tools to explore increasingly remote places. In fact, when it comes to exploration, the best is certainly yet to come. We should always resist the idea that an adventurous instinct might be foolhardy, and we should continue to value and encourage curiosity.

A rendering of the Mars Rover

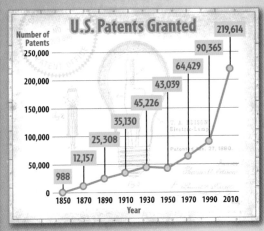

U.S. Patents Granted

Number of Patents

Year	Number of Patents
1850	988
1870	12,157
1890	25,308
1910	35,130
1930	45,226
1950	43,039
1970	64,429
1990	90,365
2010	219,614

Inventing as Fast as We Can

When the U.S. government grants patents to "promote the Progress of Science and useful Arts," it gives exclusive rights to inventors for a set period of time. The numbers of patents issued in the years from 1850 to 2010 reveals a stunning increase in the rate of technological innovations.

Make Connections

Talk about the ways in which technologies used for exploration have developed over time. ESSENTIAL QUESTION

Tell how a technological tool you use in your daily life helps you learn about your community and the world. TEXT TO SELF

Summarize

Summarizing an expository text can help you understand the information in it. As you read "Tools of the Explorer's Trade," identify the key ideas about technologies used for exploration. Use the ideas to summarize the text in your own words.

 ## Find Text Evidence

You may not be sure how to summarize the significance of the sextant as a tool for exploration. Reread the section "The Sextant" on page 368 of "Tools of the Explorer's Trade."

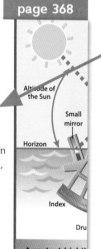

page 368

The Sextant

The sextant is another tool that used the positions of the Sun and stars to find a location on Earth. First developed in Asia Minor in the late tenth century, it was used to measure the angle between a celestial object and the horizon. When navigators considered the measurement in relation to the time of day or night it was taken, they could find their ship's location on a nautical chart. Far from **obsolete**, this technology is still used today as a backup to modern navigation technologies.

Altitude of the Sun

Small mirror

Horizon

Index

Dru

A sextant (right)

I read details about taking angle measurements and using them to find a "ship's location," both in the past and as a "backup" today. To summarize this section, I can say that an old tool, the sextant, still has value as a navigational technology.

Your Turn

COLLABORATE

What made the invention of the compass important? Reread the section "The Compass" to identify the key ideas. Then use them to summarize the section.

Author's Point of View

Authors of expository texts present primarily factual information, but their perspective, or point of view, about a topic often comes across in their writing. In nonfiction, the author's point of view is usually supported with evidence that can be checked.

 Find Text Evidence

When I reread "Tools of the Explorer's Trade," I can look for details that suggest a particular perspective on tools used for exploration.

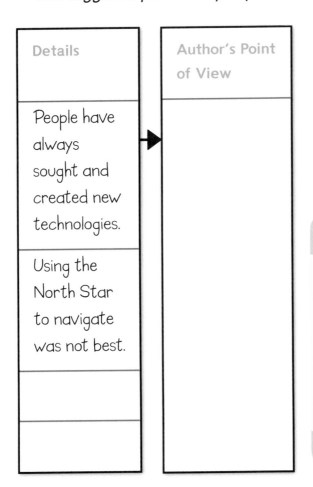

Details	Author's Point of View
People have always sought and created new technologies.	
Using the North Star to navigate was not best.	

Your Turn

Reread "Tools of the Explorer's Trade." In the graphic organizer, list more key details supporting the author's point of view. Then tell what you think the author's overall point of view is.

Go Digital!
Use the interactive graphic organizer

Expository

The informational article "Tools of the Explorer's Trade" explains the role technology has played in exploration. Expository articles may include graphs to represent concepts visually and sidebars to present opinions related to the topic.

 Find Text Evidence

"Tools of the Explorer's Trade" includes descriptions and photographs of tools that were developed for exploration. The diagram on page 368 shows how one tool works. The sidebar on page 369 presents a specific opinion supported by evidence. The information in the line graph on page 369 makes an additional point related to the topic.

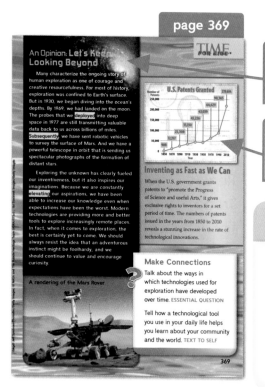

page 369

Text Features

Sidebars Sidebars provide a way to add related information, such as a definite opinion, to the text.

Graphs Graphs of numerical data often show how something has changed over time.

Your Turn

COLLABORATE

Identify two text features in "Tools of the Explorer's Trade." Then explain how the information in each feature adds to your understanding of the topic.

Connotations and Denotations

The denotation of a word is its most common dictionary definition. The connotations of a word are associations it has that are beyond its basic meaning. You may come across words whose connotations in context add meaning to the text.

 Find Text Evidence

I wasn't sure what the word antiquated *means on page 367 of "Tools of the Explorer's Trade." When I read on, I see the definition, or denotation, of* antiquated *in the next sentence: "old." The connotations in this paragraph, however, are that antiquated technologies are very out-of-date or no longer useful at all.*

> Some of them are <u>antiquated</u>. Others, though <u>old</u>, are continually improved.

Your Turn

COLLABORATE

Use context to identify the connotations of each word as it is used in "Tools of the Explorer's Trade." Tell how the connotations vary from the word's basic meaning.

spectacular, *page 369*   **adventurous,** *page 369*

stunning, *page 369*

Write About the Text

Tools of the
Explorer's Trade

Pages 366–369

Darell

I answered the question: *Is the rapid rate of technological growth a positive or a negative? Support your argument with details from the text.*

Student Model: *Argument*

Grammar

The word **worse** is the **comparative** form of *bad*.

Grammar Handbook See page 467.

Content Words

I chose to use content words such as *application* to add support to my argument.

> Some people may be overwhelmed
>
> by how quickly technology changes. They
>
> may think it's bad that a new computer
>
> may be obsolete within a year. Even worse,
>
> when they get a new phone, they know it
>
> will soon need a new application or two.
>
> That kind of change can be frustrating.
>
> Yet the rapid rate of technological
>
> growth is good because most inventions
>
> are meant to help people. Inventions such
>
> as the astrolabe and compass helped

navigators explore our planet.
Just in the last few decades, even
better technologies have allowed us to
explore far into space and deep into
the ocean. New technology helps us
communicate with each other and explore
all parts of our lives. How can easy
communication not help us live the
best lives possible?

Supporting Claims
I supported my argument with evidence from the text.

Strong Conclusion
I ended my argument with a question that will lead the reader to think about my claim.

Your Turn

Which early navigational tool was the most important invention? Explain your answer.

Go Digital!
Write your response online.
Use your editing checklist.

Unit 6

Taking ACTION

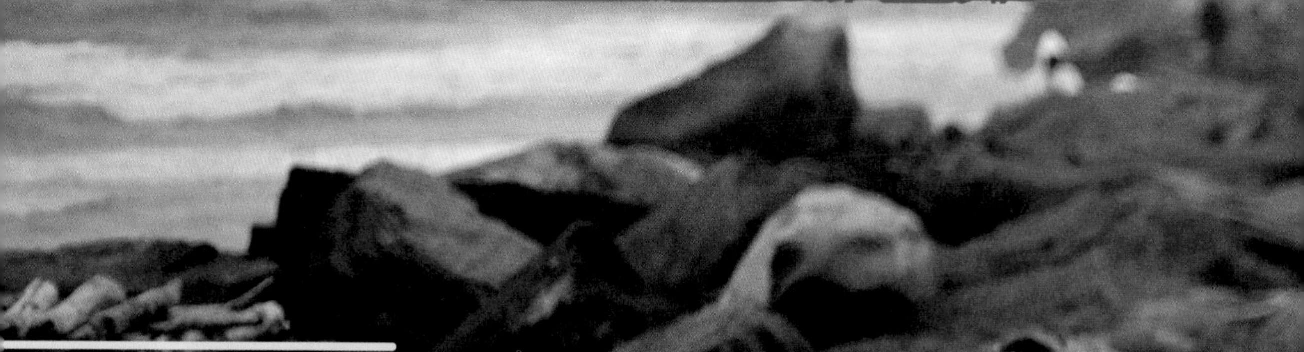

Photography by Krystin Norman/Flickr/Getty Images

One Step

Sun up, sun down
Moon up, moon down…
I continue on;
I've grown afraid—
Moments tighten, fold into habits
Sights narrow;
Though I have goals to reach,
I hesitate.

Then a sound catches me
From a lonely shadow
Off my path, outside my routine—
A muffled voice, softly calling;
I waver, am slow to turn and look;
Someone's here,
Seeking a smile, a kind word,
With eyes hopeful and wide.

In that moment I wonder:
What would I gain
By not changing my stride,
By dodging one who shares my
doubts?
So I stop to offer a nod, a word.

Soon it all comes back how simple
this can be:
One smile builds a friendship,
One laugh conquers sadness,
One step, always, begins each
journey.

—Jane Markover

The **BIG** Idea

**When is it important
to take action?**

Essential Question

How have people used natural resources?

Go Digital!

Relying on Nature

The working relationship between this masked man and his bees is a special partnership.

▶ The hives he builds on his honey farm in Missouri provide safety for the bees' queen and an environment the bees like for manufacturing their food supply.

▶ In return, the bees pollinate local crops, and this keeper is rewarded with a valuable commodity to sell: delicious honey.

More than ever, people are learning the importance of protecting such indispensable natural resources as bees.

Talk About It

Write words you have learned about natural resources. Then talk with a partner about why beekeepers are willing to risk getting stung.

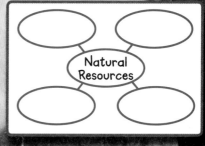

Natural Resources

Burke/Triolo Productions/Brand X Pictures/Getty Images; Ingram Publishing/SuperStock

Vocabulary

**Use the picture and the sentences to talk with a
partner about each word.**

commodity

Because of its use in food production, corn
is a highly valued **commodity** in the U.S.

Name another commodity that is
important to Americans.

distribution

The relief effort ensured **distribution** of
medical supplies to flood victims.

Describe a time when you helped with
the distribution of something.

dominant

The **dominant** wolf that leads the pack
is called the alpha male.

How would you describe the behavior of
a dominant person?

edible

All of the decorations on the cake were
edible.

How are the meanings of the words
edible and nutritious related?

impenetrable

Mario doubted that he would be able to get through the **impenetrable** crowd.

What else could you describe as impenetrable?

ornate

At the historic home, we saw several vases decorated in a complex, **ornate** style.

What is an antonym of ornate?

replenished

The water in the fountain is **replenished** by a nearby mountain stream.

How can supplies of nutrients in soil be replenished?

significant

The environment club made a **significant** contribution to the cleanup effort.

Describe something that makes a significant difference to your ability to study.

Your Turn

COLLABORATE

Pick three words. Write three questions for your partner to answer.

Go Digital! *Use the online visual glossary*

The Fortunes of Fragrance

? Essential Question

How have people used natural resources?

Read about the natural resources used in production of fragrances from ancient times to today.

Rose blossoms grown in the Atlas Mountains of Morocco

Our sense of smell plays a **significant** role in our survival. It helps us detect poisons, smoke from a fire, toxic gases, and other dangers. Our noses can tell us a great deal about something that is unfamiliar or questionable. For example, a piece of rotten fruit may look beautiful, but its smell lets us know it is not **edible**. For centuries, doctors have used their sense of smell to identify infection or disease. Fortunately, there are many pleasant odors as well. From earliest times, people have sought ways to preserve the lovely scents of flowers and herbs.

Capturing Aromas

Many plants contain volatile oils. These chemicals often repel insects, but they smell good to us. Early humans discovered them while crushing or bruising leaves, fruits, and bark. Before long, people found ways to release and use the oils. They noticed that soaking rose petals in water resulted in a scented liquid. They also learned that simply burning parts of aromatic plants would scent the air. People soon started to mix powdered resin, or tree sap, with honey to form lumps of incense. They placed the incense on hot coals or in **ornate** burners to produce a perfumed smoke. In fact, the word *perfume* comes from the Latin words *per* and *fumum*, meaning "through smoke."

Over time, people developed other means to capture fragrance from plants. They squeezed the rinds of citrus fruits or boiled the leaves of such plants as lavender and peppermint to obtain their oils. Later, they found that steam could extract oils from both fresh and dried plants. After the steam releases volatile oils from plant material inside a pressurized chamber, it passes through cooling tubes where the oils become a separate liquid. This technique of *steam distillation* is still widely used today.

Copper distilling chambers in use at a perfumery in Grasse, France

akg-images/Rainer Hackenberg/Newscom

FLOWERS
Jasmine, Rose

PODS, SEEDS
Vanilla Pod,
Anise Seed

BARK
Cinnamon,
Birch

LEAVES
Peppermint,
Patchouli

ROOTS, RHIZOMES
Vetiver Root,
Iris Rhizome

The petals of certain flowers cannot stand up to the heat of steam distillation, so people learned to press them gently into animal fat, which absorbs their fragrance. The fat is then washed in alcohol to draw out the fragrance molecules. After the alcohol evaporates, only the flower's fragrance remains as something called a *concrete*. This process, known as *enfleurage*, is both time-consuming and expensive. Today, solvent chemicals such as hexane are used to extract fragrance from delicate flowers.

Trading in Aromatics

Most fragrant plants are quite portable, so their **distribution** through vigorous trade was widespread throughout the ancient world. Depending on its availability, a treasured aromatic resource was often a more valuable **commodity** than gold or silver. Along Silk Road trade routes, Chinese merchants offered camphor for sale and purchased cinnamon and sandalwood from India. Egypt imported large quantities of myrrh. Caravans carried frankincense hundreds of miles by camel from Arabia to buyers in Greece and Rome. Eventually, Romans used so much incense that cargo ships were sent across the Mediterranean to speed up the way that supplies were **replenished**.

Trade in aromatics increased during the Middle Ages after people in Europe were introduced to the perfumes and spices of the Far East. But Europeans could buy these items only through merchants in the Middle East. Traders from that region had become the **dominant** players in the market and often charged extremely high prices. This monopoly on aromatic goods seemed **impenetrable**. So European explorers sought trade routes that went around the Middle East by sea.

The Enduring Power of Perfume

In the modern world, trade involving fragrance materials is as brisk as ever. But chemists are the new explorers. Over several decades,

WOOD
Sandalwood, Cedar

BERRIES
Black Pepper, Juniper Berry

CITRUS RINDS
Lime, Lemon

SAP, RESINS
Frankincense, Myrrh

these scientists have learned to isolate the fragrant molecules in natural plant oils and engineer synthetic replacements for others. Synthetic fragrance chemicals are derived primarily from petroleum. They are usually less expensive than natural materials, because supplies are not affected by weather conditions or crop yields.

Still, many of the highest quality perfumes require a small percentage of ingredients derived from real flowers. One perfume company maintains its own fields in the south of France to grow the special kinds of rose and jasmine needed to produce their best-selling product. Many companies use a process called *gas chromatography* to identify the molecules that make up a natural flower's fragrance. The molecules are then manufactured and blended to make a fragrance that simulates the real thing.

Demand for aromatics has only increased since ancient times. The production and sale of fragrance products make up an industry that is now worth billions of dollars. History has shown that, as long as people seek beautiful aromas, the fragrance market will continue to be big business.

Early twentieth-century perfume bottles were often works of art.

Make Connections

Talk about the developments in technology and trade that resulted from people's demand for fragrance. **ESSENTIAL QUESTION**

Describe the scent of a household product you use regularly. What do you like or dislike about it? **TEXT TO SELF**

Ask and Answer Questions

When a passage in an expository text is unclear to you, you can ask yourself questions about it and look for the answers as you read on. As you read "The Fortunes of Fragrance," pause frequently to consider what questions you have.

Find Text Evidence

After reading the first paragraph of "Capturing Aromas" on page 383 of "The Fortunes of Fragrance," you may have had questions about what it means to "capture" aromas.

page 383

Capturing Aromas

Many plants contain volatile oils. These chemicals often repel insects, but they smell good to us. Early humans discovered them while crushing or bruising leaves, fruits, and bark. Before long, people found ways to release and use the oils. They noticed that soaking rose petals in water resulted in a scented liquid. They also learned that simply burning parts of aromatic plants would scent the air. People soon started to mix powdered resin, or tree sap, with honey to form lumps of incense. They placed the incense

cooling tubes where the oils become a separate liquid. This technique of *steam distillation* is still widely used today.

Copper distilling chambers in use at a perfumery in Grasse, France

I asked myself, "What is actually being captured and how?" <u>I read that "plants contain volatile oils" and that people soaked or burnt plants to extract the oils.</u> I'll look for more explanations as I read the rest of the section.

Your Turn

COLLABORATE

What questions did you have after reading the first paragraph of "Trading in Aromatics?" Tell how you used details in the rest of the section to answer your questions. As you read, remember to use the strategy Ask and Answer Questions.

Main Idea and Key Details

The most important point an author makes about a topic is the main idea. When reading expository text, look for key details in each passage. Then think about what the details have in common to infer the main idea.

Find Text Evidence

When I reread "Capturing Aromas" on page 383 of "The Fortunes of Fragrance," I can look for key details about the topic. Then, to identify the main point the author is making in this section, I can think about how all the details are related.

> What idea connects all the key details?

Main Idea

Ever since learning that plants contain fragrant chemicals, people have found ways to extract them.

Detail

People discovered many plants that contain fragrant volatile oils.

Detail

People soaked flowers and burned plants to release their fragrance.

Detail

People used steam, animal fat, and chemical solvents to extract plant fragrances.

Your Turn

COLLABORATE

Reread the remaining sections of "The Fortunes of Fragrance." Identify key details and use them to determine the main idea of each section. Use the graphic organizer to help you.

Go Digital!
Use the interactive graphic organizer

Expository

"The Fortunes of Fragrance" is an expository text about people's use of fragrant resources.

An **Expository** text:
- May use technical terms to explain a concept or process
- May use diagrams to flesh out details in the main text

 Find Text Evidence

In "The Fortunes of Fragrance," I read facts and technical information related to people's use of plants as natural resources for making fragrances. A diagram provides organized details that add to my understanding of information in the text.

page 384

FLOWERS
Jasmine, Rose

PODS, SEEDS
Vanilla Pod,
Anise Seed

BARK
Cinnamon,
Birch

LEAVES
Peppermint,
Patchouli

ROOTS, RHIZOMES
Vetiver Root,
Iris Rhizome

The petals of certain flowers cannot stand up to the heat of steam distillation, so people learned to press them gently into animal fat, which absorbs their fragrance. The fat is then washed in alcohol to draw out the fragrance molecules. After the alcohol evaporates, only the flower's fragrance remains as something called a *concrete*. This process, known as *enfleurage*, is both time-consuming and expensive. Today, solvent chemicals such as hexane are used to extract fragrance from delicate flowers.

Trading in Aromatics
Most fragrant plants are quite portable, so their **distribution** through vigorous trade was widespread throughout the ancient world. Depending on its availability, a treasured aromatic resource was often a more valuable **commodity** than gold or silver. Along Silk Road trade routes, Chinese merchants offered camphor for sale and purchased cinnamon and sandalwood from India. Egypt imported large

quantities of myrrh. Caravans carried frankincense hundreds of miles by camel from Arabia to buyers in Greece and Rome. Eventually, Romans used so much incense that cargo ships were sent across the Mediterranean to speed up the way that supplies were **replenished**.

Trade in aromatics increased during the Middle Ages after people in Europe were introduced to the perfumes and spices of the Far East. But Europeans could buy these items only through merchants in the Middle East. Traders from that region had become the **dominant** players in the market and often charged extremely high prices. This monopoly on aromatic goods seemed **impenetrable**. So European explorers sought trade routes that went around the Middle East by sea.

The Enduring Power of Perfume
In the modern world, trade involving fragrance materials is as brisk as ever. But chemists are the new explorers. Over several decades,

384

Text Feature

Diagrams Diagrams often use visual images to explain and expand on concepts in the text.

 COLLABORATE

Your Turn

Describe a technical process that is explained in the text. Then tell your partner what information you learned from the diagram.

Latin Roots

You may not be sure of the meaning of some technical words in an expository text. Knowing common Latin roots can help you verify the meaning of an unfamiliar or multiple-meaning word.

Find Text Evidence

I wasn't sure what the word extract *means in the third paragraph on page 383 of "The Fortunes of Fragrance." If I know that the Latin root* tract- *means "pull," I can use the word* from *as a context clue to figure out that* extract *means "pull from" or "remove."*

> Later, they found that steam could <u>extract</u> oils from both fresh and dried plants.

Below are Latin roots of some words in "The Fortunes of Fragrance."

Latin Root	Meaning
-sim-	make like
-solv-	loosen
-duct-	bring, lead

COLLABORATE

Your Turn

Use the Latin roots in the chart and context clues to verify the meanings of these words in "The Fortunes of Fragrance."

solvent, *page 384*

introduced, *page 384*

simulates, *page 385*

Write About the Text

Pages 382–385

Mateo

I answered the question: *How do text features in "The Fortunes of Fragrance" support the text?*

Student Model: *Informative Text*

The text features help the reader

understand how fragrances are made.

Pictures of roses and other plants show

where different fragrances come from,

while the photo of the copper distilling

chamber shows the reader one of the

ways that perfume is made. The photos

of the artistic perfume bottles show

the importance that some people put on

Introduce the Topic

My thesis statement explains what my paragraph is about.

Vary Sentence Patterns

I used different types of sentences, such as this sentence, to make my paragraph more interesting.

Jack Hollingsworth/Photodisc/Getty Images

fragrances. The photo of the field of rose blossoms in Morocco includes artistic graphic designs that remind the reader of the aromas of flowers. The text features show that the plant parts used to make fragrances vary widely. This text would have been less informative and harder to understand without the text features.

Grammar

In this sentence, the **adverb** *widely* modifies the verb *vary*.

Grammar Handbook See page 468.

Strong Conclusion

My ending restates my topic sentence and follows logically from the evidence given in the paragraph.

Your Turn

Compare and contrast how fragrances were made in the past with how they are made today.

Go Digital!
Write your response online.
Use your editing checklist.

Essential Question

How do we learn about historical events?

Go Digital!

GATEWAYS TO HISTORY

Everyone asks about my hat. But that's good. I can use my tricorne to begin telling them about life in eighteenth-century Philadelphia.

▶ "The tricorne's shape is very practical," I say. "The upturned brims act like gutters to channel rain water. So my head stays dry!"

▶ Soon they're asking me about the rest of my gear. Before they realize it, they're learning all about militias during the crucial years of the War of Independence.

Making history come alive for people is what makes being a reenactor so much fun.

Talk About It

Write words you have learned about understanding history. Then talk with a partner about a time you learned about the past in a unique or unexpected way.

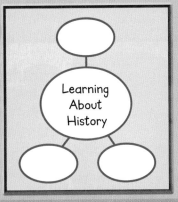

Learning About History

Vocabulary

Use the picture and the sentences to talk with
a partner about each word.

agitated

The customers became **agitated** when the line took too long to move.

Describe a situation that makes you agitated.

crucial

Getting enough sleep is a **crucial** part of a healthy lifestyle.

What other habits are crucial to staying healthy?

futile

It was **futile** to try moving the boulder, which was simply too heavy.

What is an antonym of futile?

populous

With more than 37 million residents, California is the most **populous** state.

Which U.S. cities are very populous?

presumed

Since they had arrived early to the ticket line, Jess **presumed** they would get a seat.

How are the meanings of presumed and concluded related?

smoldering

The **smoldering** coals in the barbecue were still giving off a lot of heat.

What else could you describe as smoldering?

undiminished

Despite the threat of rain, their hopes for having fun at the picnic were **undiminished**.

What is a synonym for undiminished?

urgency

Lifeguards learn to respond with **urgency** to swimmers who are in trouble.

Describe a time when you did something with urgency.

Your Turn

COLLABORATE

Pick three words. Write three questions for your partner to answer.

Go Digital! *Use the online visual glossary*

(t to b) John Eder/The Image Bank/Getty Images; Foodcollection RF/Getty Images; Anthony Collins/Alamy; Mike Harrington/Stone/Getty Images

THE GREAT FIRE OF LONDON

Essential Question

How do we learn about historical events?

Read how a fire that nearly destroyed the city of London in 1666 was recorded for history by those who witnessed the event.

London in 1666

London was by far the most **populous** city in England in 1666. And it was growing fast. Nearly 500,000 people crowded into its wooden buildings, some of which were hundreds of years old. The top floors of many houses overhung the narrow streets. Most had roofs waterproofed with tar pitch. Storerooms were brimming with flammable goods, such as oil and tallow for producing soap and candles. Open-hearth fires burned day and night for cooking, making pottery and metal goods, and providing heat.

Accidental fires were common. Some people feared that fire would someday destroy London. "Forewarned is forearmed," they said, hoping the government would take action to improve safety. Many Londoners, however, were more worried about the plague, a dreadful sickness that had killed nearly 68,000 people during the previous two years. But the summer of 1666 had been unusually hot and dry, so a single spark was all that was needed to cause disaster.

Fire Erupts

The spark occurred early on Sunday morning, September 2. Officially, the fire was **presumed** to have started in the King's bakery on Pudding Street. The baker later claimed that he had checked every room before going to bed at midnight and had diligently "raked up in embers" a fire he found in one fireplace.

Samuel Pepys, a Royal Navy administrator living in London, recorded his observations of the fire in a diary. He wrote that the baker's family had woken up choking on smoke rising from downstairs. He noted they were "in absolute ignorance how this fire should come." A strong wind then fanned the flames, sending sparks from the bakery to ignite other buildings. Fire quickly spread to surrounding streets.

In the 1600s, London had no fire department. People began throwing water on the fire from leather buckets and beat it with brooms, but these efforts were a case of "too little too late." The flames soon reached the banks of the River Thames, burning

A seventeenth-century painting depicts the Great Fire of London, 1666

St. Paul's Cathedral in flames (above); a fire syringe used to spray water (left)

warehouses and half of London Bridge. Pepys went to the river and "there saw a lamentable fire." He described people flinging goods into the water and leaping into boats to try to escape the flames. Others pulled heavily laden carts with great **urgency** to save the few belongings they could.

London Is Burning

Pepys alerted King Charles II, who sent him to the Lord Mayor with the command to pull down houses to create a firebreak. The greatly **agitated** mayor told Pepys he had already directed men to do just what the king ordered, but their efforts had been **futile**. He said the fire "overtakes us faster than we can do it." Wind spread the fire across firebreaks as wide as 20 houses. Sparks even ignited the rubble from torn-down houses, so flames were soon sent in new directions. Panic enveloped the city.

John Evelyn, a well-known writer who also kept a diary about the fire, described fighting the flames on Fetter Lane. The ground under his feet was so hot, he noted, that it "even burnt the soles of my shoes." When the fire reached St. Paul's Cathedral, Evelyn documented how the heat melted the lead roof, causing molten metal to "run down the streets in a stream" and stones from the walls to explode outward.

The incessant fire raged **undiminished** for four days.

The *London Gazette* reported that "all attempts for quenching it however industriously pursued seemed insufficient." Finally, **crucial** relief came when the fire reached a brick wall near a law school and the winds changed direction. But by that time, four-fifths of the city had become a **smoldering** ruin. In all, 13,200 houses, 87 churches, and many government buildings were destroyed. Although few deaths were recorded, thousands were homeless.

The City Rebuilds

After the fire, people wanted someone to blame. A French watchmaker named Robert Hubert became a scapegoat when he said he had set the fire. Few people believed Hubert's confession. The Earl of Clarendon called him a "poor distracted wretch." Still, he was hanged. By 1667, Parliament had formally declared the fire an accident, as "nothing hath yet been found to argue it to have been other than . . . a great wind, and the season so very dry."

Where there is life there is hope, and people began to rebuild while living in nearby fields. For safety, many new buildings were constructed of stone rather than wood. The need for businesses to recover quickly even took priority over King Charles's plans for a new city design. People could also count their blessings that the fire had destroyed the city's rats and their plague-infected fleas. The plague's devastation was finally halted.

Make Connections

Talk about the ways in which personal and official records help us understand what happened during London's Great Fire. ESSENTIAL QUESTION

Describe an event that you and others witnessed. Tell what each of your accounts added to the overall understanding of what happened. TEXT TO SELF

Ask and Answer Questions

As you read narrative nonfiction, stop to ask yourself questions about any information you may not understand. Then, as you read further, use text evidence to answer your questions.

 Find Text Evidence

After you read "London Is Burning" on pages 398–399 of "The Great Fire of London," you may have had questions about why London's fire spread so quickly.

page 398

efforts had been **futile**. He said the fire "overtakes us faster than we can do it." Wind spread the fire across firebreaks as wide as 20 houses. Sparks even ignited the rubble from torn-down houses, so flames were soon sent in new directions. Panic enveloped the city.

John Evelyn, a well-known writer who also kept a diary about the fire, described fighting the flames on Fetter Lane. The ground under his feet was so hot, he noted, that it

ndon
·iver and
·e." He
ʒoods into
boats
. Others
vith great
·longings

> I asked myself why the fire kept burning. <u>I read that fire-fighting methods were almost useless when "wind spread the fire," and that the fire stopped only when it "reached a brick wall" and the wind changed.</u>

COLLABORATE

Your Turn

What questions did you ask yourself about events that occurred after the fire was out? Reread "The City Rebuilds" on page 399 to identify details that can help you answer them.

Cause and Effect

Authors of narrative nonfiction often describe a historical occurrence by explaining how some events caused others. If the cause of an event is not directly stated in the text, look for details to help you identify why the event happened.

 Find Text Evidence

In "London in 1666" on page 397 of "The Great Fire of London," the details "wooden buildings," "flammable goods," and "open-hearth fires" tell me that London was in danger from the threat of fire.

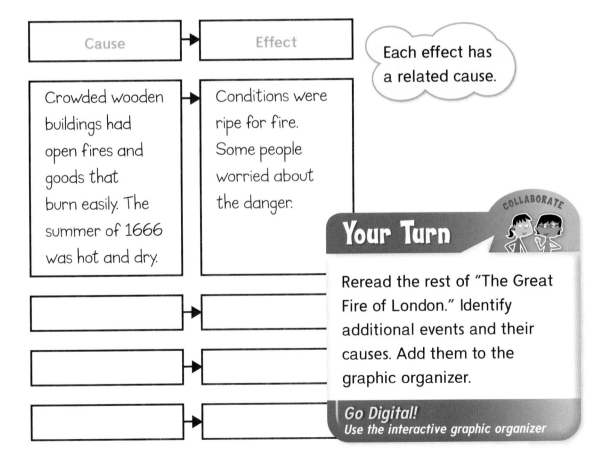

Cause	Effect

Each effect has a related cause.

Cause: Crowded wooden buildings had open fires and goods that burn easily. The summer of 1666 was hot and dry.

Effect: Conditions were ripe for fire. Some people worried about the danger.

COLLABORATE

Your Turn

Reread the rest of "The Great Fire of London." Identify additional events and their causes. Add them to the graphic organizer.

Go Digital!
Use the interactive graphic organizer

Narrative Nonfiction

"The Great Fire of London" is narrative nonfiction.

Narrative nonfiction:

- Reads like a story but tells about real events, people, and places
- Often describes events in chronological order
- May include supporting information from primary sources

Find Text Evidence

Dates and transition words in "The Great Fire of London" show that events are described in time order. Quotations from diaries of eye witnesses, a newspaper, and government records provide key details about what happened during and after the fire.

page 397

London in 1666

London was by far the most **populous** city in England in 1666. And it was growing fast. Nearly 500,000 people crowded into its wooden buildings, some of which were hundreds of years old. The top floors of many houses overhung the narrow streets. Most had roofs waterproofed with tar pitch. Storerooms were brimming with flammable goods, such as oil and tallow for producing soap and candles. Open-hearth fires burned day and night for cooking, making pottery and metal goods, and providing heat.

Accidental fires were common. Some people feared that fire would someday destroy London. "Forewarned is forearmed," they said, hoping the government would take action to improve safety. Many Londoners, however, were more worried about the plague, a dreadful sickness that had killed nearly 68,000 people during the previous two years. But the summer of 1666 had been unusually hot and dry, so a single spark was all that was needed to cause disaster.

Fire Erupts

The spark occurred early on Sunday morning, September 2. Officially, the fire was **presumed** to have started in the King's bakery on Pudding Street. The baker later claimed that he had checked every room before going to bed at midnight and had diligently "raked up in embers" a fire he found in one fireplace.

Samuel Pepys, a Royal Navy administrator living in London, recorded his observations of the fire in a diary. He wrote that the baker's family had woken up choking on smoke rising from downstairs. He noted they were "in absolute ignorance how this fire should come." A strong wind then fanned the flames, sending sparks from the bakery to ignite other buildings. Fire quickly spread to surrounding streets.

In the 1600s, London had no fire department. People began throwing water on the fire from leather buckets and beat it with brooms, but these efforts were a case of "too little too late." The flames soon reached the banks of the River Thames, burning

A seventeenth-century painting depicts the Great Fire of London, 1666

397

Text Features

Primary Sources Primary sources include official records, eyewitness accounts, and newspaper reports from the time of the events described.

Your Turn

Find and list three examples of primary source information in "The Great Fire of London." Tell your partner what you learned from each.

Adages and Proverbs

Adages and proverbs, such as "A penny saved is a penny earned," are traditional sayings about common experiences, often using figurative language. In nonfiction, such sayings can help readers understand an unusual event in a familiar way. Use context clues to figure out or verify the meaning of an adage or proverb.

 Find Text Evidence

I was unsure of the meaning of the phrase forewarned is forearmed *on page 397 of "The Great Fire of London." The context clues* people feared, hoping, *and* take action *in surrounding sentences, tell me that people who were worried about a possible fire felt that heeding warning signs could help prevent disaster.*

> Some people feared that fire would someday destroy London. "Forewarned is forearmed," they said, hoping the government would take action to improve safety.

Your Turn

Use context clues to help you determine the meaning of each adage or proverb in "The Great Fire of London."

too little too late, *page 397*

Where there is life there is hope, *page 399*

count their blessings, *page 399*

Write About the Text

Pages 396–399

Gabrielle

I responded to the prompt: *Imagine you were living in London in 1666. Which disaster would you consider worse: the plague or the Great Fire? Explain your response.*

Student Model: *Argument*

Introduce a Claim
I stated my opinion about which disaster was worse.

Style and Tone
Because of the subject, I used a formal style and maintained an objective tone by using facts from the text to support my opinion.

The Fire of London was a catastrophe that destroyed four-fifths of the city. Thousands of people were left homeless. However, I think that the plague was a worse disaster. As bad as the fire was, it caused far fewer deaths than the plague. About 68,000 people had already died of the plague before the fire started, and the city was infested with the rats and fleas

Radius Images/Alamy

that spread the disease. The fire wiped out the rat and flea populations faster than humans could, bringing the deadly plague to an end. Finally, the fire inspired people to rebuild a safer and more modern London with buildings made of stone rather than wood. As devastating as the fire was, it halted the plague, a much worse disaster.

Jackson, Peter (1922-2003)/Look and Learn/Bridgeman Art Library

Grammar

The **adverb** *faster* compares two actions.

Grammar Handbook See page 469.

Clear Reasons

I provided specific words to link my reasons with text evidence.

Your Turn

Could London have prevented the fire, or was it bound to happen eventually? Provide reasons for your response.

Go Digital!
Write your response online.
Use your editing checklist.

405

Essential Question

How can a scientific investigation be an adventure?

Go Digital!

Javier Trueba/MSF/Photo Researchers, Inc.

Scientific ADVENTURES

The Cave of Crystals was discovered in 2000 in a mine nearly 1,000 feet beneath Naica, Mexico.

▶ The crystals are a mineral called selenite. Some exceed 35 feet in length and weigh more than 50 tons. But selenite is not very resilient, so scientist must be careful while working in the cave.

▶ Geologists hypothesize that the crystals formed in a steaming hot bath of mineral-rich water over a remarkably long time—about 500,000 years. Temperatures in the cave still reach 112°F.

Studying the gigantic crystals has been a spectacular adventure for scientists!

Talk About It

Write words you have learned about scientific investigations. Then talk with a partner about what makes studying the Cave of Crystals such an adventure.

Scientific Investigation

Vocabulary

Use the picture and the sentences to talk with a
partner about each word.

alternative

When the grocery had no beets, they had
to consider some **alternative** vegetables.

What is an alternative filling for apples
in a pie?

correspond

He made sure each player on his list
would **correspond** to a key position on
the team.

What is a synonym for correspond?

extract

Drilling is the most common way to
extract oil from the earth.

How does a dentist extract a tooth?

foliage

The hungry deer ate some of the tree's
plentiful green **foliage**.

What trees do you know that have dense
foliage?

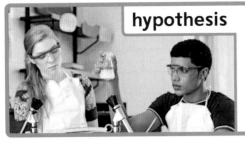

hypothesis

We had to develop a **hypothesis** before we could test it with an experiment.

How are the meanings of hypothesis and guess related?

protein

Eggs and fish are both high in **protein**.

What other foods do you know to be good sources of protein?

resilient

Many gardeners look for **resilient** plants that can survive the summer's heat.

What is an antonym of resilient?

saturated

After absorbing so much water, the sponge became completely **saturated**.

What happens when clouds become saturated with moisture?

Your Turn

COLLABORATE

Pick three words. Write three questions for your partner to answer.

Go Digital! *Use the online visual glossary*

RESEARCHER
TO THE RESCUE

(t) Jeff Foott/Discovery Channel Images/Getty Images; (b) Courtesy of Antonio A. Mignucci-Giannoni, PhD; (bkgd) Jeff Spielman/Photodisc/Getty Images

Essential Question

How can a scientific investigation be an adventure?

Read about a biologist's efforts to find creative ways to protect marine mammals.

Manatee Airlift

On a sunny December day, Dr. Antonio Mignucci is in Florida to keep careful watch as a dozen crew members lift an 840-pound manatee into the cargo hold of a National Guard plane. The scene is certainly unusual, but Dr. Mignucci has learned that saving marine mammals requires uncommon partnerships. Today's team of scientists and military personnel don't mind that their clothes are saturated with seawater. They know their unique collaboration is helping to save a life.

Transporting a manatee for treatment.

On the aircraft, everyone calls the massive six-year-old manatee "UPC" because the wounds he received when struck by a boat resemble the bar codes on store items. When they reach the Puerto Rico Manatee Conservation Center, Dr. Mignucci renames UPC Guacara, after the river where the animal was stranded. But Guacara will get more than an alternative name. He will also take on the role of surrogate parent to younger manatees recovering at the Center.

Unlike some marine mammals, manatees cannot stay submerged for long periods of time. They lack the special protein called myoglobin that enables whales and dolphins to hold oxygen in their muscles. So manatees live in shallow water, where they eat up to 10 percent of their body weight in sea grass and other underwater foliage each day. But today these coastal waters are crowded with boats that can injure and even kill the slow-moving creatures.

Manatees are naturally resilient, but they sometimes need help to recover from injuries. As a marine biologist, Dr. Mignucci recognizes when it's time to extract manatees from tough situations. For example, he knows that Guacara's injuries make him "negatively buoyant." In other words, Guacara sinks in deep water. But he can swim safely in shallow pools at the Center. There he lives a healthy life while helping to care for the younger manatees.

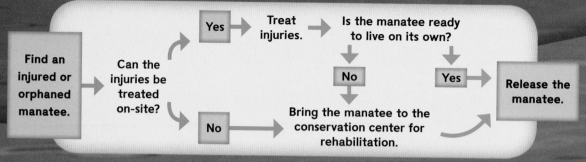

Find an injured or orphaned manatee. → Can the injuries be treated on-site? → Yes → Treat injuries. → Is the manatee ready to live on its own? → No → Bring the manatee to the conservation center for rehabilitation.

Can the injuries be treated on-site? → No → Bring the manatee to the conservation center for rehabilitation.

Is the manatee ready to live on its own? → Yes → Release the manatee.

Joining Forces

Manatees are just one focus of Dr. Mignucci's work. He investigates a wide variety of marine animals. No matter what he's studying, however, he considers collaboration to be an essential part of effective research. Working with the Seal Conservation Society of the United Kingdom, Dr. Mignucci coordinated an investigation to test the hypothesis that the Caribbean monk seal is extinct. This seal once lived in the Gulf of Mexico and the Caribbean Sea. Several unconfirmed sightings suggested that a few members of this species might still be alive. The combined research team helped to prove that those sightings almost certainly correspond with a different species, the hooded seal. Regretfully, they concluded that the Caribbean monk seal truly is extinct.

Partnerships also allow researchers to share information and expand the impact of their work. In 2010, the Manatee Conservation Center joined forces with the Georgia Aquarium in Atlanta, the world's largest. These two centers now have regular dialogues and share their knowledge of animal care, veterinary procedures, and water-quality monitoring.

Collaboration has also helped Dr. Mignucci solve some unusual problems. It is important for veterinarians at the Center to get accurate internal temperature measurements, but manatees have large molars and chew on anything you put in their mouths. So oral thermometers don't work. Dr. Mignucci sought help from a company that specializes in making animal tracking devices. The company donated microchips about the size of a grain of rice.

Jeff Spielman/Photodisc/Getty Images

Once a chip is implanted, it can be scanned with a pocket reader to obtain the manatee's body temperature.

Singing for Support

Dr. Mignucci's scientific adventures aren't limited to the laboratory. He has published books for children and even ventured into the recording studio. To spread word about the plight of manatees, Dr. Mignucci turned to another unusual collaborator, musician Tony Croatto, who was well known for his versions of Puerto Rican folk songs.

Dr. Antonio Mignucci at work

Croatto and Mignucci cowrote a song called "Moisés llegó del mar" ("Moses Came from the Sea"). Their song was inspired by the first manatee rescued by Dr. Mignucci. Moisés (Spanish for Moses) was separated from his mother when he was just two weeks old. When Dr. Mignucci's team found him, he had both external and internal injuries. After 27 months of care, they released a healthy Moisés back into the Caribbean. It was the first time a captive-raised manatee had been rehabilitated and released.

The song received plenty of airplay. Soon Moisés was a familiar icon admired by listeners around the world. Today he lives in the wild, where the Center's staff regularly monitor his progress. This was just one more way that Dr. Mignucci has brought people together to protect and care for marine life.

Courtesy of Antonio A. Mignucci-Giannoni, PhD

Make Connections

Talk about how Dr. Mignucci and his collaborators find creative solutions to the problems facing marine mammals. ESSENTIAL QUESTION

Describe how you could collaborate with others to find out more about a local species that needs help. TEXT TO SELF

413

Summarize

Summarizing the most important ideas in an expository text helps you understand the overall point the author is making. As you reread "Researcher to the Rescue," identify key details about Dr. Mignucci's work and use your own words to summarize the main ideas in each section.

 Find Text Evidence

You may not be sure how to summarize the section "Manatee Airlift" on page 411 of "Researcher to the Rescue."

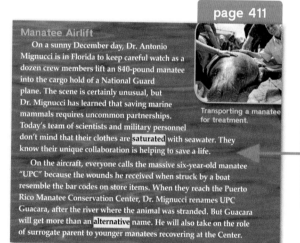

page 411

Manatee Airlift

On a sunny December day, Dr. Antonio Mignucci is in Florida to keep careful watch as a dozen crew members lift an 840-pound manatee into the cargo hold of a National Guard plane. The scene is certainly unusual, but Dr. Mignucci has learned that saving marine mammals requires uncommon partnerships. Today's team of scientists and military personnel don't mind that their clothes are saturated with seawater. They know their unique collaboration is helping to save a life.

On the aircraft, everyone calls the massive six-year-old manatee "UPC" because the wounds he received when struck by a boat resemble the bar codes on store items. When they reach the Puerto Rico Manatee Conservation Center, Dr. Mignucci renames UPC Guacara, after the river where the animal was stranded. But Guacara will get more than an alternative name. He will also take on the role of surrogate parent to younger manatees recovering at the Center.

Transporting a manatee for treatment.

I read details about flying a manatee to Puerto Rico, the diet and habitats of manatees, and the impact of Guacara's injuries on his health. I can summarize this section by saying that Dr. Mignucci and others brought an injured manatee to a place where options for treatment are optimal.

Your Turn

COLLABORATE

In what ways does Dr. Mignucci collaborate with others in order to study and help sea mammals? Reread the rest of "Researcher to the Rescue." Then summarize the main ideas in each section in your own words.

Main Idea and Key Details

After you have identified key details in a passage of expository text, you may not be able to find a sentence that directly states how they are related. In a case like this, use what the key details have in common to determine the main idea of the passage.

 Find Text Evidence

If I can't find a sentence stating the main idea for the important details I identified in "Joining Forces" on page 412, I can think of a central idea that expresses something about all the details.

Main Idea
Dr. Mignucci collaborates with many different partners to help sea mammals.
Detail
Mignucci worked with an organization in the United Kingdom to establish that monk seals are extinct.
Detail
Mignucci and the Georgia Aquarium share information about animal care.
Detail
A microchip company helped Mignucci make a manatee thermometer.

> What idea connects all the details?

Your Turn

COLLABORATE

Reread the section "Singing for Support." Is the main idea stated or unstated? What is the main idea of the section?

Go Digital!
Use the interactive graphic organizer

Expository

"Researcher to the Rescue" is an expository text about sea mammal research.

An **Expository** text:
- May use technical terms to explain scientific ideas
- May include a flowchart to describe steps in a process

 Find Text Evidence

I can tell that "Researcher to the Rescue" is an expository text because it explains some of the steps researchers are taking together to rescue and rehabilitate endangered sea mammals.

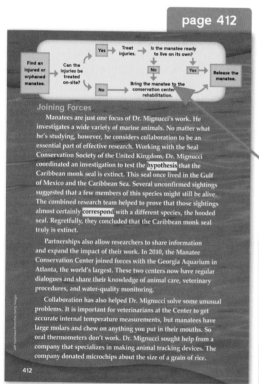

page 412

Joining Forces

Manatees are just one focus of Dr. Mignucci's work. He investigates a wide variety of marine animals. No matter what he's studying, however, he considers collaboration to be an essential part of effective research. Working with the Seal Conservation Society of the United Kingdom, Dr. Mignucci coordinated an investigation to test the hypothesis that the Caribbean monk seal is extinct. This seal once lived in the Gulf of Mexico and the Caribbean Sea. Several unconfirmed sightings suggested that a few members of this species might still be alive. The combined research team helped to prove that those sightings almost certainly correspond with a different species, the hooded seal. Regretfully, they concluded that the Caribbean monk seal truly is extinct.

Partnerships also allow researchers to share information and expand the impact of their work. In 2010, the Manatee Conservation Center joined forces with the Georgia Aquarium in Atlanta, the world's largest. These two centers now have regular dialogues and share their knowledge of animal care, veterinary procedures, and water-quality monitoring.

Collaboration has also helped Dr. Mignucci solve some unusual problems. It is important for veterinarians at the Center to get accurate internal temperature measurements, but manatees have large molars and chew on anything you put in their mouths. So oral thermometers don't work. Dr. Mignucci sought help from a company that specializes in making animal tracking devices. The company donated microchips about the size of a grain of rice.

412

Text Features

Technical Terms Technical terms are needed to explain concepts specific to the subject matter.

Flowchart A flowchart shows visually how the steps in a process are related.

COLLABORATE

Your Turn

Find a technical term used to describe a scientific concept in "Researcher to the Rescue." Tell how the text defines the term. Then explain what you learned from the flowchart.

Context Clues

When you come across an unfamiliar or multiple-meaning word, you can compare it to surrounding words. These context clues can help you figure out the word's meaning.

 Find Text Evidence

I wasn't sure what the word surrogate *means on page 411 of "Researcher to the Rescue." When I reread the paragraph, I compared* surrogate *to the words* alternative, role, *and* parent. *In this context,* surrogate *must be an adjective that means "other" or "substitute."*

> But Guacara will get more than an alternative name. He will also take on the role of surrogate parent to younger manatees recovering at the Center.

COLLABORATE

Your Turn

Make comparisons with surrounding words to determine the meanings of the following words from "Researcher to the Rescue."

marine, *page 411*

collaboration, *page 411*

rehabilitated, *page 413*

Write About the Text

Pages 410–413

Sarah

I answered the question: *How is writing a song about a manatee an effective way to raise awareness?*

Student Model: *Informative Text*

Thesis Statement

My topic sentence clearly explains how a song can raise awareness about a problem.

Grammar

The word *nothing* acts as a **negative** in this sentence.

Grammar Handbook
See page 470.

> If a song has a melody that people remember and lyrics that make them think, the ideas in that song can raise awareness about a problem. Many people know nothing about the problems that manatees face in the wild. Dr. Mignucci and Tony Croatto wrote a song to alert the public to that problem.

The song told the story of an injured baby manatee named Moisés that Dr. Mignucci and his team had to rescue. Once the song started getting a lot of airplay, more and more people learned the story of the injured manatee and of his recovery and release. The song helped the public learn how important it is to protect and help these animals.

Concrete Details
I used evidence from the text to support the topic.

Sequence
I made sure to present facts and details in a logical order.

Courtesy of Antonio A. Mignucci-Giannoni - PhD

419

Essential Question

What can scientists reveal about ancient civilizations?

Go Digital!

Astonishing Discoveries

Imagine unearthing thousands of soldiers made of fired clay, all lined up in trenches underground. That's exactly what happened in China's Shaanxi Province in 1974.

▶ This army of life-sized terracotta soldiers was created with meticulous care more than 2,000 years ago to protect the tomb of China's first emperor, Qin Shihuang.

▶ No two soldiers have the same facial features, and many carry real—still very sharp—weapons.

As excavation at the site continues, scientists are gathering fascinating facts about a long ago time.

Talk About It

Write words you have learned about discovering remarkable objects from the past. Then talk with a partner about what makes the terracotta army so extraordinary.

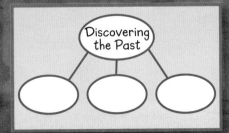

Discovering the Past

Vocabulary

Use the picture and the sentences to talk with a partner about each word.

bedrock

The construction crews were concerned about hitting **bedrock** during the dig.

How would you know if you hit bedrock?

embark

Once we have put all our luggage in the car, we can **embark** on our vacation.

How are the meanings of embark and start related?

excavation

To learn more about the ancient town, archaeologists began an **excavation**.

What is an antonym of excavation?

exquisite

The actress wore an **exquisite** gown to the awards ceremony.

What else could be described as exquisite?

intriguing

The astronomer thought that the idea of finding life on distant planets was **intriguing**.

Name something that you find intriguing.

intrinsic

Brenda admired the **intrinsic** beauty of an autumn day.

Describe something that you think has intrinsic beauty.

methodical

Lena's **methodical** preparation ensured that she had everything she needed during her camping trip.

What is a synonym for methodical?

meticulously

Leon **meticulously** painted each detail on the model.

What activity do you do meticulously?

Your Turn

COLLABORATE

Pick three words. Write three questions for your partner to answer.

Go Digital! *Use the online visual glossary*

(t to b) Baback Tafreshi/Photo Researchers/Getty Images; Lane Oatey/blue jean images/Getty Images; PhotoStock-Israel/Alamy; Fuse/Getty Images

MESSAGES IN STONE AND WOOD

Essential Question

What can scientists reveal about ancient civilizations?

Read what scientists are learning about the rock and tree art of Native Americans.

Native American petroglyphs, Canyon de Chelly, Arizona

Pete Ryan/National Geographic/Getty Images

"We Were Here"

Deep in a forest in what is now Pennsylvania, members of a hunting party were preparing to **embark** on their trip home. Only one task remained: creating a chronicle of their successful hunt. One of the hunters selected a broad oak tree, carefully made some cuts with his knife, and used the blade to peel back the bark. From a small leather bag, he shook out some powder he had ground from red pebbles. Then he mixed the powder with animal fat to make a thick red paint.

On the tree, the hunter **meticulously** painted images of a turtle and six men carrying packs and bows. Next, he drew a circle, a half circle, and six marks. Finally, he added the heads of three deer and a bear. From then on, anyone passing this spot would see from these designs that six men of the terrapin clan had hunted here. They had camped for one and a half moons, plus six days. And they had had a successful hunt.

Mysterious Markings

The first Europeans to explore North America came across many markings like the ones on that Pennsylvania tree. At first, no one understood the meanings of these mysterious *petroglyphs* (stone carvings) and *dendroglyphs* (tree carvings and paintings). Nor did they know who had created them. As time went on, however, people studying the markings, or *pictographs*, began to understand that

Petroglyph of a "Water Panther," Parkers Landing, Pennsylvania

Photo by Paul Nevin/Courtesy of the State Museum of Pennsylvania, Pennsylvania Historical and Museum Commission

they had been made by Native Americans. They concluded that the pictographs were records of hunts, battles, and clan meetings. They seemed also to serve as directions, warnings, boundary markers, and clan identifications.

When non-native people pushed farther west during the 1800s, they discovered many more of these images. In the dry desert of

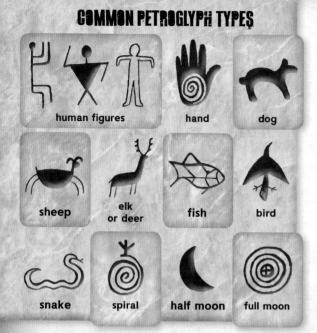

COMMON PETROGLYPH TYPES

human figures	hand	dog
sheep	elk or deer	fish	bird
snake	spiral	half moon	full moon

the Southwest, **exquisite** pictographs on rocks and cave walls appeared to be freshly made. This was especially true of carvings protected from direct sunlight. In the East, however, moisture decomposes dead tree trunks and winter ice damages rocks. Pictographs generally survive this wetter and colder climate only in sheltered spots. These spots are often outcroppings of **bedrock** that have been covered over by soil or moss. As a result, the only remaining records of many vanished pictographs are copies that were sketched by early explorers and historians.

Reading the Messages

For a long time, archaeologists made little progress in studying the rock art of Native Americans. They could not reliably date the pictographs, relate them to other human artifacts, or even agree on their meanings. But as technology improved, scientists learned much more about these **intriguing** images. For example, they used radiocarbon dating to measure the decay rate of carbon in the paint of dendroglyphs. By analyzing how rock surfaces had weathered, they estimated that some petroglyphs were nearly a thousand years old.

Although dating is now more reliable, understanding the meanings of rock images remains difficult. It is generally accepted that the people who made pictographs in open areas wanted to mark borders or record significant events. But interpreting images hidden in sheltered areas or caves has been more challenging.

Archaeologist Rex Weeks, an Echota Cherokee from Alabama, has brought an **intrinsic** cultural perspective to the scientific study and interpretation of Native American rock images. Dr. Weeks suggests that petroglyphs in secluded locations were purposely made at sites that would not be accessible to outsiders. The images were intended primarily for ceremonial use. Elders may also have used them to teach young people the beliefs and history of their clan. Weeks's research has shown that many of the symbols employed in pictographs link the cultures of ancient peoples to existing oral traditions of Native Americans. And by conducting experiments with hammer and chisel stones, Weeks has been able to demonstrate his theories about the techniques used to create rock carvings.

Dr. Rex Weeks

Courtesy of Rex Weeks

Preserving the Past

Today, many pictographs are in danger of being destroyed by natural forces before they can be documented and studied. Others are damaged when careless **excavation** by non-professionals defaces them or leaves them exposed to the elements. So experts have developed a system called the Rock Art Stability Index to assess in a **methodical** way which sites are most at risk. They also enlist trained volunteers, including native people, to record and manage newly discovered sites. One such site, a cave in the Appalachian mountains, contains fragile rock art that is more than a thousand years old. Educating the public about the importance and vulnerability of these sites is critical if the efforts of archaeologists such as Dr. Weeks are to succeed in preserving these rich cultural resources for future generations.

Make Connections

Talk about what archaeologists have learned from studying the pictographs of early Native Americans. **ESSENTIAL QUESTION**

Compare pictographs to the methods you use today to deliver messages and record events in your life. **TEXT TO SELF**

Summarize

When you summarize the information in an expository text, use your own words to restate the most important points, but do not express your own opinions.

 Find Text Evidence

You may not be sure which of the author's points in the section "Mysterious Markings" are the most important. Reread the section on page 425.

page 425

Mysterious Markings

The first Europeans to explore North America came across many markings like the ones on that Pennsylvania tree. At first, no one understood the meanings of these mysterious *petroglyphs* (stone carvings) and *dendroglyphs* (tree carvings and paintings). Nor did they know who had created them. As time went on, however, people studying the markings, or *pictographs*, began to understand that they had been made by Native Americans. They concluded that the pictographs were records of hunts, battles, and clan meetings. They seemed also to serve as directions, warnings, boundary markers, and clan identifications.

Petroglyph of a "Water Parkers Landing, Pennsy

In the first paragraph, I read that Europeans "came across many markings" and tried to understand them. In the second paragraph, I read how different climates affect pictographs. I can summarize the section by saying people learned about pictographs through years of observation in different locations.

Your Turn

COLLABORATE

What are the most important points the author makes in the section "Reading the Messages"? Reread the section on pages 426–427, and summarize the information in it. As you read, remember to use the strategy Summarize.

Sequence

Authors of expository texts organize facts and information in a logical way. They frequently use a time-order sequence to explain when things happened and why.

Find Text Evidence

When I reread the first two sections of "Messages in Stone and Wood," I can look for details about when events occurred. The section "We Were Here" does not state when the hunters lived. When I reread "Mysterious Markings," I conclude that they lived before "the first Europeans to explore North America" arrived.

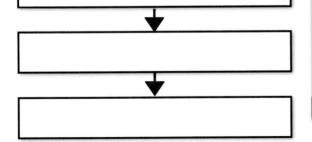

Event

Early Native Americans left apictograph describing their successful hunt.

↓

Newcomers to North America wanted to know the meanings of the mysterious markings they saw.

↓

↓

Your Turn

COLLABORATE

Reread the rest of "Messages in Stone and Wood." Identify key events in time-order sequence to list in the graphic organizer. Which parts of the sequence include activities that may be ongoing?

Go Digital!
Use the interactive graphic organizer

Expository

"Messages in Stone and Wood" is an expository text.

> An **expository** text:
> - May describe activity taking place over a range of time
> - May include photographs
> - May provide lists that display or catalogue items in an organized way

 ## Find Text Evidence

"Messages in Stone and Wood" explains what the pictographs of early Native Americans are and how people have studied them over many years. A labeled list shows me illustrations of representative items in a easy-to-understand way.

page 426

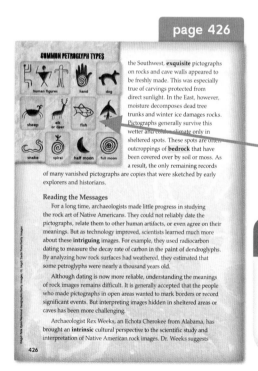

COMMON PETROGLYPH TYPES

human figures · hand · dog
sheep · elk or deer · fish
snake · spiral · half moon · full moon

the Southwest, **exquisite** pictographs on rocks and cave walls appeared to be freshly made. This was especially true of carvings protected from direct sunlight. In the East, however, moisture decomposes dead tree trunks and winter ice damages rocks. Pictographs generally survive this wetter and colder climate only in sheltered spots. These spots are often outcroppings of **bedrock** that have been covered over by soil or moss. As a result, the only remaining records of many vanished pictographs are copies that were sketched by early explorers and historians.

Reading the Messages

For a long time, archaeologists made little progress in studying the rock art of Native Americans. They could not reliably date the pictographs, relate them to other human artifacts, or even agree on their meanings. But as technology improved, scientists learned much more about these **intriguing** images. For example, they used radiocarbon dating to measure the decay rate of carbon in the paint of dendroglyphs. By analyzing how rock surfaces had weathered, they estimated that some petroglyphs were nearly a thousand years old.

Although dating is now more reliable, understanding the meanings of rock images remains difficult. It is generally accepted that the people who made pictographs in open areas wanted to mark borders or record significant events. But interpreting images hidden in sheltered areas or caves has been more challenging.

Archaeologist Rex Weeks, an Echota Cherokee from Alabama, has brought an **intrinsic** cultural perspective to the scientific study and interpretation of Native American rock images. Dr. Weeks suggests

426

Text Features

Photographs Photographic images provide documentary evidence.

Lists Lists organize and display series of items in a logical way.

COLLABORATE

Your Turn

Find and list two text features in "Messages in Stone and Wood." Tell what you learned from each.

Greek Roots

Expository texts often use scientific words that contain Greek roots. Knowing the meanings of these roots can help you figure out the meanings of unfamiliar words in context. Below are some common Greek roots in "Messages in Stone and Wood."

Root	Meaning		Root	Meaning
archaeo-	original, ancient		*chron-*	time
-graph	written		*techn-*	skill, art

 Find Text Evidence

In the first sentence of "Reading the Messages," I read the word archaeologists. *If I know the Greek root* archaeo- *means "ancient" or "original," I can use the context clue* studying *to figure out that an* archaeologist *is "someone who studies ancient objects."*

For a long time, <u>archaeologists</u> made little progress in <u>studying</u> the rock art of Native Americans.

Your Turn

COLLABORATE

Use the roots in the chart and context clues to help you define these words in "Messages in Stone and Wood."

chronicle, *page 425*

pictographs, *page 425*

technology, *page 426*

Write About the Text

Pages 424–427

Amanda

I responded to the prompt: *Explain how our understanding of early Native American cultural sites has grown over time. Use text evidence.*

Student Model: *Informative Text*

Introduce a Topic
My first sentence explains what my paragraphs are about.

Word Choices
I chose the time-order words *then, next,* and *finally* to help describe the sequence of events.

When early European explorers discovered pictographs on trees and rocks in the eastern regions of North America, at first they did not know who made them or what they meant. Then they realized that Native Americans had made the pictographs. The explorers thought the pictographs could be symbols of events such as hunts and battles.

Next, as Americans moved farther west, they discovered well-preserved

pictographs in the Southwest. When the

technology was available, researchers

used radiocarbon dating to figure out

how old the pictographs were. Finally,

Native American scientists such as

Dr. Rex Weeks began to connect the

pictographs to current Native American

cultures to understand how they

were made and what they might

mean. It is important to understand

these symbols and to protect them.

Grammar

In this sentence, *in* is the **preposition** and "in the Southwest" is the **prepositional phrase**.

Grammar Handbook
See page 470.

Supporting Details

I used details and facts from the text to support my topic.

Your Turn

Describe the effects that weather can have on pictographs. Use text evidence.

Go Digital!
Write your response online.
Use your editing checklist.

Weekly Concept Taking a Break

Essential Question

Why is taking a break important?

Go Digital!

Design Pics/Con Tanasiuk

434

A Little Time Out

It's been a busy day. . . and it isn't over yet.

▶ My best friend and I have been working pretty much *all* day. We want to make sure everything is set for the art fair tomorrow. It's a lot to deal with!

▶ Even though we each need to go home and finish our own art projects tonight, I suggested we take a breather down by the playing field.

It sure is nice just to sit for a few minutes and watch the sunset!

Talk About It

Write words you have learned about taking a break. Then talk with a partner about a time when you realized how important it was to relax for a while.

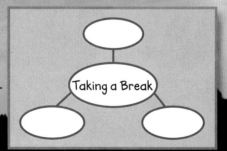

Taking a Break

Vocabulary

Use the picture and the sentences to talk with a partner about each word.

horizons

Meeting all kinds of new people helped to broaden Joan's **horizons**.

How could you expand your horizons?

incentive

He offered his dog treats as an **incentive** to do tricks.

What incentive has convinced you to do something?

recreation

For **recreation**, Carl and his family like to go hiking.

What does your family like to do for recreation?

unfettered

Unfettered by a saddle, the pony raced around the corral.

What is a synonym for unfettered?

Poetry Terms

ode

I wrote an **ode** dedicated to an unusual flower that captured my interest.

How can a poet express admiration for something in an ode?

imagery

A poem's **imagery** is developed through the use of sensory words and figurative language.

What does strong imagery in a poem help the reader understand?

repetition

A poet who uses **repetition** uses the same sounds, words, and phrases multiple times in a poem.

How can repetition affect the sound of a poem?

hyperbole

A poet uses **hyperbole** when the speaker makes an exaggerated claim about something.

How does hyperbole add to a description?

Your Turn

COLLABORATE

Pick three words or poetry terms. Write three questions for a partner to answer.

Go Digital! *Use the online visual glossary*

How Many Seconds?

Essential Question

Why is taking a break important?

Read how two poets view opportunities for rest and renewal.

How many seconds in a minute?
Sixty, and no more in it.

How many minutes in an hour?
Sixty for sun and shower.

How many hours in a day?
Twenty-four for work and play.

How many days in a week?
Seven both to hear and speak.

How many weeks in a month?
Four, as the swift moon runn'th.

How many months in a year?
Twelve the almanack makes clear.

How many years in an age?
One hundred says the sage.

How many ages in time?
No one knows the rhyme.

—Christina Rossetti

An Ode to the Wind

Ode to the wild and whistling wind,
To its power,
To its pleasures,
To the sky that it clears
And the comfort that it brings,
Revealing a warm and radiant sun.

Ode to the wind's uproar,
To its chaos and pandemonium
Unfettered by mountains and mammoth peaks,
Moving deserts and dust great distances,
Whipping snow into undisciplined drifts,
Lashing waves upon dark sand,
Driving flames through bush and bark,
Hissing and roaring like a dragon.

Ode to the wind's energy and titanic strength,
Scattering seeds as valuable as gold upon the land,
Filling square-rigged sails with billowing force,
Thrusting ships toward new horizons,
Whipping windmills to turn and generate,
Dispersing autumn leaves to replenish the earth,
To the storms it brings upon us
And the life-giving rain.

Ode to the moving air,
To the warm air rising
And the cool air that comes in to take its place,
To the sky that it cleared
And the comfort it brought,
Rustling hair, cooling fevered brows.
Wind a thousand times softer than silk
Offering a sweet incentive for recreation,
Lifting kites to the outer edge of the stratosphere.

—Jonathan Moss

Make Connections

Talk about the way each poet expresses
an understanding of how people may
take time to relax. ESSENTIAL QUESTION

How might experiencing the sensations
of a windy day help when you feel the
need to take a break? TEXT TO SELF

Lyric Poetry and Ode

Lyric Poetry:

- Expresses the speaker's personal thoughts and feelings
- Often has a musical quality and doesn't always rhyme

An **Ode:**

- Is a type of lyric poem with a pattern of stanzas
- Praises a person, natural phenomenon, object, or concept

 Find Text Evidence

The title of "An Ode to the Wind" and its pattern of stanzas tell me that it is an ode. The speaker praises different qualities of the wind. It is also a lyric poem, because it suggests the speaker's feelings.

page 441

Ode to the moving air,
To the warm air rising
And the cool air that comes in to take its place,
To the sky that it cleared
And the comfort it brought,
Rustling hair, cooling fevered brows.
Wind a thousand times softer than silk
Offering a sweet incentive for recreation,
Lifting kites to the outer edge of the stratospher

—Jonathan Moss

This ode praises the wind, which is a natural occurrence. The choice of words shows the speaker's feelings about the subject.

Your Turn

Reread "How Many Seconds?" on pages 438–439. Use the poem's structure and any feelings expressed by the speaker to determine whether it is lyric poetry, an ode, or both. Explain your reasons.

Theme

A poem's theme is the overall idea, or message about life, that the poet wants readers to understand. To determine the theme, look for clues that show how the speaker feels about the topic.

 Find Text Evidence

When I reread "How Many Seconds?" I can look for details that reveal the poet's attitude toward the subject. Thinking about all the details together helps me identify the poet's message.

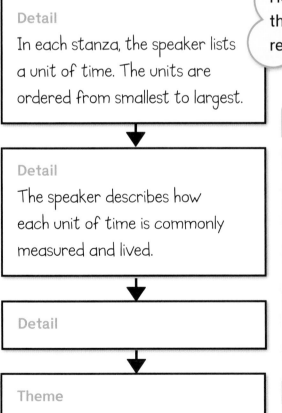

Detail

In each stanza, the speaker lists a unit of time. The units are ordered from smallest to largest.

How are all the details related?

Detail

The speaker describes how each unit of time is commonly measured and lived.

Detail

Theme

Your Turn

Reread "How Many Seconds?" to find other details about the poet's attitude toward the subject. Use all the details to identify the theme. Use a second graphic organizer to list details from "An Ode to the Wind" and identify its theme.

Go Digital!
Use the interactive graphic organizer

Repetition and Imagery

Poets repeat words and phrases for emphasis. Repetition also affects how the poem sounds when read aloud. Poets use images to paint a picture in the reader's mind. A pattern of sensory images often suggests a mood or feeling.

Find Text Evidence

Reread "An Ode to the Wind" on pages 440–441. Identify words and phrases that are repeated. Then look for images, words and phrases that appeal to the senses.

page 440

An Ode to
the
Wind

Ode to the wild and whistling wind,
To its power,
To its pleasures,
To the sky that it clears
And the comfort that it brings,
Revealing a warm and radiant sun.

Ode to the wind's uproar,
To its chaos and pandemonium
Unfettered by mountains and mammoth peaks,
Moving deserts and dust great distances,
Whipping snow into undisciplined drifts,
Lashing waves upon dark sand,
Driving flames through bush and bark,
Hissing and roaring like a dragon.

440

Each stanza begins with the words "Ode to" and tells about a different aspect of the wind. In the second stanza, the poet uses images of snow, waves, and fire to help the reader "feel" the wind's fearful strength.

Your Turn

Reread the first two stanzas of "An Ode to the Wind." Find examples of repetition and imagery. What ideas about wind do they emphasize?

444

Figurative Language

Poets use figurative language to create images in the reader's mind. Poets may emphasize a point by using **hyperbole**, which is exaggeration that is not meant to be taken literally. The phrase *hotter than a million suns* is an example of hyperbole.

 ## Find Text Evidence

When I read the line Wind a thousand times softer than silk *on page 441, I realize that the poet who wrote "An Ode to the Wind" was exaggerating to emphasize how soft wind can be. We can't actually feel something a thousand times softer than silk.*

> **Wind a thousand times softer than silk**
> **Offering a sweet incentive for recreation**
> **Lifting kites to the outer edge of the stratosphere.**

Your Turn

Reread "An Ode to the Wind." Find another example of hyperbole and explain how the exaggeration adds to or strengthens the poem's praise of the wind.

Write About the Text

Pages 438–441

Russell

I responded to the prompt: *Write a poem about your favorite class. Use rich vocabulary.*

Student Model: *Narrative Text*

I love Mondays and Wednesdays

Most of all;

That's when the music room

Sends out its call.

We gather in that dusty room without

A view,

There to learn songs old and new.

Our voices catch the soft morning air,

Then explode into a happy roar.

Listen how we harmonize

Grammar

I **combined the sentences** and used an adjective to avoid repeating words.

Grammar Handbook
See page 469.

Sensory Language

I used the *connotation* of the word *explode* to add excitement to this line of the poem.

Santiago Bañón/Moment/Getty Images

446

And tap the rhythm on the floor.

We sang a brand new song today

And then a sad old melody.

When it was time to go outside,

My heart was still singing deep inside.

I love Mondays and Wednesdays

Most of all,

Because I love music,

Any and all.

Figurative Language
I used a metaphor to describe how much I love to sing.

Narrator
I identified how I felt about music class, and I repeated it for emphasis at the end of the poem.

Your Turn

Write a poem to the Sun or the Moon. Use rich vocabulary.

Go Digital!
Write your response online.
Use your editing checklist.

Christopher Futcher/Getty Images

447

Table of Contents

Sentences

Nouns

Verbs

Pronouns

Adjectives

Adverbs

Negatives and Prepositions

Mechanics: Abbreviations

Mechanics: Capitalization

Mechanics: Punctuation

Sentences

Sentences and Sentence Fragments

A **sentence** is a group of words that expresses a complete thought. A **sentence fragment** is a group of words that does not express a complete thought.

My mother builds a shed. (complete sentence)

the size of the shed (needs a predicate)

stores tools and supplies (needs a subject)

Your Turn Write each group of words. Write *sentence* or *fragment* next to each item. Then rewrite each fragment to make a complete sentence.

1. Built a fence.
2. We all helped decide what to plant.
3. A great harvest in the fall.

Kinds of Sentences

There are four different types of sentence. Each begins with a **capital letter** and ends with an **end mark**.

A **declarative sentence** makes a statement. It ends with a **period**.	*We watched the snow fall.*
An **interrogative sentence** asks a question. It ends with a **question mark**.	*How much will we get?*
A **imperative sentence** tells or asks someone to do something. It ends with a **period**.	*Listen to the forecast.*
An **exclamatory sentence** shows strong feeling. It ends with an **exclamation mark**.	*Snow days are my favorite!*

Your Turn Write one sentence of each type. Use the correct punctuation. Trade with a partner to check your sentences.

Subjects and Predicates

Every sentence has two important parts: the **subject** and the **predicate**.

The **subject** tells *whom* or *what* the sentence is about. The **complete subject** is all the words in the subject part. The **simple subject** is the main word or words in the complete subject.

> *The strongest <u>swimmers</u> crossed the bay.*

The **predicate** tells what the subject *does* or *is*. The **complete predicate** is all the words in the predicate. The **simple predicate** is the main verb in the complete predicate.

> *The strongest swimmers <u>crossed</u> the bay.*

Your Turn Write each sentence. Draw one line under the simple subject. Draw two lines under the simple predicate.

1. Their friends cheered them on.
2. My brother led the way in a boat.
3. He helped anyone in trouble.
4. Luckily, the water remained calm all morning long.
5. Next year my friends will swim for the first time.

Combining Sentences: Compound Subjects

A **compound subject** has two or more simple subjects that share the same predicate. Use the **conjunction** *and* or *or* to join the parts of the compound subject.

> *Brett volunteered at the rally. Diane volunteered at the rally.*
> *Brett and Diane volunteered at the rally.*

Your Turn Combine the sentence pairs to form one sentence.

1. Adam ran onto the field. Lisa ran onto the field.
2. Mom watched them play. Dad watched them play.
3. My brother enjoyed the game. I enjoyed the game.
4. Mom started to shout. My brother started to shout.
5. Did Adam score a goal? Did Lisa score a goal?

Sentences

Combining Sentences: Compound Predicates

A **compound predicate** has two more simple predicates that share the same subject. Use the word *and, but,* or *or* to join the parts of a compound predicate.

> Mom *docked the boat.* Mom *went ashore.*
> Mom *docked the boat and went ashore.*

Your Turn Combine the sentence pairs to form one sentence.

1. I stayed behind. I watched the ducks.
2. The ducks paddled around. The ducks shook their feathers.
3. They flapped their wings. They flew away.
4. My mother returned. Mom started the engine.
5. The engine sputtered. The engine didn't stop.

Combining Sentences: Compound Sentences

A **compound sentence** has two or more complete thoughts about different subjects. The **coordinating conjunctions** *and, but,* and *or* can be used to connect the complete thoughts in a compound sentence. Use a comma before the conjunction. The **correlative conjunctions** *either/or* and *neither/nor* can also be used in a compound sentence.

> My brother likes to swim, **but** I prefer riding my bike.

Your Turn Combine the sentence pairs to form one sentence. Circle each coordinating conjunction.

1. My tire was flat. I learned how to fix it.
2. I asked my father. He showed me how to do it.
3. Now the wheels are fine. The brakes don't work.
4. A cable is broken. A bolt is loose.
5. We'll take it to the shop. They'll fix it tomorrow.

Combining Sentences: Complex Sentences

An **independent clause** can stand alone as a sentence. A **dependent clause** cannot stand alone and begins with a **subordinating conjunction**, such as *after, although, as, before, because, if, since, until, when, where,* and *while.* A **complex sentence** has an independent clause and one or more dependent clauses.

We drove west until we saw the mountains.

Use a **comma** after dependent clauses at beginnings of sentences.

As we climbed higher, the temperature dropped.

Your Turn Combine the sentence pairs to form a complex sentence. Circle the subordinating conjunction you used.

1. We reached the summit. It began to snow.
2. Dad drove slowly. The road was slippery.

Run-On Sentences

A **run-on sentence** contains two or more independent clauses without the proper conjunctions or punctuation. A **comma splice** joins two independent clauses without using a conjunction.

I heard a noise I called the police, they came quickly.

Break the independent clauses into separate sentences.	*I heard a noise. I called the police. They came quickly.*
Create a compound subject or compound predicate.	*I heard a noise and called the police. They came quickly.*
Create a compound sentence using coordinating conjunctions.	*I heard a noise. I called the police, and they came quickly.*
Create a complex sentence using subordinating conjunctions.	*When I heard a noise, I called the police, and they came quickly.*

Your Turn Use strategies above to correct the run-on sentences.

1. An officer saw a raccoon it ran under the porch.
2. She shined a light on the raccoon, it hissed.
3. It took an hour they finally caught it, I was so happy!

Nouns

Common and Proper Nouns

A **common noun** names a person, place, thing, or idea. A **proper noun** names a particular person, place, thing, or idea. A proper noun begins with a capital letter.

> The **professor** pointed to the **country** on the **map**. (common)
> **Dr. Jenkins** located **Brazil** in **The Explorer's Atlas**. (proper)

Your Turn Write each sentence. Underline each noun. Tell whether it is common or proper.

1. My grandparents were born in Ethiopia.
2. Their attic is filled with boxes of photographs.
3. Dad found a picture of their old house.
4. A scrapbook showed their trips to Europe and Asia.
5. Would Grandpa talk about Africa to my class?

Concrete and Abstract Nouns

A **concrete noun** names a person, place, or thing that physically exists and can be perceived with the senses. An **abstract noun** names a quality, concept, or idea that does not physically exist. Many abstract nouns have no plural form.

> **Dad** took his **guitar** out of the **case**. (concrete)
> The **music** he played filled me with **joy**. (abstract)

Your Turn Write each sentence. Underline each noun. Tell whether it is concrete or abstract.

1. Strange noises filled the house.
2. My brother had bought an accordion.
3. My family hoped he would take lessons.
4. My sister put plugs in her ears.
5. He feels no guilt at all for causing discomfort.

Singular and Plural Nouns

A **singular noun** names one person, place, thing, or idea. A **plural noun** names more than one. It is usually formed by adding *-s* or *-es*.

Singular nouns: boy   horse   boardwalk   chapter
Plural nouns: girls   foxes   beaches   stories

Your Turn Write each sentence. Draw one line under each singular noun. Draw two lines under each plural noun.

1. Flames leapt into the sky as the firefighters arrived.
2. Reporters noted that the fire was out an hour later.

More Plural and Collective Nouns

If a noun ends in a consonant + *y*, change *y* to *i* and add *-es*.	ladies, berries, skies, libraries
If a noun ends in a vowel + *y*, add *-s*.	boys, monkeys, essays
If a noun ends in *-f* or *-fe*, you may need to change *f* to *v* and add *-es*.	chefs, roofs, leaves, hooves, knives
If a noun ends in a vowel and *o*, add *-s*.	studios, trios, duos, zoos
If a noun ends in a consonant and *o*, add *-s* or *-es*.	pianos, echoes, cellos
Some nouns have the same singular and plural forms.	deer, sheep, moose, fish, elk
Some nouns have special plural forms.	men, women, children, feet

A **collective noun** names a group acting as a single unit. Collective nouns can also have plural forms.

Dad's **band** will take the stage after two other **bands**.

Your Turn Write each sentence. Change the singular noun in parentheses ( ) to a plural noun. Circle any collective nouns.

1. The coach spoke to the (child) on the team.
2. She had recorded (video) of their last two games.
3. Our (life) would be easier if we didn't practice so often.
4. How many (trophy) do you think our squad can win?

455

Nouns

Possessive Nouns

A **possessive noun** names who or what owns or has something. Add **'s** to a singular noun to make it possessive. Add just an apostrophe (') to most plural nouns ending in *-s* to make them possessive. Other plural nouns add **'s**.

The **teachers'** cars were parked in the **school's** lot.

Your Turn Write each sentence. Change the word in ( ) into a possessive noun.

1. The (store) owners looked at the crowds.
2. People lined up to buy the (author) new book.
3. All the (newspapers) reporters wrote about it.
4. Did you get your (parents) permission to buy one?
5. You should see the expressions on the (children) faces!

Appositives

An **appositive** is a word or group of words that identifies or tells more about another nearby noun. Use commas to set off most appositives from the rest of the sentence. You can use an appositive to combine two sentences into one.

Sid Phillips, **last year's winner**, spoke about the contest.

Your Turn Use an appositive to combine the sentence pairs into one.

1. This year's winner is Jada. She is a poet from Guam.
2. Ginny knows Jada. Ginny is my oldest cousin.
3. They went to Bickham together. Bickham is a summer camp.
4. I submitted my poem. It is a limerick about stars.
5. Will it arrive by the final date? The final date is May 14.

Verbs

Action Verbs

An **action verb** is a word that expresses action. It tells what the subject of the sentence does or did.

*My dog **chased** the turkeys.*

Your Turn Write each sentence. Underline each action verb.

1. The turkeys trotted across the ice.
2. They slipped and slid all over the place.
3. I laughed when I saw them.
4. Did anyone take a picture of them?
5. They disappeared before I found my camera.

Direct and Indirect Objects

A **direct object** is a noun or pronoun in the predicate that receives the action of the verb. It answers the question *"what?"* or *"whom?"* after an action verb.

*Mom bought **tickets**.*

An **indirect object** usually comes before the direct object. It answers the question *"to what?"*, *"to whom?"*, *"for what?"*, or *"for whom?"* after an action verb.

*Mom gave my **sister** the tickets.*

Your Turn Write each sentence. Circle each verb. Draw one line under each direct object. Draw two lines under each indirect object.

1. My sister created a costume.
2. My brother gave my sister advice.
3. The actors rehearsed their lines before the show.
4. The comedian told the audience funny jokes.
5. Who handed the singer flowers as she performed?

Verbs

Verb Tenses

A **present-tense verb** shows action that happens now.
> *My family **plans** its vacation.*

A **past-tense verb** shows action that has already happened.
> *Last year we **sailed** to an island.*

A **future-tense verb** shows action that may or will happen.
> *This summer we **will fly** overseas.*

Your Turn Write each sentence. Underline each verb. Then tell the tense of each verb.

1. My mother studies a foreign language.
2. Both of her parents often talked in Swedish.
3. By next summer, my mother will speak fluently.
4. Who helped her with her pronunciation?
5. I hope that someday I will know a new language.

Subject-Verb Agreement

A present-tense verb must **agree** with its subject. Add -*s* to most verbs if the subject is singular. Add -*es* to verbs that end in *s, ch, sh, x,* or *z.* Do not add -*s* or -*es* if the subject is plural or *I* or *you.*
> *Jenny **catches** the ball. Her friends **race** off the field.*

When parts of a compound subject are joined by *or, either...or,* or *neither...nor,* the verb agrees with the subject that is nearer to it.
> *Either Jon or Ellen **writes** the daily column.*

Your Turn Write each sentence. Use the correct present-tense form of each verb in parentheses.

1. The pilot (check) the instrument panel.
2. Green lights (verify) that everything is normal.
3. The other pilots (communicate) over the radio.
4. The lead jet (rush) down the runway.
5. You (consider) enrolling in flight school some day.

Main Verbs and Helping Verbs

A **verb phrase** is a verb that contains more than one word. The last word in a verb phrase is the **main verb**. All other words in a verb phrase are **helping verbs**. A helping verb helps the main verb show an action or make a statement. The verb *be* is often used as a helping verb with a **present participle**, or a verb ending in *-ing*. The verb *have* is often used as a helping verb with a **past participle**, or a verb ending in *-ed*.

*Our family **will watch** the shows we **have recorded**.*

Your Turn Write each sentence. Underline each main verb and circle the helping verb.

1. My sister has followed this program for years.
2. The series will reach its conclusion next spring.
3. They may release a movie shortly after that.
4. We will be checking the magazines for news about it.
5. I should pay that much attention to my studies.

Progressive Forms

The **present progressive** form tells about an action that is continuing (or in progress) now. Use the helping verb *am, is,* or *are* followed by a **present participle**. The **past progressive** form tells about an action that was continuing at an earlier time. Use the helping verb *was* or *were* followed by a present participle.

*I **am counting** the days until vacation.*

*I **was reading** about our destination.*

Your Turn Write each sentence. Use the progressive form of the verb in parentheses ( ) that makes the most sense.

1. We (hope) that we can visit the famous fountains.
2. Last year, the park's staff (repair) them all summer long.
3. People complained that the water (look) discolored.
4. Reports say that the fountains (attract) huge crowds.
5. My father (explore) other options just in case.

Verbs

Perfect Tenses

The **present perfect tense** tells about an action that happened in the past. It also tells about an action that began in the past and continues in the present. Use the helping verb *have* or *has* followed by a **past participle**, which is usually the *-ed* form of the verb.

*I **have performed** in two plays this year.*

The **past perfect tense** tells about one past action that occurred before another past action. Use the helping verb *had* and a past participle to form the past perfect tense.

*At this time last year, I **had performed** in four plays.*

Your Turn Write each sentence. Use the present perfect or past perfect tense of the verb in parentheses.

1. I (rehearse) my lines for the show every day this week.
2. Last week we (worry) there wouldn't be enough time.
3. My teachers and parents (assure) me that I would do fine.
4. For years now my brother (promise) to support my acting.

Linking Verbs

Some verbs do not express action. A **linking verb** links the subject with a word in the predicate. This word can be a **predicate noun**, which renames or identifies the subject, or a **predicate adjective**, which describes the subject. Some common linking verbs are *be, seem, feel, appear, become, smell, stay,* and *taste.*

*Luke **is** a fine cook. His soups **taste** delicious.*

Your Turn Write each sentence. Circle each linking verb. Underline the predicate noun or predicate adjective that follows it.

1. My father is a student in a cooking class.
2. His rice pilaf smells strange.
3. He was nervous about adding too much salt.
4. This meal seemed difficult even for a master chef.

Irregular Verbs

The past tense or past participles of **irregular verbs** do not add *-ed*.

Present	Past	Participle (with *have*)
be (am/are/is)	was/were	been
bring	brought	brought
buy	bought	bought
catch	caught	caught
come	came	come
do	did	done
draw	drew	drawn
drink	drank	drunk
eat	ate	eaten
give	gave	given
go	went	gone
grow	grew	grown
hide	hid	hidden
read (/rēd/)	read (/rĕd/)	read (/rĕd/)
ride	rode	ridden
run	ran	run
say	said	said
see	saw	seen
sell	sold	sold
sit	sat	sat
take	took	taken
teach	taught	taught
tell	told	told
think	thought	thought
write	wrote	written

Your Turn **Write each sentence. Use the correct form of each verb in parentheses.**

1. Yesterday the scientists (go) to the new laboratory.
2. A guide (bring) them to see the new equipment.
3. Some of them had (take) a tour of the building before.
4. "They (think) about it but decided not to," the guide (say).

Pronouns

Pronouns and Antecedents

A **pronoun** is a word that takes the place of one or more nouns. A pronoun must match the number and gender of its **antecedent**, which is the noun (or nouns) to which it refers.

*I passed the camera to my sister. **She** used **it** to take a picture.*

Your Turn Write each sentence. Underline each pronoun. Circle the antecedent.

1. Kendra photographs everything she sees.
2. Dad takes the best pictures and puts them in frames.
3. People can see the photos if they visit this Web site.
4. Dad told Kendra he would look for a better camera.
5. Mom took Kendra shopping and let her try the new model.

Subject, Object, and Indefinite Pronouns

A **subject pronoun** is used as the subject of a verb. The pronouns *I, you, he, she, it, we,* and *they* are subject pronouns. An **object pronoun** is used as the object of either an action verb or a preposition. The pronouns *me, you, him, her, it, us,* and *them* are object pronouns.

*My sister made a video for our cousins. **She** sent **it** to **them** last night.*

An **indefinite pronoun** refers to someone or something that is not known or specific, such as *anyone, anything, all, both, everybody, everything, everywhere, none, no one, somebody, somewhere,* or *something*.

*My aunt sang **something** that **everyone** would enjoy.*

Your Turn Write each sentence. Replace the words in parentheses with the proper pronoun.

1. (All of the people) clapped along to the music.
2. Dad decided that (Dad) needed to get his guitar.
3. Mom helped (Dad) look for the guitar in the closet.
4. My sister told (Mom and Dad) that she had the guitar.
5. (Not one person) sang until my parents found (the guitar).

Homophones

Homophones are words that sound the same but are spelled differently. Some commonly confused homophones are *it's/its, you're/your, they're/their/there,* and *there's/theirs.*

> **They're** proud of **their** cooking over **there**.

Your Turn Write each sentence. Choose the correct word in parentheses to complete the sentence.

1. (You're, Your) phone is over on the table.
2. Have you checked (it's, its) batteries lately?

Reflexive and Intensive Pronouns

A **reflexive pronoun** tells about an action that a subject does for or to itself. (Singular pronouns take *-self*; plural pronouns take *-selves*.)

> He talked **himself** into it. We blamed **ourselves** for the mess.

An **intensive pronoun** takes the form of a reflexive pronoun. It adds emphasis without changing the meaning of the sentence.

> The principal **herself** handed me the trophy.

Your Turn Write each sentence. Underline each reflexive pronoun. Circle each intensive pronoun.

1. My mother and I gave ourselves plenty of time.
2. The signs themselves said we were on the right trail!

Possessive Pronouns

A **possessive pronoun** shows who or what owns something. *My, your, her, his, its, our,* and *their* come before nouns. *Mine, yours, hers, his, its, ours,* and *theirs* can stand alone.

> They like **their** music, but I like **mine** better.

Your Turn Write each sentence. Replace the words in parentheses with a possessive pronoun.

1. My family visited (my family's and my) hometown.
2. Luckily, my mother could do (her job) from anywhere.

Pronouns

Pronoun-Verb Agreement

A present-tense verb must **agree** with its subject, even if the subject is a pronoun.

> *I **am** happy. He **is** delighted. He and I **are** cheerful.*

Your Turn Write each sentence. Use the correct present-tense form of the verb in parentheses.

1. She (catch) the train into the city.
2. They (meet) at the aquarium.
3. I (be) waiting for them near the shark tank.
4. They ask if you (be) curious about the penguins.
5. I point at the octopus, and it (scurry) behind a rock.

Relative and Interrogative Pronouns

A **relative pronoun** shows how a dependent clause relates to another noun or pronoun already mentioned in the sentence. *That, which, who, whose,* and *whom* can be used as relative pronouns. An **interrogative pronoun** asks a question and has no clear antecedent. *What, which, who, whom,* and *whose* can be used as interrogative pronouns.

> ***Who** owns the dog **that** ran past our house?*

Your Turn Write each sentence. Underline each relative pronoun. Circle each interrogative pronoun.

1. What startled the dog in the first place?
2. The dog ran into a store that had its door open.
3. The man who owns the store chased the dog out.
4. Which of these streets did it run down?
5. What was the name of the boy whose dog was missing?

Adjectives

Adjectives

Adjectives are words that modify, or describe, nouns or pronouns. Adjectives tell *what kind, which one,* or *how many.* A **predicate adjective** follows a linking verb and modifies the subject.

*I am **curious** about the **three red** tents in **that** field.*

Your Turn Write each sentence. Underline each adjective.

1. The circus had arrived in this town for two weeks.
2. The performers' costumes were bright and colorful.

Articles: *a, an, the*

The words *a, an,* and *the* are special adjectives called **articles.** Use *a* and *an* with singular nouns only. Use *a* if the next word starts with a consonant. Use *an* if the next word starts with a vowel.

***The** artists will host **an** afternoon talk at **a** gallery downtown.*

Your Turn Write each sentence. Choose the correct article.

1. Mom wanted to hang (a, an) abstract drawing in the hall.
2. My sister visited (an, the) folk art museum.

Demonstrative Adjectives

Demonstrative adjectives, such as *this, that, these,* and *those,* tell *which one* or *which ones.* Use *this* to point out a nearby person or thing. Use *that* to point out a person or thing that is farther away. Use *these* to point out two or more nearby people or things. Use *those* to point out two or more people or things farther away.

***This** ring on my finger is shinier than **those** rings on display.*

Your Turn Write each sentence. Choose the proper demonstrative adjective to complete the sentence.

1. (That, Those) pile is larger than the other one.
2. What is (this, these) box of magazines doing here?

465

Adjectives

Comparative and Superlative Adjectives

A **comparative adjective** compares two people, things, or ideas. Form comparative adjectives by adding *-er* to most one-syllable and some two-syllable adjectives. A **superlative adjective** compares more than two things. The superlative is usually formed by adding *-est*. If an adjective ends in a consonant and *y,* change the *y* to *i* before adding *-er* or *-est.* If an adjective ends in *e,* drop the *e* before adding *-er* or *-est.* If an adjective has a single vowel before a final consonant, double the final consonant before adding *-er* or *-est.*

*Ted is a **faster** runner than Cal. Reg is the **thinnest** boy on the team.*

Your Turn Write each sentence. Use the correct form of the adjective in parentheses.

1. My brother is a (calm) person than I am.
2. Dad is the (quiet) one in our whole house.
3. I talk with a (loud) voice than my sister.
4. We had the (lively) discussion ever last night!

Comparing with *More* and *Most*

To form comparative and superlative forms of most adjectives with two or more syllables, use the words *more* and *most* instead of the endings *-er* or *-est.* Never use *more* or *most* in front of adjectives with *-er* or *-est* endings.

*That lion has a **more ferocious** roar than the other one.*
*The largest lion has the **most ferocious** roar of all.*

Your Turn Write each sentence. Use the correct form of the adjective in parentheses.

1. This zoo has (interesting) exhibits than that one.
2. They have the (diverse) collection of reptiles in America.
3. Does the gray iguana look (frightening) than the green one?
4. What is the safest, (sensible) place to see the snakes?

Comparing with *Good* and *Bad*

The comparative and superlative forms of some adjectives, such as *good* and *bad*, are irregular. The comparative form of *good* is *better*. The comparative form of *bad* is *worse*. Their superlative forms are *best* and *worst*.

> Rex is a **good** dog. Spike is a **better** dog than Rex. Fido is the **best** dog of all.
>
> Mom has a **bad** cough, but Dad's cough is **worse**. I have the **worst** cough of all.

Your Turn Write each sentence. Use the correct form of the adjective in parentheses.

1. I had the (good) time ever at last night's movie marathon!
2. We watched some of the (bad) films ever made.
3. The first movie had a (good) plot than the second one.
4. The longest film also had the (bad) acting.
5. Do you think there is a (bad) movie than the last one?

Combining Sentences: Adjectives

You can combine sentences by leaving out repeated words and moving an adjective into one of the sentences.

> We caught a fish. The fish was **huge**. We caught a **huge** fish.

Your Turn Combine each pair of sentences by moving adjectives.

1. We stepped into the boat. The boat was small.
2. I looked up at the clouds. The clouds looked fluffy.
3. Waves rocked the boat. The waves were gentle.
4. We rowed to an island. The island was rocky.
5. Fish swam past. They were light blue.

Adverbs

Adverbs as Modifiers

An **adverb** can modify, or tell more about, a verb. Many adverbs end in *-ly*. Adverbs often tell *how, when,* or *where* an action takes place. Adverbs can also modify adjectives and other adverbs. Some adverbs called **intensifiers** add emphasis to a description.

*Lightning **most certainly** poses a **very** serious threat **today**.*

Your Turn Write each sentence. Underline each adverb. Circle any intensifiers that are used.

1. Heavy rains fell outside.
2. People were most definitely worried about flooding.
3. The reporter spoke excitedly about the emergency.
4. We listened closely and promptly gathered supplies.
5. People who lived nearby called often to check on us.

Adverbs' Positions

An adverb can come before or after the verb, adjective, or adverb it modifies. It can also come in another part of the sentence.

*The **intensely** bright light **suddenly** moved **away**.*

Your Turn Write each sentence. Add the adverb in parentheses ( ).

1. We called the professor. (immediately)
2. He didn't sound concerned at all. (very)
3. We thought we had seen a spacecraft. (overhead)
4. He explained that it was a police helicopter. (probably)
5. One had flown close to his house as well. (incredibly)

Using *Good* and *Well*

The adjective *good* tells more about a noun. The adverb *well* tells more about a verb. The comparative and superlative forms of *well* are *better* and *best*.

> The **good** food made us feel **well**.

Your Turn Write each sentence. Choose the correct word to complete the sentence. Underline the word being described.

1. I didn't sleep (good, well) last night.
2. I had a (good, well) reason to stay up late.
3. I would have done (better, best) if I hadn't been tired.

Comparing with Adverbs

Use *more* or *less* before most adverbs to compare two actions. Use *most* or *least* before most adverbs to compare more than two actions. Add *-er* or *-est* to shorter adverbs to compare actions.

> Lea spoke **louder** and **more fluently** than Hal.
> Owen spoke **softest** and **least fluently** of all.

Your Turn Write each sentence. Use the correct form of the adverb in parentheses.

1. You read your speech (confidently) than I did.
2. Of all the speakers, we listened (intently) to her.
3. Were you seated (close) to her than I was?

Combining Sentences: Adverbs

You can combine sentences by leaving out repeated words and moving an adverb into one of the sentences.

> We ran to the store. We ran **quickly**. We ran **quickly** to the store.

Your Turn Move an adverb to combine each pair of sentences.

1. I remembered our meeting. I remembered it suddenly.
2. I turned around. I turned immediately.
3. I walked to the bus stop. I walked directly.

Negatives and Prepositions

Negatives

A **negative** is a word that means *no* or *not*. Other examples are *never, barely, hardly,* and *scarcely*. Negatives may appear as the contraction *-n't* (short for *not*). Correct a **double negative** (two negatives) in a sentence by changing one into a positive word.

*Nobody wants bad news. I **didn't** want to hear it.*

Your Turn Write each sentence. Correct the double negative.

1. I couldn't see nothing outside our tent.
2. Hardly no one wanted to investigate the noise.
3. Nobody couldn't sleep that night.

Prepositions and Prepositional Phrases

A **preposition** is a word that relates a noun or pronoun to another word in the sentence. A **prepositional phrase** is a group of words that begins with a preposition and ends with a noun or pronoun. The **object of a preposition** is the noun or pronoun that follows the preposition. When a prepositional phrase acts as an adjective or an adverb, it can be called an **adjective phrase** or an **adverb phrase**.

*Musicians **in the band** (adjective) rested **during breaks** (adverb).*

Common Prepositions: about, above, across, after, against, along, among, around, at, before, behind, below, beside, between, by, down, during, for, from, in, inside, into, near, of, off, on, out, outside, over, through, to, under, until, up, with, without

Your Turn Write each sentence. Underline each prepositional phrase and circle the object of each preposition. Tell whether the phrase is used as an adjective or an adverb.

1. The birds swooped above the trees.
2. My mother took a video of the flock.
3. Did you see how they formed patterns in the sky?

Mechanics: Abbreviations

Organizations

In both formal and informal writing, use abbreviations for certain organizations and government agencies. These abbreviations usually have all capital letters and no periods.

United Nations - UN   Federal Bureau of Investigation - FBI

National Aeronautics and Space Administration - NASA

Your Turn Write each sentence. Change each word or group of words in parentheses into its abbreviation.

1. My aunt applied for a job with the (Central Intelligence Agency).
2. He wrote a report on the (Environmental Protection Agency).
3. The (United Service Organizations) put on a show for the troops.
4. My brother did well on his (Scholastic Achievement Test).
5. We visited the (United States Postal Service) headquarters.

Internet Addresses

Use abbreviations at the end of Internet addresses.

.com (commercial)   .edu (educational)   .gov (government)

.org (organization)   .net (network)   .info (information)

Your Turn Write each sentence. Change each word in parentheses into its abbreviation.

1. I found a space program time line at www.nasa.(government).
2. My mother checked www.mayoclinic.(commercial) for health information.
3. I used www.humanesociety.(organization) to research animal adoptions.
4. Dad looked at www.mta.(information) to see if the subway was on schedule.
5. We looked at the available courses at www.harvard. (education).

Mechanics: Abbreviations

Units of Measure

Use abbreviations for units of measure. Most abbreviations are the same for singular and plural units.

in.—inch(es)	*lb.—pound(s)*	*km.—kilometer(s)*	*L—liter(s)*
ft.—foot (feet)	*kg.—kilogram(s)*	*oz.—ounce(s)*	*hr.—hour(s)*

Your Turn **Write each sentence. Abbreviate each word in parentheses ( ).**

1. My cousin is now 6 (feet) tall.
2. I weighed 7 (pounds), 2 (ounces) at birth.
3. We worked for 7 (hours) in a row yesterday.
4. My tomato plant grew 8 (inches) last week.
5. It took us 3 (hours) to drive 130 (kilometers).

Time

Use the abbreviation A.M. (*ante meridiem*) for times before noon and P.M. (*post meridiem*) for times after noon. Abbreviations for years are B.C. for "Before Christ," A.D. for *anno Domini,* (Latin: "in the year of the Lord") B.C.E. for "Before Common Era," and C.E. for "Common Era."

Your Turn **Write each sentence. Add time abbreviations wherever possible.**

1. I went to bed at 10:30 last night.
2. Sunrise is scheduled for 6:32 tomorrow.
3. This piece of pottery from 365 is over 2,000 years old.
4. My complete birth date is October 23, 1999.
5. We worked by moonlight alone from 9:45 until 5:30.

Mechanics: Capitalization

Mechanics: Capitalization

Proper Nouns: Names and Titles of People

Capitalize the names of people and the initials that stand for their names. Capitalize titles or abbreviations of titles when they come before or after the names of people. Capitalize the abbreviations for Junior (Jr.) and Senior (Sr.).

Mrs. Foss took Dr. Ann J. Rice to see Gov. Tim Bell, Jr.

Capitalize an official title when it comes before a person's name or when it is used in direct address. Do not capitalize the title if it comes after or is a substitute for the person's name.

Cheryl, the club's president, introduced Mayor Watson.

Capitalize words that show family relationships when used as titles or as substitutes for a person's name. Do not capitalize words that show family relationships when they are preceded by a possessive noun or pronoun.

Aunt Pat gave my mother a painting of Grandpa.

Capitalize the pronoun *I*.

I will practice my guitar until I can play the song well.

Your Turn Write each sentence. Correct any errors in capitalization.

1. I volunteered to work at the p. j. Diego Foundation.
2. I had an interview with mr. culver.
3. My uncle knows professor Rita Stewart, the director.
4. She is also friends with mom and aunt Iris.
5. Dad and i spoke to Tim Flynn, sr., the senator from Ohio.

473

Mechanics: Capitalization

Other Proper Nouns and Adjectives

Capitalize names of cities, states, countries, and continents. Do not capitalize articles or prepositions in those names. Capitalize names of geographical features but not compass points showing direction.

Juneau, Alaska   United States of America   Miami is south of Boston.

Capitalize the names of buildings, bridges, and monuments. Capitalize street and highway names, either whole or abbreviated.

Golden Gate Bridge   Air and Space Museum   Keene Blvd.

Capitalize the names of stars and planets. Capitalize *Earth* when it refers to the planet but not when it is preceded by the article *the*.

We felt the earth shake. We hope one day to travel to Mars.

Capitalize the names of schools, clubs, teams, organizations, institutions, businesses, political parties, and products.

Stargazers' Club at Fletcher Elementary School

Capitalize names of historic events, periods of time, and documents.

Battle of Bunker Hill   Declaration of Independence

Capitalize the days of the week, months of the year, and holidays. Do not capitalize the names of the seasons.

Labor Day is the first Monday in September.

Capitalize the names of ethnic groups, nationalities, and languages. Capitalize proper adjectives formed from those names.

Most Swiss citizens speak either Italian, French, or German.

Capitalize the first word of main topics and subtopics in an outline.

1. Products and Industries
   A. Technology

Your Turn Rewrite each sentence. Capitalize words as needed.

1. The foreign cinema club watched a spanish film.
2. It was shown at starlight theater on oak ave.
3. An upcoming mexican film depicts the battle of the alamo.

Salutations and Closings

Capitalize all the words in the greeting of a letter, including the title and name of the person addressed. Capitalize only the first word in the closing of a letter.

Dear Ms. Sullivan: *Sincerely yours,*

Your Turn Write each sentence. Use capital letters correctly.

1. dear aunt beverly,
2. yours truly,
3. dear dr. grimes and associates:
4. with our deepest gratitude,
5. to whom it may concern:

Titles of Works

Capitalize the first, last, and all important words in the title of a book, play, short story, poem, movie, article, newspaper, magazine, TV series, chapter of a book, or song.

Mom hummed "Ship on the Water" while I read <u>Treasure Island</u>.
I wrote the "This and That" column for the <u>Boyden School Herald</u>.

Your Turn Write each sentence. Use capital letters correctly.

1. The glee club sang "only our best" for their audition.
2. They were featured on the show "an ear for talent."
3. Did you see the headline in <u>the foxpaw courier</u>?
4. They set my poem "winds and waters" to music.
5. It was inspired by the book <u>two boats in the bay</u>.

Mechanics: Punctuation

End Punctuation

To end declarative sentences, use a **period**; interrogative sentences, a **question mark**; imperative sentences, a period or **exclamation mark**; exclamatory sentences, an exclamation mark.

Do you know how to ski? Look out for that tree! The snow is deep.

Your Turn Write each sentence. Add correct end punctuation.

1. How cold will it be today
2. My feet feel like blocks of ice

Periods

Use a **period** at ends of abbreviations; after initials; in abbreviations for time or units of measure; after numbers and letters in an outline.

Dr. B. Waters will arrive at 3:15 P.M. on Feb. 12.

Your Turn Write each sentence. Insert periods where needed.

1. Mom had an appointment at 11:30 AM on Oct 5.
2. I spent 2 hrs and 35 min taking notes.

Hyphens, Dashes, and Parentheses

Use a **hyphen** or **hyphens** in certain compound words (including numbers) or to divide a word between syllables at the end of a line.

Her real-life columns are based on stories of thirty-eight wild horses.

Use a **dash** to set off expressive or clarifying information.

We set off on the trail—the most scenic trail, by all accounts.

Use **parentheses** to set off non-essential information.

The largest horses (among those on the trail) stopped often.

Your Turn Write each sentence. Insert hyphens, dashes, or parentheses where needed.

1. We had ninety five minutes left until sunset.
2. It can get cold very cold in the mountains at night.

Colons and Semicolons

Use a **colon** to separate the hour and minute when you write the time of day. Use a colon after the greeting of a business letter. Use a colon to introduce a list of items that ends a sentence. Do not use a colon if the list immediately follows a verb or a preposition.

Use a **semicolon** to combine parts of a compound sentence when a conjunction is not used.

> *Dear Professor Lightman:*
>
> *I will be late for tomorrow's 8:30 class; I should be there by 9:00.*
>
> *I will bring the following: paper, three pencils, and an eraser.*

Your Turn Write each line of the printed letter. Insert the correct punctuation where needed.

1. Dear Ms. Alton and Staff
2. Please find enclosed the following pins, badges, stickers.
3. We had more than enough these are the extras.
4. We handed them out until 1130 last night.
5. People shared these comments more variety, brighter colors, less text.

Apostrophes

Use an **apostrophe (')** and an *s* to form the possessive of a singular noun. Use an apostrophe and an *s* to form the possessive of a plural noun that does not end in *s*. Use an apostrophe alone to form the possessive of a plural noun that ends in *s*. Do not use an apostrophe in a possessive pronoun. Use an apostrophe in a contraction to show where a letter or letters are missing.

> *She'll ask the boys' parents about their behavior.*

Your Turn Write each sentence. Insert apostrophes where needed.

1. We worked all day in a farmers field.
2. The suns rays made us hot and thirsty.
3. We couldnt wait to swim in the pond.
4. My two sisters friends enjoy working with farmers.
5. Theyll join us at the pond when theyre finished.

Mechanics: Punctuation

Commas

Use a comma between the name of a city and the complete name of a state. Use a comma after the name of a state or a country when it is used with the name of a city in a sentence. A comma between the name of a city and the postal service abbreviation for a state may be omitted.

>*We flew from Miami, Florida, to Venice, Italy.   We live in Nome AK.*

Use a comma between the day and the year in a date. Use a comma before and after the year in a sentence, when the year is used with both the month and the day. Do not use a comma if only the month and the year are given.

>*We moved on May 12, 2004, and returned in March 2008.*

Use a comma after the greeting in a friendly letter and after the closing in all letters.

>*Dear Aunt Sally,*   *Very truly yours,*

Use a comma before the conjunction *and, but,* or *or* when it joins simple sentences to form a compound sentence. Use a comma after a dependent clause at the start of a sentence. Use a comma after introductory words or phrases at the start of a sentence.

>*When Dad came home, the dog barked, but the cat just sat there.*

Use a comma to set off a direct quotation. Use a comma to set off a noun of direct address. Use a comma to set off an appositive within a sentence.

>*"Ben, in that picture," Dad asked, "can you find Jim, your cousin?"*

Use commas to separate three or more items in a series. Use commas to separate three or more subjects in a compound subject. Use commas to separate three or more predicates in a compound predicate.

>*The article told about the rains, high winds, and flooding.*

Use commas to set off words that interrupt the flow of thought in a sentence. Use commas to separate nonessential words and clauses from essential words and clauses.

I thought her idea, which was silly, would cost too much.

Use a comma after the words *yes* or *no* or other introductory words at the beginning of a sentence. Use a comma before a tag question that comes at the end of a sentence. Use a comma before the word *too* when it means "also."

Hey, Jules, you know that song, don't you? Yes, and I can sing it, too.

Your Turn **Write each sentence. Add commas where needed.**

1. This park has the best views in Boulder Colorado.
2. We couldn't decide whether to ski skate or snowshoe.
3. Dad said "Kids let's take our sleds up that hill."
4. When we reached the top the slope looked much steeper.
5. I slid down first and my sister brother and father followed me.

Quotation Marks in Dialogue

Use **quotation marks** before and after a direct quotation, the exact words that a speaker says or writes.

Use a comma or commas to separate a clause, such as *he said,* from the quotation itself. Place the comma outside the opening quotation marks but inside the closing quotation marks.

Place a period inside closing quotation marks. Place a question mark or exclamation mark inside the quotation marks when it is part of the quotation.

"Why are you out of breath?" my brother asked.

"I ran back," I replied, "because I thought I saw a bear."

Your Turn **Write each sentence. Add punctuation where needed.**

1. My mother asked Did you bring a flashlight?
2. It's right here in the tent I replied.
3. Oh my! Did you hear that? my brother shouted.
4. Go back to sleep my father said. It's nothing to worry about.
5. If it doesn't stop my mother said I'm calling the ranger.

Mechanics: Punctuation

Titles

Use italics or underlining for the title of a book, movie, television series, play, magazine, or newspaper. Use quotation marks around the title of a short story, song, short poem, print article, online article, or chapter of a book. Remember to capitalize all of the important words in a title.

> *I finished my poem, **"Along the Old Path."***
> *My father has a column in **<u>The Hometown Gazette</u>**.*

Your Turn **Write each sentence. Apply the correct treatment of titles where needed.**

1. A writer for The Travel Show spoke at our school.
2. She also wrote the article Packing your bags.
3. I submitted a story to Teen Travel magazine.
4. They changed the title to eight days in Delaware.
5. Have you ever read The Incredible Journey?